The Primal Runes

Archetypes of Invocation and Empowerment

By Roger Calverley

LOTUS
PRESS

COPYRIGHT © 2005 by Roger Calverley. ALL RIGHTS RESERVED. No part of this book may be reproduced in any form or by any electronic or mechanical means including information storage and retrieval systems without permission in writing from the publisher, except by a reviewer who may quote brief passages in a review.

Page Design/Layout: Paul Bond, Art & Soul Design
Cover Design: Mary Sullivan

First Edition, 2005
    Printed in the United States of America
    The Primal Runes: Archetypes of Invocation and Empowerment

ISBN-13: 978-0-9409-8583-4
ISBN-10: 0-9409-8583-7
Library of Congress Control Number: 2005920018

Published by:
Lotus Press
P.O. Box 325
Twin Lakes, Wisconsin 53181 USA
web: www.lotuspress.com
e-mail: lotuspress@lotuspress.com
800-824-6396

Table of Contents

Acknowledgements vi
Foreword vii
Preface ix

Chapter 1: Rune Magic 1
Chapter 2: The Primal Runes 11
Chapter 3: People of the Moon 27
Chapter 4: Moon Magic 33
Chapter 5: Archetypes 41
Chapter 6: Runelore 49
Chapter 7: Ancient Powers 65
Chapter 8: Rune Profiles 75
    Field 76
    Seeding 82
    Gestation 86
    Emergence 91
    Thunder 95
    Growth 98
    Challenge 103
    Fire 108
    Choice 113
    Karma 119
    Creativity 125
    Grace 130
    Love 135
    Courage 141
    Fullness 146
    Descent 153
    Wisdom 158

Mastery	164
Lake	169
Transmission	174
Dreamweaver	181
Water	188
Crisis	193
Sacrifice	198
Knot	205
Mountain	210
Transformation	215
Merging	221
Primal Light	226
Primal Dark	232
Source	236
Chapter 9: Making the Runes	243
Chapter 10: Using the Runes	247
Chapter 11: Chanting the Primal Runes	265
Chapter 12: The Sacred Sounds	271
Field	271
Seeding	272
Gestation	272
Emergence	273
Thunder	273
Growth	274
Challenge	274
Fire	275
Choice	275
Karma	275
Creativity	276
Grace	276
Love	277
Courage	277
Fullness	278

Descent 278
Wisdom 279
Mastery 279
Lake 279
Transmission 280
Dreamweaver 280
Water 281
Crisis 282
Sacrifice 282
Knot 283
Mountain 284
Transformation 284
Merging 285
Primal Light 285
Primal Dark 285
Source 286
The Wisdom Cycle 286

Chapter 13: Bard of Runes 289

Appendix 1: Old Europe 305
Appendix 2: A Sacred Script 311
Appendix 3: Cultic Symbols 315
Appendix 4: The Lunar Law 319
Appendix 5: The Cypriot Syllabary 331

Bibliography 337

Acknowledgements

I wish to extend my sincere thanks to all who have contributed to this book with their time, energy and skills. Thanks firstly to Maneesh Rampersad for his work in computer formatting, and thanks to Mary Sullivan for her work on the cover design. Thanks to Mary Lucas Emerson for her insights into the sounds of the runes (chapter 10) and her Foreword. Also, my gratitude to Rig Svenson for his thoughtful advice and his Preface. Finally, thanks to Paul for his contributions of talent and skill in formatting, and to Santosh for his many thoughtful and timely emails. Your help, all of you, has helped to make the book possible.

Foreword

When I move in consciousness to connect with teachers from the past, I begin to see images in my mind of mountains and glaciers, with pools of energy swirling through time. My heart opens, the Creator's love comes to me in a vessel of thought, and I know my existence to be very old. I remember the ancient world, the world which has disappeared. I remember how light danced over the pyramids, filling the temples by the riverside with beauty. Those moments are still present in my memory. It was a time when those who had the gift imparted their teaching so that we could become wise.

We would gather in sacred glades and listen to the masters. They moved in silent places. When we came together, they would share their lives and teachings with us. Their words and energy would flow into my mind, and then into my infinite consciousness. To this place I can still go, and there I recall the ancient memories to life.

I knew a master then, and I have given myself the privilage to meet him in this life. I know him now as Roger Calverley, and it is a renewal of an experience that I had when I knew him so many moons ago. The words he speaks carry a familiar message. He lifts me up to sing my infinite heartsong. He is a musical tone that rings out to embrace the morning sky. His words slip between the sun's rays to convey the light of spirit which he calls HOME.

I am like a butterfly. I float along in the gentle currents of the warm wind and I wait on the flowers drinking from the dew. I watch the earth shift, and I can hear Roger passing through the veils to visit his spirit home before he begins his daily rituals. Once again we begin to sing our songs and share our words. We gather like moths to a great light and when we meld together we become the perfect tone of velvet light. Roger moves with the great ones and sits in council with the Ancients. He touches the human domain of life with ceremony and blesses the earth with an initiate's prayer. He knows the way to the old worlds and he drinks from the sacred waters of antiquity. He clears a path for others and shares the wisdom of the beyond with love and joy.

I am old now, and I will dance my way home to my people. I

will laugh in the light of the stars and sing the song of life here on the breast of Mother Earth, the friend of my worship. Roger, the Master of the Eternal Flame, is a brother to my inner soul, and a friend of Earth. His light is immense and his spiritual family move in various reaches of the planet, exploring new domains of consciousness and expressing new ranges of insight about the unfolding adventure of life. When the seekers' hearts are open, he is moved to speak, and his words fill our minds with encouragement. His hands of grace point our world toward perfection. His harp notes draw the spirit out from its hidden domain to dance in the clouds.

Bless you, bless your heart dear Roger. We were in danger of becoming so shy that we could no longer play in our own dreamfields. But I have awakened at last, and I thank you for seeing and embracing my light in such a way that the rainbow spirit is again resurrected. You are giving us an opportunity to understand ourselves in a deeper and more profound way than ever before. You challenge us to learn more about who we really are.

The world is different now, not like the ancient times. We are experiencing many new things. The primal vibrations are still here with us, and we can access them to explore our past or glimpse the fast approaching future. Your book is a vital vehicle to assist us in this attunement of awareness. Through you we can reach new realms of awareness and information. You help us see and feel the unconditional love that supports all of our aspiring endeavours. You show us a way of thinking that can change reality, a path to self-mastery. Our past and our future fold together like a sacred cloth which you carefully place on the altar of the Most High. We have the growing courage to seek out our elders and our master teachers in order to confirm what we already know, deep down in reaches of our being, things that we have hidden even from ourselves. We are here, beautiful and profound, spiritual beings with only one limitation: an open heart too polite to admit to ourselves how glorious we really are. You unveil the mystery. You show us ourselves, and we thank you, Roger.

There is but one Truth. And you are right, we are all one family. We will treasure what you have shared in this book, *The Primal Runes*, and what you will be sharing with us in the future.

Mary Lucas Emerson
Janetville, Ontario
September 14, 2004

Preface

by Rig Svenson

In the world of runelore, it is refreshing to be able to say that a recent contribution to the field is completely new and different. To understand that difference, it might help to understand the wide range of the author's interests. Roger Calverley is currently the director of a meditation centre in Lindsay, Ontario, Canada. He has lectured all around the world and across North America on meditation, and has authored a number of books on various aspects of self-development, including: *The Healing Gems, The Language of Crystals, Crystal Spirit, Mantric Music, Radionics and Self Development,* and *Ancient Mysteries Tarot*. Roger also composes and performs harp music in the ancient Celtic and Bardic tradition. His CD's include: *Celtic Mysteries, Avalon, Celtic Mysteries II, The Celtic Mysteries Collection,* and *Bard of Hearts*. He uses his own mystical harp music to open spiritual hearts when he is called on to teach meditation. Additionally, Roger Calverley is a poet, artist (designer of *The Ancient Mysteries Tarot Deck*), and a triple initiate in the Andean tradition. His travels to Egypt, Greece, Crete, India, SE Asia and to Inca temples in South America have helped to deepen his understanding of the Mystery School Tradition, and of his many past-life connections with this field. His current writings are devoted to transmitting the essence of the ancient wisdom teachings in a form which speaks to the realities of the modern world.

This background certainly shows in his new release, *The Primal Runes*. This is a book which explores a set of runes which may well have been the progenitors of all subsequent runes. It also explores the relation of these earliest runes to the mystical wisdom of the Moon, the Great Goddess, and the civilization of Old Europe, which predates the Sumerians by millennia. As a student of history, spirituality and esoteric tradition, Calverley weaves together the available facts and insightfully adds his own reasoning as well as some judicious speculation. In the end, he achieves a kind of revelation, a runic system which is truly "primal", and which may indeed be the archetypal grandparent of all subsequent runelore.

To read and comment on a book like this requires me to draw on my own background in the field of runic studies. I am a well traveled lay scholar, researcher, lecturer and author of *Elder Futhark Runes* taking my sources where possible from archaeology with a growing interest in the history and development of what I believe to be **proto runes** and the cryptography behind these ancient symbols. I have been in this field for over 20 years and have lectured on the subject of runes throughout Britain for about 12 years.

In my opinion, the word rune (Old English run) stirs the imagination and conjures up many possible connotations, such as 'whisper'; 'mystery'; and 'secret', suggesting that the symbols were originally used for magical or mystical rituals (an aspect which receives much attention in *The Primal Runes*). However, the modern English term 'rune' is not a survival of the Old English word, but actually a later borrowing from Norse via Latin. For the modern, magical sense of *rune* we need observe the Scandinavian rather than the Anglo-Saxon traditions.

1. Proto-Indo-European echoic base, **reu-* 'to give hoarse cries, mutter'
2. Proto-Germanic **runo*
3. Old Norse **ru:n**
4. Old English *run* which didn't survive,
5. Middle Dutch *rune*
6. Old High German *runa,*
7. Gothic *runa.*
8. Old Norse **ru:n** is the source for some borrowings: *rune* in modern English (via *runic* in Latin) and Finnish **runo** 'poem', 'canto'.

Since Calverley gives considerable importance to the sounds of his 'primal runes', I want to point out that the evolution of runes is the story of the sounds of runes. As the Germanic peoples migrated, so did the runes. However, not only did they spread, but they <u>*developed!*</u> The way in which this progressed is fundamental to understanding the runes themselves. For example, most of the runic ideographic associations that changed with the development of the runes did so in accordance with the laws of phonetic mutation. For example, the Germanic Rune ansuz **'A'** meaning **"God"** became **'O'**, **'A'** and **'Æ'** in Saxon meaning **"Mouth"**, **"Oak"** and **"Ash"** respectively. This can be shown in most cases to be responsible for the changing shape of the runic figures.

The fundamental meaning of historiography is to perceive history not just as it's written, but to gain insight and understanding of the writings through the acquired knowledge of the anthropological essence of the period of time in which the writing occurred. Symbols are as old as antiquity itself and I suggest that what we understand to be runic writing long existed before the Aesir war bands had ever heard of them. It is plausible that Odin afterwards adapted the oldest runic symbols he came across in the land of the Vanir, thus creating and further developing these ancient symbols until they eventually developed into the well known Elder Futhark. It is with this thought that I would like you to consider the notable, very new and exciting developments worked out by Roger Calverley in his new book, *The Primal Runes*.

Calverley's *The Primal Runes* takes the reader on a fascinating journey into the past, back to the dawn of antiquity where rune linguistics and phonetics must originally have evolved. This is no simple task given the complexity and obscurity of the field, the research involved, and the vast scope of subject matter. It is an ambitious and challenging attempt at piecing together all the feasible evidence into a very plausible synthesis, combining both archaeology and Marija Gimbutas' thoughts on the original Goddess-centred culture, known as "Old Europe".

The sacred signs of Old Europe which Calverley calls 'primal runes' are possibly the oldest of all known runes, many being in constant use from Paleolithic times. As a consequence, no written documents from the time prior to the Indo-European invasions exist. This book is very concerned with the archetypal process, and Calverley, like most of us, feels that archetypes can and do work through symbolic images. I also am one of those who agree that these images organise, direct and specify the unconscious content of the human mind, enabling us to have a more conscious and enriching interaction with them. The runes have always contained this embodied in their own consciousness. Calverley's unique contribution to the field is to unveil a set of 31 ancient runic symbols, along with a revelation of their energies, powers and meanings, so that they could be used for pathworking, divination or initiation. He links this to the mysterious energy and wisdom of the Moon, and the Goddess, which gives his primal runes a very interesting magic and charm. They are likely to appeal not merely to scholars, but to actual practitioners, with wide interest in the New Age community.

This book is no neophyte's guide to primal runes but rather a Journeyman's insight to a whole new perspective on kernel runelore, developing a detailed exposition of Cypriot syllabaries into a well thought out primal runic system. There are, by the way, four types of syllabaries developed from the seven ancient logographic systems: cuneiform syllabaries from Sumerian, West Semitic syllabaries from Egyptian, the Cypriot syllabary from Cretan. Cuneiform syllabaries derived from Sumerian include those for the extinct languages Urartian, Elamite, Hattic, Hurrian, Luwian, and Palaic. West Semitic peoples of Syria and Palestine created an open syllabary from the Egyptian hieroglyphic system by leaving out logograms and the signs for more complex syllables. While Calverley does not go into this background in extensive detail, he does make very sensible comments and extrapolations focused on the Cypriot syllabary, which is his main focus.

The author's underlying field area has been both studying and practicing in the spirit of the spiritual teacher for the better parts of three decades, and it is no surprise to see elements of spirituality reflected throughout his book. I personally find his research a refreshing change from the many "clone stereotypes" regurgitated rune works that I have come across by many of the better known New Age rune authors. Having said that, this book's timeline is based on pre-historical runelore and therefore very unique and far removed from any futhark styled rune research I have yet come across.

Calverley suggests that a rune has four values: Visual symbol, sound, cosmic meaning and lastly as an esoteric tool. He is building on solid ground here. C Marstander (1925e: 164) suggests that "runology is paleography, linguistics, ethnography and mythology". The question as to the origins of runic writing would take up several libraries worth of books to fully detail all arguments and this is not possible to do within the covers of any single book. The common accepted timeline for the futhark based runic alphabet is around 2nd – 3rd century CE. The time line of runes is moving even further back as new theories come to light, and *The Primal Runes* is an important contribution to this evolution.

The Primal Runes goes way back to Neolithic times to the culture of Old Europe, and dates from a period of several thousand years prior between 7,000 and 1,500 BCE. Although Calverley does not mention it in his new work, there is much support for his approach among other scholars like Kjell Aartun, a doctor of philosophy and language-researcher who claims that he has proven that the runes were not inspired by the Greek and Latin alphabets. He argues that it is the opposite, maintaining that the Norwegian runes are identical with runes which were used in Semitic language areas such as Trojan Asia Minor and Canaan (Palestine) as far back in history as 2000 BCE. Calverley's new book lends persuasive support to the idea that runes have a very ancient origination indeed.

These very ancient proto-runes, Aartun claims, are the basic platform by which the Greek and Latin alphabets later developed. Additionally, he writes that he can prove that the first Norwegian runic inscriptions were written in a Semitic language. According to Aartun, new archeological finds show that many people from the Mediterranean Sea area, and especially the Cretans (who were Semitic), often traveled to the north on trading tours. Although Calverley's aim was not to explore the supporting scholarhip in detail, his approach and conclusions harmonize well with the thinking that others are currently doing. It must be added, however, that Kjell Aartun's theories are not yet accepted by all Norwegian runeologists.

For Calverley, the symbols of Old Europe, and especially those of Vinca are of central importance. Vinca symbols have been found in south-eastern Europe, in particular from Vinèa near Belgrade, but also in Greece, Bulgaria, Romania, eastern Hungary, Moldova, southern Ukraine and the former Yugoslavia. The artifacts date from between the 7th and 4th millennia BCE and those decorated with these symbols are between 8,000 and 6,500 years old. Vinèa symbols may well represent the earliest form of writing ever found, predating ancient Egyptian and Sumerian writing by thousands of years. Since the inscriptions are all short and appear on objects found in burial sites, and the language represented is not as yet known or deciphered.

Common symbols used throughout the Vinèa period

To further give credence to Calverley's primal runes being based in the Caucasus region, there is strong evidence that our Swedish predecessors were migratory Thracians, an aggressive seafaring race who first came from the ancient city of Troy. Located in northwest Asia Minor (present-day northwest Turkey), the ruins of Troy were discovered in 1870. This was estimated to be during the period beginning about 2500 BC. Historians refer to the Aesir people as the Thraco-Cimmerians, since the Trojans were of Thracian ancestry. The locals named the Trojan conquerors the "Aes", meaning "Iron People", for their superior weaponry. The tribes of Trojan Aes would eventually move north, settling in present-day Scandinavia. The Aes or Aesar (plural) subsequently became known as the Svear, and then Swedes. Historians refer to the Aes people as "Thraco-Cimmerians" due to their Trojan ancestry. Other tribes of Thracians remained a culture in Asia Minor and southern Europe until the 5th century CE. Many present-day Bulgarians claim to be direct descendants of ancient Thracians.

Roger Calverley's work on proto-runes is highly illuminating and challenges us to deepen our understanding of these ancient symbols. With so much poorly written, mass produced material on the runes today, the need for well-researched, intellectually challenging and thoroughly original work is very welcome. There are no absolutes in anything today, but if you are the inquisitive sort, with a spirit of adventure in your heart, you will certainly enjoy *The Primal Runes;* it is a well-referenced book with excellent footnotes. It is the kind of writing which will encourage the reader to use runes in a variety of ways, including their sound-power, for self-development. In this sense, it really does bring the most ancient energies of the Goddess and Her Lunar Law into play for modern man.

CHAPTER 1

Rune Magic

*T*here is a river that flows through forested lands where sometimes I go to be alone. The water runs below high, granite cliffs where pines and oaks have established themselves. There is a quiet bay beneath the rocks there, and the deep waters in that spot call to my mind and spirit with special fascination. Where the waters of the river move relentlessly forward, all is astir, but in the bay, beneath the looming granite rocks, all is still. It is a hollow into which words or thoughts drop and disappear like pebbles. I become silent whenever I spend time here, especially in summer when the afternoon sun draws out the fragrance of the pine needles, and suffuses the air with golden warmth.

The revelations of ancient runelore must have started here, for it is in this place that I first truly experienced the primal archetypes of earth, water, air and fire. I would spend long periods in stillness, hearing the sounds of nature, watching, taking in different kinds of invisible influences, absorbing the spirit of the land, listening to the music of the wind in the trees, dissolving in the glow of the late afternoon sunlight. At first, it was not in my mind to write, only to experience, to experience and remember. But somewhere, deep in my heart, seeds of attunement were being sown, and by the time I had visited the sacred valley in Peru, and awakened the ancient memories, and returned home again to my forest retreat, the urge to write was there. The inner knowledge, soon to unfold as a book called *The Primal Runes*, was coming to the fore. The awakening process was itself a long gestation, for the sacred elements still had much to teach me.

The cliffs in my solitary nature retreat seem to be whittled out of silence, and if you sit there for a while, their silence will envelop you. But inside the silence I began to hear the sound of voices, voices that echoed from east to west, from the hills and valleys, from the swirling river and the dark caverns, from the hidden places where sunlight never reaches. Then came a moment when my heart felt the emptiness of its days. I was carried back to the shores of my own awareness. The silence had begun to weave together various strands of the unlit mind, and slowly, very slowly, something new was revealed, a new mind that could touch a leaf, a mountain, a seed, and know it, and become it. From this new mind, in time, would emerge an innate knowledge of the earliest runes, ancient signs filled with the magic of moonlight and water, the power of stone and of fire, wind-music and ethereal mystery. This was still to come. But the seeds of it were being sown in solitude and unknowing.

I must try to tell you what this time of gestation in nature is like, to convey some notion of what went into the birthgiving of the runes. You begin by carving out time to be alone, and finding a place that speaks to your spirit, a place of buried memories, a place that calls to you as if it were home. You go there, to embrace the solitude and the spirit of the land. Time passes, and it is ordinary, seemingly uneventful. Then, you find yourself searching within, until you touch once more the wordless awareness, the inner law that binds stone to water, sky and wind. You begin to sense in all things an ancient sleeping power, their innermost law. And then, as if from timeless submerged memories, the mind begins to weave again the bindings of awareness to knowledge and knowledge to fate. Slowly, slowly comes this linking of mind to rocks, trees, rivulets, searching into the dark heart of the hills, spinning tendrils of thought into a web that reaches over fields, forests and lakes. It traces its movements slowly outward, seeking, seeking to reveal something long obscured, something wild in the dark heart of earth, a forgotten mystery scribed in stone by the law of fire. Time flies. The mind melts into silence, timeless silence and darkness.

In this place, some years ago, I built a home from pine logs. I took my harp there, to be alone, to give myself plenty of time and space so that I could become attuned to the music of nature. I learned to listen. And when I listened, I saw how music fills the empty spaces which nature has made. I could hear it as the whispering of flames, the shivering of leaves, the sighing of wind, the babbling of water, the murmuring of insects. This music is deep, wide, beautiful, slow, full of exaltation, yet blended with immeasurable sorrow, majestic. This is music that foreshadows things which are as yet unformed, unseen. This music alchemizes passion into ecstasy, and transmutes fear into longing. It inspires songs which are filled with the sound of waves, and in imagination you touch the distant shores of dream-vision.

It is the wind which taught me my earliest songs. Among the trees there is always a rustling and a murmuring of breezes. Seldom are the forest glades windless. I would go to the top of a hill to feel the winds, to hear their voices. The winds touch everything in their boundless curiosity, telling of places they have visited, carrying fragrances that haunt and awaken and vitalize the heart.

The winds that come out of the west and south often smell of ploughed earth and sunlight. The wild, ancient voice of the north wind brings coldness and rainclouds, a looming darkness under leaden skies and a promise of storms. The soft morning winds speak a language my mind has never learned. They come sighing through the tops of the trees with a thousand names and memories. From the east sometimes would come a rousing wind, sweet-smelling, empty, stalking the woods like a hunter, seeking something nameless, absent. I breathe the loneliness of the wind, ever unsatisfied. I allow it to hollow me into something as nameless and empty as itself.

In my place overlooking the river, the wind sighs through the pines and rustles the oak leaves. It whispers in the tall grasses. Sometimes, I take my harp to the hill, and when the wind blows across its harpstrings, a strange, ethereal sound can be heard, lifting the spirit up towards the stars, as if to contemplate the music of the spheres.

At my log home in the woods, not long ago, I brought together a circle of friends, nineteen in all. From Peru came Kamaq

Wageaq (also known as Regis Llerena), an Andean Spiritual Master, and his apprentice Diane Dunn. Also present were my sister Rosemary, and a circle of a dozen people who meditate with me on a weekly, and in some cases, daily basis.

At one point, Regis asked us to lie on the granite rocks and to put our ear against the stone to hear its message. As we did this, our minds became still, and our intuitive senses entered into the darkness of the ancient stone. For most of us it was a remarkable and totally new experience. For some, it carried the consciousness far beyond its normal boundaries, to the very gateway of initiation.

The ancient granite yields a space which mind can hardly penetrate as it feels its pathway deeper and deeper into the dim silence below. At first we are blind in the darkness. But when we breathe the blackness of stone into ourselves, it begins to seep into the neglected corners of our mental restlessness, and our thoughts reach out to merge with what they touch. We enter an endless night, expanding through hollows of silence into vast gulfs, moving into a bottomless abysm where we pass through timeless darkness.

By the time this experience ended, we were very quiet and recollected, all nineteen of us. After a short while, Regis asked us to go and place our feet in the running water. We were instructed to open our hearts and listen to the music of the water as it rushed over stones and boulders. In our imagination, we were to become the flowing of the water and merge with it.

I can recall the experience quite clearly. I am sitting on a rock with my feet in the cool, flowing water, not far from a set of rapids. I watch the swirling of the stream, and listen to its endless voices, I am drawn into the spell. The moving waters are unquiet, teaming with strange shapes even in their lightless depths, murmuring, undulating, rushing forward impetuously.

Then, in the self-sounding of the water, I heard the echo of the music through which all things were brought into being. I came to know how the children of the forest listen to the voices of the brooks and rivers and the wave-lapping of the lakes, knowing not for what they listen, but knowing still that they have heard and been touched. The touch is there. None can quell the music of the streams and rivers, nor can any fully comprehend it.

Rain comes, a sound of water falling over stone, a primal music, old as time. And the rivers gather the rains and carry them to the distant sea. And by the side of the river, I watch and listen. My feet are in the river, but my mind has become the river's flow, winding its long course back to its eternal home. My heart is hungry for the sea, and is longing to return home. I become the flow that pours down the mountains, into the rivers, then into the vast ocean. I become the music of water which runs through all the veins of the world in sorrow and in joy, the fountain that rises to the sun in merriment, and the hidden wells of sorrow unfathomed at the foundations of the earth.

I can neither explain nor control their music as it penetrates my spirit. Salt tears well up in my eyes and drop into the stream, to merge and be carried away. I know that the harp music which I inwardly hear and create from deepest feeling comes from this ancient womb, the watery web of moon-magic. I am carried to the sea, to the shores where waves pound against rocks and shoot their spume into the air. The sea's language is whispered there to the ears of my heart, just beyond hearing, a tangle of power and memory on the verge of definition, yet always full of mystery.

This music takes us to our ancient home in the depths of the spiritual heart. We overhear it and become poets; we dream it and awaken as mystics; we dance it and we know love. In the soundless deep of the sea is something beyond comprehension, a longing, a loneliness, wordless understanding to caress the dark rim of the mind. All these I felt as I entered into the mystery and magic of water.

Out of a world beyond eyesight, a world beyond hope, comes a mingled, fragile sound as of harp notes, almost lost in the brush of rain over the sea, in the flow and ebb of the tide. Then, I notice that the others have finished their meditations, and are getting ready to leave. Reluctantly, I return to the outer world.

That night, we assemble around a campfire, to share experiences of the day. Fire has its own tale, a glory of light in the story of nature. You must go out into the lonely places if you want to prepare to hear the tale that fire can tell. You don't understand fire until you forget yourself and become fire. Being in the woods for days on end can help bring about this forgetting.

The story fire tells is a tale so familiar that we mostly no longer value it. It is simply there, like the air we breathe, the sunlight in the corner of the eye ... but one day we look into its deep beauty and see as we have never seen before. Seeing thus becomes the one thing in the world that has meaning any more. This fire into which we gaze with eyes made new is an epiphany of the ancient power still locked within the stones, buried and hidden in coldness and in wetness, but ready to blaze forth in a splendour no less magical than earth and water.

In time, the soft rustlings of fire become a language, a language older than the memories of men. Hearing this language, the wordless knowledge of fire fills the heart. Fire, the incessant weaving of a purpose, a word. Faces appear there, shadows beyond recognition, forming and then vanishing in the gentle pressure of the mind's probing. Something undefined, unexpected begins to take form. The fire blossoms into flowers that melt away, then fiery birds that take wing and disappear. Through and beyond them all, the life behind the mind begins to sense its own form and presence. One becomes dimly aware of powers intangible, shadows in the mind, primal beings that cannot be grasped or controlled

To see fire, to know it, to know the essence of fire, to hold it in the mind's eye, to melt into its great beauty, even to become fire, to find within yourself the power that is able to know and accept without fear, without question the power of the ancient law – slowly, slowly all this becomes possible. Out of the fire rise fragments of knowledge, weaving back and forth into one shapelessness after another. Long, long, the gazing on fire continues in the silent evening, and then one by one we begin to speak and to share our experiences.

My friend Grace Richardson speaks words of special meaning. She has seen signs, carved by the forefathers, and she has drawn what she has seen on a piece of paper. There are seven glyphs in all. She has taken great pains to record the vision. The paper is passed to Regis. He meditates on it. Then, he begins to speak.

"In the first glyph, the time of creation is shown. People have begun to populate the earth. They live lives of harmony through long ages in the early part of mankind's history.

In the second glyph, there is progress being made. Evolution is taking place, and the human mind has become capable of evaluating its progress. Many tribes are now living in the land, and they have become different from each other. Some are good in their intentions, but others are aggressive. The aggressive ones have become more numerous than the good ones.

In the third glyph, a time has come when men must choose their way of life. They must take great care to do what is right. They build and use temples. They hide behind masks. They become complex, their paths being complicated like labyrinths which seem to have no exit. But there is one path which ascends and has an exit, and it resembles the Andean Cross, the chakana. For the time being, there is a balance between the aggressive energies and the good energies, but things are changing.

In the fourth glyph, the fate of man hangs in the balance. A giant has been created. It will meet its end, submerged in water. People of good principles have contributed to the creation of this giant. Will they end up like him, facing death by water? Even the people who created this giant cannot save him.

In the fifth glyph, tremendous growth has taken place in the upper portion of the planet earth. It is disproportionate to the balance of earth energies. The people are dwarfed by their own creation, and live like pygmies in its shadow. Some of the people, however, are spiritual in nature and live in connection to a higher set of energies. Collapse is inevitable because of the actions of the aggressive people.

In the sixth glyph, the disaster has come. What was built up has fallen. A period of darkness has descended upon the earth. The people of good faith survive, at least some of them.

In the seventh and last glyph, an ordered existence has been restored. Resources are distributed with fairness and equity. There is equilibrium, and the centre is strong, holding all things in balance."

This vision was channeled at the end of June, 2004, by Grace, and interpreted by master Kamaq (Regis), with all 19 initiates in attendance. It was one of the very special moments which emerged in five days of attunement to the sacred elements of earth, water, air and fire. Regis said that it was a very solemn revelation from a higher source, and that it should be shared with the world at large.

8 THE PRIMAL RUNES

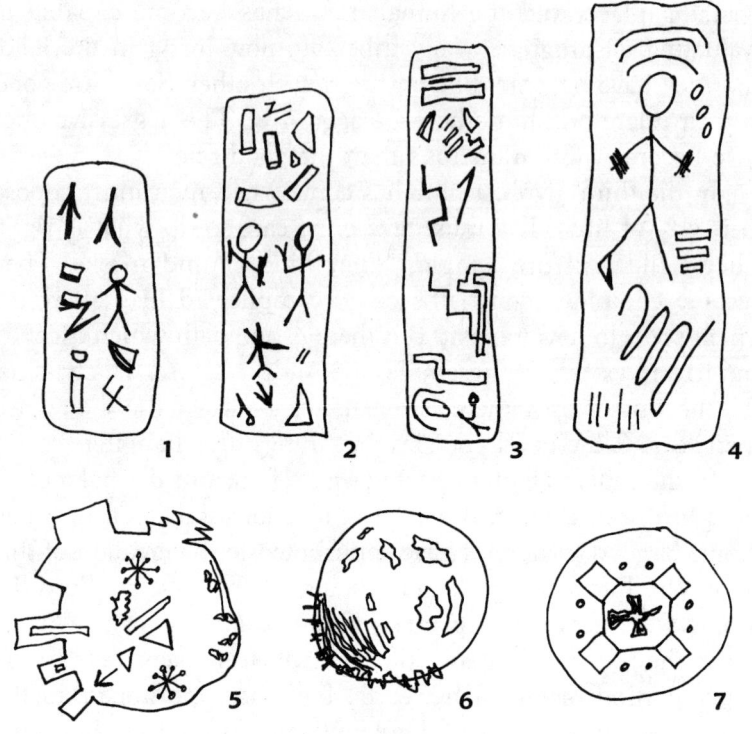

Fig. 1: The Images Channelled by Grace Richardson

In sharing this material, there is another revelation at work, a revelation concerning the living magic of runes and their self-communication to the human mind and spirit. From time to time, contemplatives experience the runes in the inner world as a language by which archetypal truth can reveal its workings to human understanding. They do so in remarkable and unpredictable experiences like that of Grace. And they do so in more extended and detailed ways such as the process by which the present book, *The Primal Runes*, has taken shape over many months of inner gestation.

This book, *The Primal Runes*, and Grace's vision, as interpreted by master KamaqWageaq, have something very important in common. They are both archetypal revelations. They are communications from the beyond which come forward at this historic time because humanity has need of the wisdom that they contain. Both revelations are transpersonal. They do not come from the individualized mind, imagination or ego structure of the recorder. Rather they enter into the seer's mind from the beyond, and demand thoughtful study to develop an adequate understanding and articulation of their import. For this reason, I asked Grace, and she kindly consented, to include her revelation at the very beginning of this work, as an example of the wonderful possibilities which are stirring all around us as the once and future wholeness of humanity's spirit rediscovers itself.

What happens when you have had an inner revelation? You are left with a nameless question inside your mind and heart. There is a tale that needs to be told if you would dare to answer that question. And the telling of the tale may take you to places you never dreamed. As I write this book, Grace and her husband are booking a flight to Cusco, Peru, for a rendezvous with the initiates of Andean spirituality. I will be joining them there on an adventure whose parameters I have no way of pre-judging. It was a year ago in Cusco that my interest in divining with stones first awakened, at a time when I had just finished writing *Ancient Mysteries Tarot*, but had yet to complete the artwork for the deck of cards which would accompany it. Revelations take you to strange places, and every journey opens doorways for further revelations in an upward spiral of spiritual awakening. I climbed one day to the ancient Inca ruins of the Temple of the Moon above the village of Pisac, near Cusco, and I prayed to be granted the true knowledge of the ancient archetypes according to the Lunar revelation. This temple had two doorways and seventeen alcoves, with an altar in one corner of the interior space. I prayed at each of the alcoves, and in each I found a small pebble. These, I gathered and placed in a box of stone which is now on an altar in my home in Lindsay, where the days and weeks of writing unfold. In those moments of contemplative prayer, as once before when I was carried up into a vision of the world of the Moon, my spirit ascended to touch the primal realities so that I could later give them expression in words. There was no one else there, I was the only one; and when the ritual had ended, I went away satisified in spirit.

In my home in Canada, I still go to my special places in nature as often as I can. There, I discover the uncorrupted energies that renew my spirit. The wind sighs through the pines and rustles the oak leaves. It whispers in the tall grasses. Sometimes, I take my harp to the hill, and when the wind blows across harpstrings, the strange, ethereal sound is renewed and the mind reaches up towards the stars as if to contemplate the music of the spheres.

I still find moments to lie on the grass and place my ear to the soil. Earth, good earth, dark earth, fragrant Mother Earth. You show us that through darkness one may come to the light. Your voice comes from the foundations of time. You are still. You are deep. You hide many secrets. You give birth and then you bury all that you have blessed. You support life and you swallow it. You give from your bounty, then you take back all. Your surfaces are full of the sun, but your hidden deeps are impenetrable and dark. The wind and the rain and the frost carve your body. Your mountains are ground to dust over long eons, but you are there, enduring, sometimes desolate, sometimes full of promise, but present through the long ages of time. Beneath the mysterious silver light of the moon, you spin through space – your dance of self-revelation attracting even the angels who envy your radiant mystery. Child of mystical possibilities, mother of our ancient dreams, you are the tablet on which the signs of our destiny are cyphered.

The magic which the elders set down in runes, first conceived under the moonlight in silent contemplation, by firesides and riverbeds when time seemed to stand still, again speaks to us. We contemplate the revelation and become silent in awe.

CHAPTER 2

The Primal Runes

"*The Supreme, having decided to create a universe, took a certain inner attitude which corresponded with the inner manifestation (unexpressed) of the divine Mother, the supreme Shakti. At the same time, he did this with the intention of its being the mode of creation of the universe he wanted to create, the creative power of the universe. Hence, first of all, he had to conceive the possibility of the divine Mother in order that this divine Mother could conceive the possibility of the universe. ... So we may very well say that there is a transcendent Divine Mother, that is, independent of her creation. She may have been conceived, formed (whatever you like) for the creation, with the purpose of creation, but she had to exist before the creation to be able to create, else how could she have created? That is the transcendent aspect, and note that this transcendent aspect is permanent. We speak as though things had unfolded in time at a date which could be fixed: the first of January 0000 for the beginning of the world, but it is not quite like that! There is constantly a transcendent, constantly a universal, constantly an individual and the transcendent, universal and individual are co-existent. That is, if you enter into a certain state of consciousness, you can at any moment be in contact with the transcendent Shakti, and you can also, with another movement, be in contact with the universal Shakti, and be in contact with the Individual Shakti, and all this simultaneously – that does not unfold*

> *itself in time, it is we who move in time as we speak, otherwise we cannot express ourselves. We may experience it but we can express it only by saying one word after another (unfortunately, one cannot say all the words at the same time; if one could say them all at the same time, that would be a little more like the truth). Finally, all that is said, all that has been said, all that will be said, is always only an extremely clumsy and limited way of expressing something which may be lived but which cannot be described. And there is a moment, when one lives the thing, in which one sees that the same thing can be expressed almost with the same exactness or the same truth in religious language, mystical language, philosophic language and materialistic language and that from the point of view of the lived truth, it makes very little difference. It is only when one is in the mental consciousness that one thing seems true to you and another does not seem true; but all these are only ways of expression. The experience carries in itself its absolute, but words cannot describe it – one may choose one language or another to express oneself, and with just a very little precaution, one can always say something approaching the Truth in all instances."*
>
> – The Mother (*Collected Works*, Vol. 4, p. 394)

The sacred 'Primal Rune' symbols are a language of revelation, the first and most ancient revelation of the Divine Mother to her human children. They evolved in prehistoric Europe as tools of ritual power, divination and teaching. Taken together, the Primal Runes are a summation of the Lunar Law and its wisdom; they tell the way of the divine unfolding and reveal the energies of transformation by which the light of consciousness grows, matures, and ultimately merges in its Source.

For several thousand years prior to the Aryan invasions, in fertile valleys near the Mediterranean Sea and in other regions across Eurasia, the Divine Mother was venerated as the giver and taker of all life. A wealth of archaeological evidence indicates that the matriarchal culture of Old Europe (see Appendix One) was centred on the Goddess, whom we also call the 'Great Mother'. For our earliest ancestors, the Moon was one of the greatest embodiments of the Mother; she was the weaver of destiny, the channel through which the light of life was measured out to all living beings on earth.

The term Old Europe was coined by the famous archaeologist Marija Gimbutas and refers to a Goddess-centred culture which flourished in the Danube Basin and elsewhere in Western Europe prior to the Indo European invasions. The word Europa means "full Moon" and the goddess Europa was an ancient "Moon cow". In the 1960's, a combination of radiocarbon and tree-ring dating made it possible to establish a reliable chronology for this earliest chapter of the history of Europe between about 7,000 BC and about 3,500 BC. Archaeologists working on that period have uncovered extensive evidence of a widespread ancient civilization that may be the oldest on earth. It is now, in fact, fairly common for archaeologists to refer to Old Europe as "the world's oldest civilization"[1] and there is a growing belief that the glyphs and signs used on pottery and elsewhere were the earliest form of writing on earth.

The richest finds have come from the region of the Danube Valley where some of the earliest human settlements in existence have been uncovered. Even as early as 5 to 7 thousand years BC, we find symbols related to the cult of the Goddess engraved on pottery, spinning whorls and objects like the Lepinski Vir stone, which is believed to have been a tool for divination. A number of experts claim that the runes of Old Europe constitute the earliest script in existence (see Appendix Two). These symbols pre-date anything that has been found in Sumer or in Mohenjo-Daro, India. However, since we cannot decipher them, and may never know the language(s) spoken prior to the invasions, there is some dispute as to whether or not these signs constitute writing, as we know it. Beyond dispute is that these signs were used for sacred purposes, that they were central to the religious beliefs and cosmology of the earliest Europeans.

In all, archaeologists have found several hundred signs which together they call the Old Europe Script. These signs are ancestral to writing systems such as Linear A, Linear B and the Cypriot Syllabary (also called the Cypro-Minoan Script), the Etruscan alphabet and the later Futhark runes. A syllabary is a set of signs that designate syllables (like "pa, po, pi, pe, pu") rather than alphabetic sounds. The Cypriot Syllabary, used as a form of writ-

14 THE PRIMAL RUNES

CLASSICAL CYPRIOT		OLD EUROPEAN	CLASSICAL CYPRIOT		OLD EUROPEAN	CLASSICAL CYPRIOT		OLD EUROPEAN
SA	∨	∨	PE	⌇	⌇	LO	+	+
SE	⊢⊢	⊢⊢	PI	⌄⌄	⌄⌄	LU	⌒	⌒
SI	⇧	⇧	PO	⌇	∼ψ	RA	⊓	○
SO	≋	≋	PU	⊕	⊕ψ	RE	⇧	⇧
SU	⋇	⋇	NA	T	T	RI	Ⴢ	Ⴢ m
KA	⇧	⇧	NE	⎮ᛋ⎮	⎮ᛋ⎮	RO	⛬	⛬
KE	⋇	⋇⋇	NI	⇶	⇶	RU	)(	GC
KI	⋔	⋔	NO	⋀	⋀	WA	⋈	⋈
KO	∩	∩	NU	⋗⌇	⋗⌇⋇	WE	I	I
KU	⋇	⋇	MA	⋇⋇	⋇⋇	WI	⋇	⋇
TA	⊢	⊢	ME	⋇	⋇⋇	WO	⇧	∧⎞
TE	⋇	⋇⋇	MI	∿	∿	ZA	⋇	⋇
TI	↑	↑	MO	⊕	⊂⊃	ZO	⌇⌇	⌇⌇
TO	F	F	MU	⋈	⋈	XA	)(	⊃
TU	⍓	⍓	LA	⋁	⋁	XO	(+	⇥
PA	⊹	⊹	LE	8	8			
			LI	⋜	⋜⋁			

**Fig. 2: Syllabary Correspondences
Based on Research by Marija Gimbutas**

ing on the isle of Cyprus up to the time of Alexander the Great, is particularly interesting because it is obviously drawn from the sacred signs of Old Europe. The late Marija Gimbutas, the foremost expert in the Goddess cult of prehistoric Eurasia, has prepared a table of correspondences showing how the Syllabary of ancient Cyprus derives from the much earlier script of Old Europe. Figure 2 illustrates the high degree of iconographic continuity between the two. The Cypriot Syllabary, (sometimes called the Cypro-Minoan Script) was in use at least as early as 1,500 BC. Its early forms are sometimes called Cypro-Minoan to distinguish them from the Cypriot script used for writing the Greek language after 1,200 BC. These early inscriptions form a vital link to the Old Europe traditions that predate the Aryan invasions.

As a writing system, the Cypriot Syllabary was not ideal for use with Indo-European languages such as the various Greek dialects. Thus, when Greek became the dominant language in the Middle East, following Alexander's conquests, it died out. Because the symbols themselves have had a remarkably long continuity of use, spanning thousands of years, we may speculate that the sound associated with each sign might have remained constant until the Cypriot Syllabary fell into disuse. As a subset of the Old Europe symbols, the Cypriot Syllabary is a valuable but little-recognized link to the earliest magical traditions of the Great Goddess.

The symbols, or "runes" that I focus on in this book as 'Primal Runes' are a subset of twenty eight (plus three) taken substantially from the Cypriot Syllabary. They are virtually identical in form (and very likely in pronunciation too) to the signs used in Old Europe from about 6,500 BC onward. The most common term used to refer to the glyphs of Old Europe is the "Vinca Script", a name deriving from location of one of the more important archaeological digs in the Danube Valley.

To understand primal runes, we need some understanding of the ancient cosmology, or wisdom-tradition within which they evolved. (see Appendix Three) In this regard, we are on very firm ground when we take the Moon as centrally important to the ancient spirituality of prehistoric Europe, as well as the Middle East, India and China. Broad consensus has established the lunar months as a time period of 28 days divided into four seven-day weeks. In reality, the lunar cycle is 29.5 days, however various traditions handled the extra day and a half in a variety of ways. Approximately thirteen lunar months make one lunar year, or 364 days. Thus, one lunar cycle provides us with 28 phases of waxing and waning light from the darkness of the New Moon to the brightness of the Full Moon and back again.

The Aryan (also called Kurgan, or even Indo-European) invasions brought upheaval and disruption to the culture not only of Old Europe, but also of Sumeria, which seems to have been similarly Goddess-centred in its earliest phases. The nomadic invaders introduced a fundamentally different way of seeing life which in time became the dominant paradigm and supplanted the old world-view centred on the Goddess. They had a fixed religious belief about the fundamental opposition between the powers of light and darkness, whereas the older view had been a holistic vision where both light and darkness played complementary roles in a cyclically changing relationship. In the lunar mythology of Old Europe, the disappearance of light had to do with a movement of life from the visible to the invisible planes of reality, not its cessation, and by no means its annihilation. But the Aryan view tended to see darkness as that which was *not* light or life, that which was intrinsically evil. Death also was seen as part of the great evil, not a natural transition. In the new Aryan paradigm, as also in post-regnum Semitic invasions of the Middle East, death was something final and to be feared, whereas in the older view death was part of an eternal cycle, and carried a promise of rebirth. When violence and the sword prevailed, as it increasingly did under the invaders, life was felt to be something untrustworthy, fleeting and precarious. This was a momentous change from the compassionate bonding of Divine Mother to her human children, which was the paradigm of life in the older, pre-Indo-European world-view.

For the invaders, the sacred and the profane were quite separate spheres of reality. This led to a desacralization of the routines of the normal working life, and a growing, though not yet absolute, division of life into two spheres, the "sacred" and the "profane". The Neolithic farmer had lived close to the soil and had been able to feel the rhythms of the Goddess as a palpable reality, immanent in all aspects of life. The invaders established a caste of priests and another caste of warriors, making the farmers little more than serfs under their control. Prior to the Aryan invasions, when religion and spirituality had been largely, though probably not exclusively, managed by women, there is no evidence of rigid separations of the people into higher and lower castes, or of life being bisected into separate categories of "sacred" and "profane".

For the invaders, the important gods were of the sky, not of the earth. There was a gulf of complete separation between earth-bound humanity and the heavenly powers which was a radically different understanding from that of the stone-age agriculturalists of Old Europe. After the Indo-European conquests, the sense of humanity being separate from and dominant over nature came into play, replacing the attitude that life and work were a service of the Mother and a participation in her unfolding miracle of nature.

In *The Myth of The Goddess*, Baring and Cashford write:

> The tribal migrations changed the character of the early Bronze Age and had a lasting effect on the evolution of consciousness in the civilizations that followed them. Their legacy lives on in pervasive attitudes and structures of response to life that have not been questioned and still have a controlling influence on the psyche today. Since this was a profound change for the worse, it is essential to make a distinction between the vision and values of the Aryan and Semitic tribes and those of the people who had been settled agriculturalists for thousands of years, apparently more or less peacefully. No less a question than our vision of human nature is involved here... As the inheritors of both the Neolithic and Bronze Age experience – in what proportions relative to each other is inevitably unknowable – we have two 'historical souls' in us, one with the vision of life that prevailed before the Bronze Age and the other with the vision that was forged in the crucible of that terrifying age. We may have accepted uncritically only one of these visions as being intrinsic to human nature – the paradigm of 'the victors' – rather than asking whether it was something imposed upon us so long ago that it now seems 'natural'. (pp 157-158)

This passage gives a very direct insight into why the wisdom of the Primal Runes is so important in our own age. These oldest of symbols embody the original path to wholeness, the ancient teachings of the Divine Mother. They convey a vision of humanity's innate oneness with nature, a relationship of service and reverence, not based on struggle or the need for conquest and domination. As living signs and powers of the path of integral transformation, the Primal Runes have a very important energy to impart, and at no time has it been more needed than at this critical juncture of earth's troubled history.

When we rediscover the primal unity of creation and the ancient traditions that bond all beings in unity, a complete reversal of mind can take place. In his book *Secrets of the Talking Jaguar*, Martin Prechtel describes this process:

> Somewhere during the course of my initiation as a shaman, I came across a startling and troubling realization that every human being alive today modern or tribal, primal or overdomesticated, has a soul that is original, natural, and, above all, indigenous in one way or another. And like all indigenous peoples today, that indigenous soul of the modern person has either been banished to some far reaches of the dream world or is under direct attack by the modern mind. Since the human body is the world, every individual in the world, regardless of background or race, has an indigenous soul struggling to survive in an increasingly hostile environment created by that individual's mind, which subscribes to the mores of the machine age. Because of this, a modern person's body has become a battleground between the rationalist mind and the native soul. As a shaman, I saw this as the cause of a great deal of spiritual and physical illness. Over the last two or three centuries, a heartless culture-crushing mentality has incremented its progress on the earth, devouring all peoples, nature, imagination, and spiritual knowledge. Like a big, mechanized slug, it has left behind a flat, homogenized streak of civilization wherever it passed. Every human on this earth ... has ancestors who at some point in their history had their stories, rituals, ingenuity, language, and lifeways taken away, enslaved, banned, exploited, twisted, or destroyed by this force. Now what is indigenous, natural, subtle, hard to explain, gen-

erous, gradual, and village-oriented in each of us is being banished into the ghettos of our hearts. (pg. 281)

William Butler Yeats coined a beautiful phrase: "the rag and bone shop of the heart" to convey just this idea. The power of the Primal Runes is ready to be re-discovered. These forgotten archetypes speak to us about a magic that is still possible if we can only remember the broken paradigm and renew the flow that unites earth to heaven through the *axis mundi*.

If we want to look more deeply into the ancient lunar cosmology, it helps to be aware of fundamental beliefs that have come down to us from Mesopotamia, Egypt and Greece. We know that earth, water, fire and air were held from the earliest times to be primary manifestations of the Goddess, and this fourfold manifestation can also be seen as a function of the lunar time cycle. Moon time, as experienced in Old Europe, was not merely a neutral set of evenly measured hours. The Moon imparts varied kinds of energy in each phase of her waxing and waning light. This gives significance and quality to various days of the 28-day cycle. The sacred elements are depictions of primary modalities of the Goddess – for example Air is the world of mind, measure, logic and judgement, while Fire imparts energy of dynamism, initiative, will and creativity. Just as each day of the week was held to be under the influence of one of the planets (Sun-Day, Moon-day, Saturn's Day, etc.) so too the four weeks of the lunar month can be correlated to the energies of the sacred elements - earth, water, fire and air.

The time of the New Moon is a period of darkness, and diminished energy, hence Earth. The growing light of the First Quarter Moon is a time of increasing radiance, and hence comes under the influence of Fire. Fire warms and germinates the seeds of earth, and celestial fire develops the potentials latent in human consciousness. The period of the Full Moon and several days on either side of it is the fullest revelation of the celestial influence, or Air. Air exalts what Fire has developed. And finally, the passing away of the light is a return to the primal ocean or Water. Water dissolves and disperses what has been developed. Different traditions place the elements in differing positions, and each can be valid from its own perspective.

It is important to keep in mind that cosmologies and attributions are not absolutely fixed, they vary from culture to culture and from age to age. Like mythologies, they talk *about* Truth, but do not attempt to limit and define it in any absolute, dogmatic way. This is one significant difference between myth and theology. In ancient times, we see the Goddess appearing with many forms, names and qualities. All these attributions could and did generate means of glimpsing or expressing Truth. In different ways, ancient cosmologies provided patterns of wholeness and meaning for our early ancestors. Each world-view had its own internal integrity and resonance; each was an epiphany of primal archetypes. Moon is the mother of many of the archetypes. She creates a lunar month of 28 days divided into four seven-day weeks in a world dominated by her four sacred energies. She moves from darkness to light and back again, dying and being reborn. This lunar pattern of birth, growth, death and rebirth is the first and most ancient plot from which all others derive. The Primal Runes are signposts of experience that mark the stages of this voyage from darkness to light in repeated cycles of revelation. These cycles are actually part of a spiral that carries consciousness beyond its limitations until it is able to re-unite with the Source. The runes embody the wisdom of The Goddess as she weaves and reveals the fate of all living beings on earth. Moon and earth are one reality in two forms, and what is revealed there as energy unfolds here below as fate.

The New Moon, the First Quarter Moon, the Full Moon and the Last Quarter or Waning Moon are the four most obvious phases of the lunar revelation. They have a special relation to the four sacred elements. However, between these four phases we have four other lunar stages, namely the Crescent Moon, the Gibbous Moon, the Disseminating Moon and the Balsamic Moon.

Astrology is an excellent source if we want to develop a deeper understanding of the lunar plot line, and Dane Rudyar, author of *The Lunation Cycle*, has done as much as anyone to explain the varied forces at work in the eight phases. Rudyar's thoughts have been augmented by other thinkers in the field, and in the decades since his book was published, a broad consensus has been achieved concerning the meaning of the Moon's eight principle phases. The **New Moon** is a time to project oneself into the world, to find a sense of purpose or meaning. Inner forces are at work below the threshold of consciousness. This is the seeding time that makes new life begin to stir under the mantle of winter. The **Crescent Moon** struggles to bring the new possibility which has been seeded into human consciousness up above the threshold of obscurity and into the light so that it can be revealed to the outer world. However, the heaviness of earthbound inconscience cannot be surpassed without some struggle. In this phase, the soul's inner life is beginning to warm up and to show some signs of future promise.

The **First Quarter** is seen by Rudyar as a crisis of action where a new sense of possibilities is glimpsed. Here one needs willpower and energy to eliminate obstacles and move the revealed possibilities forward. There is more light and consciousness at this stage, but still almost half of the moon's face is darkness. The **Gibbous Moon** has abundant light, and by this time personal development is well established. The energies are mostly turned outward to the world in order to gather and test varieties of experience, and there is increased dynamic activity because the fire element is increasing. The **Full Moon** achieves clear consciousness and a confirmed purpose. Here the Moon radiates as much light as she possibly can. The growing seed of purpose and possibility which entered the world at the **New Moon** becomes fully conscious and can be applied or communicated to the wider world. The abundance of light supports intense activity. The **Disseminating Moon** projects its energy and desires to embody its clear purpose in a focused way. The light has begun to wane; the energy is moving from summer to autumn, and the fruits of previous endeavour are ripening. The **Last Quarter** is a time of crisis when the coming dissolution of structures is foreshadowed. The hero of the cycle must face the approaching darkness and find meaning beyond life's outer appearances or fleeting successes. Fulfillment must now be sought within the limits of the diminishing light and energy, for the cold begins to exceed the warmth and the glow of life is starting to fade.

The **Balsamic Moon** is introverted and future-oriented. Now there is little more to do concerning the central project but to arrange for a long rest. The time of seeding has come, and passed. One can sense the outlines of a greater destiny ahead, beyond this world, as the darkness closes in. Autumn fades into the cold and quiet of winter and a long rest comes on. The Moon disappears as its light is extinguished for three days, and the cycle returns to the time of the New Moon, when a new seed is planted and a new stage of life initiated. This is the primal plot revealed by the Goddess of the Moon through eight phases of elapsing time.

The Moon Goddess is sometimes pictured as a Triple Goddess and the waxing, full and waning stages of the Moon are her principle manifestations. The Triple Goddess reveals herself in three aspects, as a maiden, as a mature lady and as an elderly crone. In Greek myths and elsewhere we have a number of examples of goddesses in all three of these aspects. For example, Demeter is a Lady, but Persephone is a Maiden when we first meet them, prior to the descent into the underworld. Hekate, on the other hand is a manifestation of the old, darkened form of the Goddess.

The Moon Goddess has historically been the revealer of all forms of divination. She can unveil destiny because she weaves it in the first place. Like Odin, who learned divination from the goddess Freya, the seeker who would release the meaning of the runes and bring the light of wisdom to the world must undergo a time of withdrawal and testing. Only by releasing the old, worldly way of seeing (the symbolic loss by Odin of one eye) can the initiate or seer cultivate a new and deeper vision. The archetype of the Goddess has within it many other archetypes which represent varied aspects of its manifestation. Since the Moon gives pattern and measure to the alternating phases of light and dark in the night sky, thus furnishing the fundamentals of cosmology and mythology, her revelation is the first and primal plot that the mind of man has apprehended. In astrology, Moon means the personal way in which a human being shapes and handles the impulse to realization. The forms one accepts in the mind, the emotions of the heart, the kind of physical body that one develops, and the timing of each step forward in the evolution of consciousness - all of these come under the sway of the Moon. The early seers and sages in the dark reaches of what we call prehistory evolved a language and symbology to express the revelations of the Great Mother, and her lunar epiphany, and from this come the Primal Runes.

A true rune is a symbol whose form expresses a primal, archetypal energy. The realities signified by true runes are powers of consciousness. They exist beyond this material world in a dimension of their own, but their energies enter into our human lives and become manifest in our personal experience. A true rune is magical, it is a charged with potency to effect change, and overlaid with information to empower wise choice. A rune's form embodies and expresses its energy and its meaning. Runes can be engraved on gems or carved onto objects for protection, empowerment, prosperity, fertility, or for other energies which they embody and express. The archaeological finds from the time of Old Europe (roughly 2,000 to 7,000 BC) tell us that our ancestors did just this from the very earliest time periods for which we have evidence. Of course, one of the principal uses to which runes have been put is divination. They reveal patterns of energy and meaning which are going on beyond the threshold of our conscious intellect, and thus they help us to understand our lives in a deeper way. The ancients knew more than we do about the powers of sound associated with each of the signs, and about the application of symbols to ritual magic. However, *The Primal Runes* brings us closer to an understanding of how the ancient symbols may be resurrected and put to use in terms meaningful to our own present reality and awareness.

Each rune has a set of associations which derive from its historic use, the shape of the symbol itself, (which is to say its iconography), the rune's relation to the underlying lunar paradigm (which I sometimes call the Lunar Law), and any previous associations it may have had with magical practice, alchemy, sacred alphabets, religious symbolism, mythology, divination, oracles, dream-symbols, Jungian psychology and ancient or modern cosmology.

The shape of a rune is of primary importance. Its physical form reveals the heart of its meaning. Images help those who contemplate them to go beyond mere verbal understandings of meaning to an intuitive and imaginative grasp of a living truth's very essence. The forms of runes must be contemplated to attain this deep insight. Once penetrated by the contemplative mind, a rune's visual form will reveal its character, and its possibilities.

In divination, one is sometimes led to select a single rune appropriate to the prevailing influences of the moment. Alternately, one may toss the runes, all 28 and more, to observe the pattern they form. Typically, some will be facing up, showing that their energy is active, while others may face downward, indicating that their powers are latent. The cloth onto which the runes are tossed may have a pattern that helps to interpret the runes by means of placement. This pattern may also be a mandala of the lunar phases. The wisdom teaching of the moon can be called the Lunar Law because it provides order, measure and structure to the dance of Light and Dark. From the Lunar Law, philosophers in later eras developed concepts of what they referred to as 'natural law'; but it is safe to say that humanity's earliest understanding of natural law was imparted through a relationship to the goddess of the Moon.(see Appendix Five).

For those who want to study and practice seriously with runes over an extended period of time, there is no substitute for wide reading and deep meditation. By studying the tales, legends, beliefs and rituals that underlie the runes, one may access a world of archetypal power and knowledge. At this point, having contacted sources of wisdom-light, and having deepened the inflowing insights in contemplation, the initiate truly draws living water directly from pure sources.

Myth sets symbols in motion. The words and music of a true bard bring the runelore to life. Through bardic performances, long before Homer's Iliad was being recited to the descendents of Hector and Achilles, mythic beings moved, spoke, interacted and revealed the archetypal possibilities of life to human seekers. Many runes are associated with gods and goddesses, or with hero and heroine archetypes who are hidden powers in the hierarchy of our own microcosm. To the extent that these latent powers and beings awaken within our consciousness, we experience life more richly and deeply. To be a king, a sage, a mystic or a warrior, we have only to activate and live those archetypes. Runes are tools of activation, doorways into worlds of archetypal experience, whereby powers and presences of mythic proportion intersect and enrich the life-scripts we live.

The ultimate aim of using runes is to personalize their meanings, internalize their powers and become a living embodiment of their dynamic play. As we bring our inner cosmography fully to life, the runes help us peer into the hidden depths of the scrying pool of destiny. They enhance our powers of intuition and our psychic capacities. With heightened awareness and sensitivity, we are able to attune to subtle energy-flows that underlie and give rise to the material world which so monopolizes our attention. As magical glyphs, the Primal Runes actually embody and communicate the archetypal forces that were active in the golden age of mythology. These energies have been neglected, but they have never completely died away. Rather it is we who have dimmed our minds by forgetting the celestial powers and ignoring the mystic lights of lunar revelation. Consciously or unconsciously, everyone who has awakened the hearts of others through words of poetry or strains of music has been gifted by one or another of the Muses, the nine powers of inspiration who are epiphanies of the Moon.

Writing about the FUTHARK runes in *Rune Magic*, Donald Tyson said:

> Gone are the techniques for applying runes to life situations. Gone are the all-important chants which empowered them and made them function. All that survive are a few pathetic folk charms. References in the heroic sagas of the Norsemen where occasional hints are given as to the use and power of runes. A scattering of historical references. Monuments erected long after the magical use of runes was forgotten. A few riddling rune poems. A small number of artifacts discovered in burial mounds and under bodies of water where they had rested the centuries undisturbed. When you have studied these fragments, you have all that remains of rune lore. Far from being a discouragement, this should provide a challenge to the modern student who has on his side the magical methods of the past and a knowledge of symbolism to help him reconstruct from these hints the full glory of rune magic. Runes operate according to the universal laws of magic. A skilled Magus can reconstruct from his own

> practical experience the ritual methods the teutonic pagans probably used. More importantly, he can create a fully functional system of rune magic that is effective in the present day. (pp. 26 - 27)

Undoubtedly Tyson is right. The occult laws that govern the working of the universe remain constant even as cultures rise and fall. Rune masters open a way into the inner temples where the tablets of life and fate are written in the language of symbolism. The Primal Runes speak not only of our most ancient past, but also of the present and the future, and not only do they speak, they sing. The ancient sounds of power can be used as effectively today as they were thousands of years ago, by the Teutons, and by the children of the Goddess whom they displaced.

The ancient Sumerians record that at the dawn of human history the Goddess Inanna brought the Tablets of Destiny from their hiding place and made them available to mankind. The Primal Runes are an equally ancient set of keys to mystical learning, a primer of revelations which can be carried in the memory and activated in many surprising combinations. Magic and divination are two common ways of employing runes, but the thing to remember is that the mind of the user who follows the path to its end becomes progressively sensitized, purified, widened, illumined and empowered. From the central paradigm of the core tradition, individual variations and creative contributions accumulate as more users achieve creative breakthroughs and the Muse fosters and multiplies the richness of the possibilities.

The sacred lore associated with runes speaks of our earliest awakening when the powers of the Goddess and the working of her magic were alive and fresh. To ponder the runes is to become aware of archetypal reality, and thus to shift consciousness to a higher domain of awareness. When we take this step, our understanding is elevated beyond the contingencies of binding karma and we discover that the wonders of myth and legend express our very own adventure of consciousness.

---

[1] Haarmann, Harald *Early Civilization and Literacy in Europe* (Berlin, 1996) pg. 5.

CHAPTER 3

People of the Moon

In the beginning, only the Great Mystery existed. It was One. There was no other to know it. It has been called the Source, but in truth it cannot be named because it has no form, and is not separate from all that is. This sublime unknowable Source exists beyond time and beyond our capacity for understanding. It simply was and is. Before any names and forms came into being, This has always been. It precedes time and space but holds them both within Itself as a tiny fragment of Its infinite life. Somehow, mysteriously, in the secret heart of the original One, a need was born, a hunger for experience. From this came creation, the 'he' of it and the 'she' of it, the light of it and the dark, the over and the under, heaven and earth. Heaven and earth between them brought forth life, which is the dance of their eternal love. Although they are now two, they want to join as One. From their desire to join, they beget the many, and this is the dance of creation. Hence come all the stories that have ever been, and all the languages to tell them. Of this the poets sing. For this we laugh and weep and dance and procreate. We become lovers because of this memory we have, and this need in our hearts to be re-united with the Source. Even in our forgetfulness of the Source and the true way of return, we have this need to embrace the dance of life and love.

All that is to be known and felt and seen and lived between heaven and earth, the glory of it, the agony, the mystery, lies hidden in the heart of humanity, to be brought forth and given birth in form. The stories of our lives are chapters in the love-epic of heaven and earth. In this context, the timeless Primal Runes came into being at a point in time earlier than recorded human history can document. They are a part of what heaven has to say to earth, modes of the dance that life and love do together to express the eternal in the temporal.

My own personal connection with the Primal Runes unfolded in the context of my inner connection to The Mother (Mirra Alfassa), and her guidance has been so important in all aspects of this work that it would be impossible to go further without explaining her role. In the course of a lifetime of spiritual seeking, I was very fortunate to discover the work of Sri Aurobindo and The Mother and to spend time living at their Ashram. The Mother collaborated with Sri Aurobindo to bring down a very high consciousness which they called the Supermind into the earth atmosphere. They knew that if they succeeded it would change the course of spiritual evolution on earth and open a new chapter of higher possibilities for mankind. Sri Aurobindo spent the last 24 years of his life in seclusion, working inwardly to bring down the Supermind, and he passed away in 1950. In 1956, The Mother told her immediate circle of devotees that a door in the inner world had finally opened and that the golden light from above had begun to descend into the earth. From that time to this, momentous spiritual changes and shifts in consciousness have been taking place all around us as evidence of this spiritual dawning, right down to the mutation of human DNA from its normal two strands upward toward twelve. This was touched on in my earlier work, *Ancient Mysteries Tarot*; now, in exploring the Primal Runes, another ancient field of wisdom, rich in potential both for divination and initiation, has been taken up and opened up in light of the continuous forward momentum of this new spiritual awareness.

Who is The Mother? Perhaps her own words are the most eloquent answer to this question:

> In the terrestrial evolution, man who is emerging out of the inconscience and ignorance, is guided by the Supreme. And the Supreme, in order to manifest His reign upon earth, labours to uplift the human consciousness so as to

establish the Divine Consciousness; and for this, He does not delegate someone but He Himself manifests physically, even in the Ignorance, to accomplish His work. And it is I who have been appointed to raise up man and the creation out of this Inconscience. My child, I am the Unknown that is unseizable, yet I consent to be seized; I am the Unknowable, yet men pretend to know me. I am the infinite but I am constrained to limit myself in a physical body by time and space. I am the Eternal who has submitted itself to be bound in the evolution. I am Immortality which awakes in its innumerable aspects that perish, in order to climb back towards the One, and which has consented to a birth, in order to suffer the terrestrial consequences. I am the Nihil where everything disappears; the Inconscience that denies my presence, yet each atom of this mass of ignorance palpitates with my consciousness. I am the Mystery – the great terrestrial and cosmic evolution. My child, I am the Cause, the great Creatrix from whom everything emanates. All that you can conceive of is created from me, by me and for me it exists. Nothing is which is not in me. You understand, it will take you hundreds of births to understand what I am. And yet I reveal myself to my devotees who love me; and still I shall remain unseizable.

– The Mother, *(The Supreme* pp 5 – 6)

When a part of the Supreme incarnates in human form, humanity is afforded an unparalleled opportunity to choose a higher level of consciousness. All the traditions and disciplines by which this can be accomplished are of immediate concern to The Mother, for her work is to nurture humanity's spiritual aspiration and bring it to its fulfillment in spiritual realization. In particular, however, Sri Aurobindo and The Mother encouraged an integral spiritual practice whose goal was not to escape from worldly ignorance, but to transform it into divine fullness. But how does The Mother's work relate to this study of the Primal Runes?

As a writer, my inspiration usually comes from an inner glimpse of a seed possibility which wants development. It is a revelation from the Muse, which is an aspect of The Mother's creative inspiration, known from the most ancient times. This seed must then be nurtured and developed into some manifest form, in words, in structured thoughts, in harmoniously organized and balanced presentation. I credit the source of my inspiration, the guidance in the work of expressing it and the results it will bring directly to The Mother's guidance. The eternal Mystery of this divine guidance will always elude the logical mind's clutches, but by following the intuitive and inspirational thread inwardly, some very stiking results invariably emerge.

I have pointed out that the Primal Runes are permeated by the living power of the Goddess, humanity's ancient archetype of the Divine Mother. The Moon, from the very earliest times, was the central revelation of what the Goddess had to say to earth and its children. Therefore, the 28 runes which are presented in this book represent the phases of the lunar revelation, and a further three runes representing Primal Darkness, Primal Light, and the Source have been added for a total of 31. These are organized into categories of Earth, Water, Fire, Air and Ether and can best be pictured laid out in a circle, moving from the New Moon up to the Full Moon and back again into darkness. Humanity's earliest archetypes, myths, rituals, religious and spiritual and occult practice, as well as art, divination and agricultural practice were based on the phases of the Lunar Law, which was the revelation of the power and presence of The Goddess.

We know that the earliest forms of human society all over the world gave central importance to the Goddess, and to the Moon as her prime epiphany. But the Primal Runes are rooted in the societies of Old Europe of whom the Pelasgians are one of the better known. These runes were the sacred symbols of the Pelasgians, a people whose culture was already dying out when the Parthenon was being erected in Athens. (See Appendix Four) For thousands of years this culture used the Primal Runes as part of its sacred and occult ritual. But of course, in those days, science, religion, occultism, politics and agriculture were not separated. They were all part of one life lived in the web of destiny woven by the Goddess and her principal emanations. It is still possible to walk the ruins of Knossos and feel and see the elements of one descendent of this earliest civilization, for it does not require much imagination to visualize the ruins as they were several thousand years ago, full of life and colour. These days, after a rainfall, you will find hundreds of potsherds littering the grounds, some with bits of mysterious symbols that derive from the Primal Runes of Old Europe. Through these symbols, humanity expressed its earliest experience of the gods, its interactions with the cosmic archetypes, and its vision of man's place in this world as well as the nature of our relation to the world beyond.

The Old Europe culture, centred on the Danube River, was primarily agricultural. It seems to have developed as a self contained entity, without importing substantial influences from the outside. The core elements of the Aegean culture, including ancient Greece, are no longer seen to have derived from Asia, but rather from Europe. Furthermore, the formative period of Greek culture can confidently be pushed back to the third millennium B.C.,[1] Linear writing may well be one of the early "exports" which moved from Europe to Anatolia and Mesopotamia rather than the reverse.[2] The Greeks of Homer's Illiad had a civilization based on very early elements of Old Europe and more recent developments from the Indo-European invasions.

The culture now called Old Europe is believed to have had a relatively undisturbed development from 5,000 or 6,000 BC right up to 3,500 BC, and the archaeological remains show unbroken continuity through this entire period.[3] The Vinca script which was used through this entire time is so far undeciphered, which means that historians have little to go on and little interest in making any attempt to document what happened. But those who are interested to explore the world's earliest culture and possibly its first recorded religion, will find a wealth of material in the extensive research done by Marija Gimbutas, who almost single-handedly defined the parameters of what we now know as the civilization of Old Europe. Some of the most interesting discoveries undoubtedly lie ahead of us in this new and exciting chapter of our ancient past.

---

[1] Renfrew, c, *The Emergence of Civilisation,* The Cyclades and the Aegean in the Third Millennium B.C. London.

[2] Haarmann, Harald, *Early Cililization and Literacy in Europe,* (Berlin, 1996) pg. 7.

[3] Haarmann, op. cit. Pg. 8.

The Primal Runes

The Field	Seeding	Gestation	Emergence	Thunder
Growth	Challenge	Fire	Choice	Karma
Creativity	Grace	Love	Courage	Fullness
Descent	Wisdom	Mastery	Lake	Transmission
Dreamweaver	Water	Crisis	Sacrifice	Knot
	Mountain	Transformation	Merging	
	Primal Dark	Primal Light	The Source	

CHAPTER 4

Moon Magic

From the earliest times, creation tales have spoken about the emergence of this world and all its living creatures from the original matrix. The word "matrix" itself comes from the same root as "mother" or mater (matter). The oldest creation tales indicate how the Great Mother gave birth to all we see around us. There are common elements in all the tales: a primal void or obscurity; a stirring of existence; an emergence of a divine primal being; the being's will to create; the act of creation, often by means of sound; the devolution of creation from the archetypal domains into a multiplicity of forms, and in the end the emergence of mankind. Details may vary from age to age and culture to culture, but this is the central pattern.

In most tribal societies, the great beings we know as the four sacred elements were among the first to appear on the scene. The original Divine Mother gave birth to them at the dawn of creation. They were considered gods, and were personified. Thus the Lord and Lady of Water and the Lord and Lady of Fire, and so on, were given many names in different ages and cultures, but their importance at the starting point of creation was always acknowledged.

Every soul born into this world as a human being has had to pass through the various layers of creation, one layer at a time. In each of these stages, the soul receives an essential dimension of its constitution. After having lived in these layers or lives in the inner world, the child is given final form and born into this physical layer of the earth, the world of material form. In this way, all souls relive the history of the world, and we are each a diminutive microcosm with everything inside us that is writ large in the greater universe around us.

Often, in the oldest myths, it is the weaver-goddess, or sometimes a triple-goddess, the three Fates, who work up (spin and weave) the substance and the destiny of a soul which is about to incarnate. Yin and Yang energies are the warp and woof of the loom of creation. There are many variations to the tale, but the soul receives its fire (soul, will, creativity) in the world of fire, its mental gifts from the kingdom of air, its emotional makeup from the world of water, and its physical constitution in the world of earth. Sometimes a fifth substance or dimension, that of ether, is referred to. This is equivalent to spirit, the heavenly kingdom, the abode of the Great Goddess. But it too is often pictured as a multi-layered kingdom.

From the kingdom of fire you get all the fiery powers. On the physical level, the warmth of the blood and the digestive fire are two examples of this. On the emotional level, a hot temper or an ardent emotional nature would derive from fire; on the intellectual level, creativity, enthusiasm and initiative are fiery in nature; and on the plane of spirit, aspiration and heroic endeavour come from fire.

From the kingdom of air come the airy powers. Air conveys the fiery power and facilitates its embodiment. It is a vehicle of co-ordination and communication. The Breath-Spirit (pneuma) is the medium through which the fiery soul can unite with the Primal Mud (water-earth). Air is moist and warm whereas fire is warm and dry. The moist aspect of air gives it the power of flexibility; its warmth gives it the ability to bring about differentiation. Thus, air represents a capacity for active change of form. Those who have a strong air endowment, for example, are nimble in analysis, flexible in discrimination, and fertile in ideas. Air separates things, creates divisions and distinctions, puts limit to the unlimited, brings things together in a higher, spiritual unity, and ultimately brings individuated souls into oneness with the world soul. Air's influence can be active not only on its own natural level, which is the world of mind, but also in the world of soul (sometimes called spirit), in the realm of emotions (astral), and on the physical level.

The essence of water is to mix and hold together while being changeable in shape. Water is primarily cool (giving it ability to bind things together), but secondarily moist (giving power to dissolve structure and form). Water permits the growth and development of form; it is characterized by passive change of form. This is how the astral world appears, a fluid flow of forms, in contrast to the physical world which has enough of the earth element to give fixity and stability. The dissolving power of water comes about because its cool (uniting) quality allows it to attach to solid matter of all sorts, but its moist (conforming, flexible) qualilty causes the result to have no fixed form. In water all things lose their rigid structure and form and identity. A passive loss of form is typical of water's action. Water thus represents the spiritual principle of flexible union which permits both dissolution and transformation. On the emotional level, water is connecting and relating (cool) as well as conforming and empathetic (moist). It gives us an ability to relate, to feel emotion, to have an inner flow of feeling-attunement which can blossom into intuition (when rightly blended with fire).

Earth is passive and form-imposing. It is an inflexible synthesis of energy, quite stable and inert. Earth tends to crystallise things, like molten wax which has been poured into a mould. Earth is cool and dry. Its dry power causes things to fix their form and structure; it gives shape, structure and solidity. Psychologically it results in a character that is stubborn, purposeful, dependable, practical, rigid, unreceptive, inflexible, strict, concrete and grounded. Earth's cool power unites things. It mixes, joins, synthesizes and relates things of different kinds as it contracts. It is inward directed, concentrated and quiet. It makes for formations that are stable, steadfast and enduring. The psychology of an earthy nature would be indecisive, undiscriminating, nurturing, careless, sympathetic, co-operative and loving. An "earthy" type of person who is the "salt of the earth" or who is a "pillar of strength" embodies many of these characteristics. They may have earthy energy on the spiritual, the mental, the emotional or the physical level, although earth's fixed nature is most evident on the physical plane.

In the creation stories, there are sometimes two deities, male and female, who assemble humans before they are born. But sometimes the tales tell of three beings, and very often there is only one. On each of the four levels (five if you include ether) the deity or deities assemble a part of your being. They utter special magical words or syllables, and these words become the very things they designate. There is a magical language where vibrations correspond exactly to the energies they designate. The gods have this language at their command, and when they utter a thing, it is manifest. Thus, the weaving of spells by means of sound, the magic of the creative word, is the process by means of which the divine ones assemble us. The spark of divine fire, or soul, is invested with its fiery qualities such as will, creativity, enthusiasm; then it is given its airy qualities, its water qualities, earthy qualities, and finally its physical body.

The spell-weaving of the divine assemblers never ends, it goes from one layer to the next. We are put together with word-magic. These words are places in our physical being, in our psyche, and on the earth too. The incarnating soul is passed down from one level of creation to the next, from fire to air, from air to water, and from water to earth, and slowly all the capacities and gifts are added to it until physical birth takes place.

The moment of birth is significant, because the configuration of the planets and stars is an exact description of the nature and destiny of the new human being. Astrology and mythology are intimately related, and they tell in complementary ways about our origins and potential. When you are born, a little of the magic still remains, but slowly as you grow up, it wears off.

Each of us enters into spiritual amnesia and for the rest of our lives we try to remember who we are and where we came from. Knowing this, we can discover our purpose for living and our ultimate goal. This knowledge is power. The runes are a symbolic language of empowerment. The rune symbols and their corresponding sounds hold keys to the process by which we are created and also the conditions which allow us to unfold and realize our full potential.

For example, the Gestation rune signifies a time of integration with the matrix, the womb, the original physical ground of being. The Emergence rune and the Thunder rune herald entry into the outer world and catalyst of change that lead to the Growth rune. Growth inevitably requires coming to terms with challenges, and the Challenge rune leads on to Fire, which is energy and clarity, and futher to the Choice and Karma runes. There is a natural progression of experience in this sequence, an outer pattern that reflects an inner unfolding.

The Primal Runes picture a world in which the Great Mother presides over creation through its many planes and processes. She gives life and takes it away. She imparts form and dissolves it. She is often pictured as the triple goddess, meaning that she has (apart from her fourfold manifestation as earth, air, fire and water) three faces. She is a maiden, a mature lady and an old crone. In these three aspects she concerns herself with different phases of creation and life-experience.

We have a hint of this in Tarot, especially with the court cards. The four suites represent the four sacred elements. Pentacles are Earth; cups are Water; swords are Air, and wands are Fire. There are four queens, namely the queens of Earth, Air, Fire and Water (or pentacles, swords, wands and cups) and each queen is associated with a consort, who is her king. She is also associated with a knight, or warrior, who is her champion, or hero, and also with a page, or youth, who is under her tutelage, whom she educates and fosters. Thus, for example, the Queen or Lady of Water is matched with the King or Lord of Water. They are defended and served by the warrior or hero or knight of Water. And they nurture and foster the child of Water, who is the page. This symbolic structure which we find in the court cards of Tarot has its roots in the most ancient myths and legends.

Consider The Mother's symbol. At the centre there is a circle, representing the Absolute, the Source, The Great Mother beyond form. From this come four petals which are her four primary manifestations. These can be termed the four sacred beings or primal elements, namely Fire, Air, Water and Earth. From each of these four petals come three further petals, which we can see as the triple form of the goddess, namely the maiden, the lady and the crone. The Mother's symbol (shown below) has three layers, first the central circle of infinity; second the four primal elements represented by four petals, and thirdly the twelve petals, three each for the four elements.

Fig. 3: The Mother's Symbol

The Moon cycle has two phases. From the New Moon to the Full Moon is a time of increasing light. From the Full Moon to the New Moon is a time of waning light. These two phases are divided into four quarters: from the New Moon to the First Quarter; from the First Quarter to the Full Moon; from the Full Moon to the Third Quarter; and from the Third Quarter to the New Moon. Each quarter is a unit of seven days. Each seven day period is, of course, a week. Thus a seven-day week is a fundamentally lunar unit of time – the word "month", which is a period of four weeks, also reflects this.

The Moon is the Goddess as she appears in the night sky. From her come measurement, time, and its cyclic patterns. This is part of her magic and power, to govern all things by placing them in the web, or net of time. The energies of four, seven and twenty-eight are part of the Great Mother's cosmology. Three and nine are also important numbers for the Great Mother, examples being the Triple Goddess which we have mentioned, and the nine Muses. The waning and waxing of light as reflected by the Moon is also a story fraught with meaning, and this story is fundamentally important for our human experience as it relates to divination and initiation.

If we want to recognize and understand the primal patterning of energy and life that we experience as human beings on earth, we must reckon with the given elements of the universe. On earth, from the most ancient times the Goddess, her representative the Moon, time and its cycles, sound, symbolism and sacrifice have basic components of human experience. The Primal

Runes reflect an ancient and timeless wisdom, a symbology of revelation by means of which the mind can see beyond appearances to glimpse the inner patterning that makes a human destiny. The Fullness rune is not only a time when light is most abundant in the night sky, it is also an opening of energetic passages to higher consciousness, a time for contemplation, ritual and magic, as ancient societies have always known. Water is much more than dyhydrogen oxide. Water is a power of purification and dissolution, a memory-holding matrix of life and consciousness, all of which is embodied in the Water Rune. Mountain (in the Mountain Rune) is much more than simply a geological upheaval. Mountain is lofty power and presence, spiritual sanctuary and stillness. Mountains feed the lowlands below with life-giving streams of water. All of this the Mountain rune expresses in only a few deft lines of engraving. The more deeply we study the ancient runes, the more clear it becomes that symbols are tools not only for the attainment of understanding, but also for changing consciousness. Knowledge is power to shape and transform destiny so that it follows our ideals and our intent. Initiation is a choice of higher destiny which The Goddess will support if we approach her in the right way.

The bards were the ancient voice of the mystical beyond. They were trained to hear and to celebrate the great archetypes of creation, and this they did through their inspired words and music. Often prophetic, always powerful and deeply moving, their ability to evoke the primal magic has never been lost. Bards are still with us, though rarely accorded official recognition as in times gone by. Not long ago, I wrote this bardic expression of the many roles that the Mother can play in our lives. It may suggest some of that wonder that we still feel when we gaze on the Moon.

> She shines in the power of being, as mother, queen, womb,
> As lilt in the laughter of children,
>   And love that shapes their doom.
> As dream finding form, or as light in the mist,
> She does and undoes all things that exist.
> From the heart to the smile, so swift and unseen,
> Her breath is the spirit of all that has been;
> From the soul to the tear, so subtle and sure,

Her presence is beauty in all that is pure.
She is queen of the forest, the magic in trees,
The voice of the brook, the caress of the breeze;
Her heart is life's goodness, her wisdom its Way,
Her peace is its twilight, her power its day.
She planted the rose in the heart of the child,
And buried the petals that time had defiled;
She reaps what is sown, and attracts to her heart
The lives and the loves that have broken apart.
She is all that embraces, and all that draws home,
The sleep at the end of the paths that we roam;
In the power of Being, the Mother of all
Is the unfolding soul, and the unending call.

CHAPTER 5

Archetypes

"Do we ever understand what we think? We understand only such thinking as is a mere equation and from which nothing comes out but what we have put in. That is the manner of working of the intellect. But beyond that there is a thinking in primordial images – in symbols that are older than historical man; which have been ingrained in him from earliest times, and, eternally living, outlasting all generations, still make up the groundwork of the human psyche. It is possible to live the fullest life only when we are in harmony with these symbols; wisdom is a return to them. It is a question neither of belief nor knowledge, but of the agreement of our thinking with the primordial images of the unconscious. They are the source of all our conscious thoughts, and one of these primordial images is the idea of life after death."

– Carl Jung, *Modern Man in Search of a Soul*, pgs. 129 – 30.

The myths, legends, cosmologies and divinatory systems of humanity give name and form to the archetypes in an external way. But the source of their inspiration is an inward image which is at work in the depths or heights of the human psyche.

When we speak of archetypes, we are discussing not only: a) the consciousness which is the primary reality, but also b) the symbolic expression and material forms through which this can be rendered, and lastly c) the content, or structure of the archetype insofar as it can be grasped by the mind.

An archetype such as that of the hero may be traced through history. It may be expressed in different forms in different cultures, which means that its symbolism can vary. However changeable the forms may be, the core reality of the archetype consists of its emotional-dynamic content, the energy processes which the archetype awakens within the human psyche.

It is quite clear that different archetypes have different effects, and we can see from these effects that each archetype embodies a different kind of consciousness. Some psychologists go so far as to say that when a mood takes hold of the entire personality it is evidence of the dynamic impact of an archetype. The conscious mind may not know the theory of archetypes, the thought processes may not be able to articulate what is at work, but this does not matter. The existence and action of archetypes does not depend on human belief or recognition.

When an archetype is at work, it manifests in one way or another in the lived, personal experience of a real human being. The congruence of symbols, images and archetypal experience is well known. Quite often, the mind may become aware of a psychic image related to whatever archetype has been activated. Different archetypes evoke different images. These images are most often experienced in dreams, and their forms may be quite other than what we can see and touch in the physical world of our normal waking consciousness.

Archetypes have a strong emotional component and impact. When they are at work, there is a compelling dynamic that seizes upon the individual and brings about changes in his or her instincts, passions, affections and in the overall feeling-tone of the personality. This can be thought of as the *action of the archetype*. Archetypes pre-exist human individuals and lend or impart their specific qualities when they come to the fore.

The unconscious content of an archetype only becomes fully conscious for us when it can be represented, which means expressed in the form of an image. When understood rightly, the image or symbol evokes an awareness of the reality to which it refers. A true image or symbol is one which mediates the *full energy and consciousness* of the archetype. Such a symbol firstly attracts our attention, and then it produces its impression. We feel different when we experience a true symbol in a complete way. Through the symbol, we glimpse the reality to which it refers.

This hidden reality may be fascinating, impressive, terrible, overpowering, compelling or enchanting, but above all a genuine and primal archetype will have a sense of power and potential.

We humans are made in such a way that the unformed instincts within our inner psyche must be 'outered', which is to say given expression by significant forms, if we wish to understand, work with and eventually master them. To express the unconscious content of our inner psyche in true and powerful forms is what great art attempts to accomplish. A true artist must simultaneously be aware of an inner, instinctive power or drive which is experienced through the intuitive feelings, and an outer set of images, forms, rhythms or colours which arrest and command attention. Archetypes have this same dual nature. They are inwardly dynamic, powerful and activating, and outwardly they are mediated through significant forms.

Carl Jung says that the archetypes "exist pre-consciously, and presumably they form the structural dominants of the psyche in general."(*Trinity*, p. 148). This suggests that archetypes are present and at work within us even though we are not aware of them. They act to magnetize and energize the behavior of the outer personality. Archetypes speak their presence through urges, intimations, instincts, intuitions, and processes of feeling-attunement.

At the same time, archetypes can work through symbolic images because these images organize, direct and specify the unconscious content of the archetypes, enabling us to have a more conscious and enriching interaction with them.

In many cases a significant archetype is expressed by a group or constellation of symbols. The more developed our awareness becomes, the more clearly we can differentiate the meanings and powers of the various symbols within such a group. As we refine and order our powers of awareness, and as our ability to distinguish a variety of subtle energies grows, we have fuller access to experiences of the archetypes. We may then begin to work with archetypes consciously, intelligently and co-operatively. As our awareness grows, we fit the archetypes and their symbols into a unified understanding of the universe, a cosmology in which each part has its place. The opposite polarities of light and dark, male and female, high and deep all find a place within the pattern of the whole.

Symbols, like the archetypes themselves, are conduits of living force. Outwardly symbols and images are physically embedded and fixed, but inwardly, as experienced in our consciousness, they can be dynamic and empowering. When symbols have been organized by the mind into a system, a picture of the world and how it works, what we have is a cosmology.

Symbols and cosmologies not only inform the mind, but more significantly they empower it. Primal images have an uncanny ability to take hold of the human personality and arouse it, fascinate it, energize it, and draw it into new levels of awareness. Sometimes through this process the human mind can learn to have a conscious interaction with the unseen powers of the beyond, and when this happens our understanding of life and its complexity is considerably deepened and widened.

Once aroused by a symbol, the awakened human consciousness can direct its attention and interest toward the core of the symbol's energy and meaning, in an effort to attain full understanding. The symbol thus sets the mind in motion; it is a catalyst or activator. A profound transformation of energy takes place in human consciousness as the meaning of archetypal symbols is contemplated and assimilated.

Archetypes, when correctly approached through their images and symbols, can alter and mould consciousness. The awakening mind, in an attempt to become fully aware of its own unconscious content and capacity, may begin to explore images, myths and cosmologies of the ancient world. In the end a seeker may discover that the hero, the quest, the great goal and the unfolding adventure are all parts of the reader's very own story. The gods, devils and sublime powers are all facets of one's own microcosm.

If we want to evolve in consciousness, we must develop a new mode of being aware. The pattern and meaning of our personal experience in this three-dimensional time-space continuum becomes more clear to us as we explore the meanings of symbols. As we extend our awareness, we experience things, their arrangements in space, their inter-relations with each other and with ourselves, their colours, forms and names as pointing beyond the multiplicity of many separate parts to a vision of integrated wholeness. Contemplating symbols, the cosmology they shape, and our own place in the greater whole, we go beyond fragmentation toward a mystical experience of oneness.

Those who journey this path often set aside some of their social, cultural and mental conditioning. Many seekers begin to let go of their educational heritage of intellectualism, materialism, and positivism; they no longer want to limit their experience of the universe to what can be processed by the five senses and the rational mind. Such seekers transcend a merely rational or verbal interaction with reality in favour of direct experience and this leads to profound personal insight.

Slowly or rapidly it dawns on such a seeker that only a non-materialistic, a spiritual, point of view can release the mind from the limitation of its mental conditioning and propel it to a wider realization. Sometimes quickly, at other times slowly, the seeker learns that concentration, meditation, ritual and intuitive attunement are powerful means to open deeper modes of knowing, seeing, feeling. Thus, in time, one comes to experience the wider world of the spirit.

Archetypal images and symbols communicate to us in accordance with the kind of consciousness we use in experiencing them. When we see, feel and relate to sacred space and its symbolic contents in the right way, we experience an inner transformation. Contemplating THAT which lies beyond appearances, one comes know Self in all things, and all things within the Self. In ancient times, the Chinese sage, Huai Nan Tzu wrote :

> The masters of the secret teaching say:
> "That the truth learned from another is of no value,
> And that the only truth which is living and effective,
> Which is of value,
> Is the truth which we ourselves discover."

When we contemplate an archetype, our inner psyche assimilates the contents of its symbol or image. This assimilation generates views, visions, perspectives and understandings that were not evident before. A vast number of forms, forces, images, viewpoints, aspects, concepts and insights may pour into the consciousness when one connects inwardly with a significant archetype, such as that of the Goddess. Long before one can describe or even grasp what an archetype is, or what a particular archetype means, one may experience this enrichment on the energetic and intuitive level. The diversity of our experiences and the sometimes contradictory nature of the energies at work can be bewildering. It becomes necessary to find a story or a cosmology or a paradigm to bring order and meaning to this multi-faceted process. When we do this, we grow in knowledge and in wisdom.

It can and does sometimes happen that an archetype may appear spontaneously and express itself in the consciousness of an individual quite by surprise. It may operate independently of the individual's mental notions and opinions, independently of the situation where the occurrence takes place, and beyond the mentality of the group with which the individual is affiliated. An archetype may function as an autonomous force that determines the actual situation which is unfolding on the human level. It may appear as a living presence that intrudes unpredictably, with the strangeness and unfamiliarity of something quite other than what is considered to be normal. But for the most part the nature of the archetype will be related to the race, the group, the historical epoch, the actual situation of the collectivity, and the unique circumstances of the individual to whom it appears. For this reason, Jung refers to archetypes as part of the 'content of the unconscious'.

The ego as the centre of consciousness does not actively and knowingly participate in the genesis and emergence of a true symbol or archetype; the individual consciousness cannot "make" a symbol or "choose" an experience of an archetype. One kind of archetypal experience may illustrate this point. It is sometimes said that early man experienced a paradoxical simultaneous presence of good and evil together, friendliness and terror mixed, in the godhead. Then, as consciousness developed the good and the bad were separated from each other and worshiped as separate beings. It may therefore come as a complete surprise when the modern mind experiences an inner presence at once terrible and blessingful, menacing but inviting, numinous but dark because this is no part of our religious training or experience.

Myth is the language natural to the archetypal dynamic, and symbol is the original language of the unconscious mind. Symbols contain both conscious and unconscious elements. They relate not to the individual ego, but to the whole of the psychic system, on many levels of energy and awareness. Some elements of a symbol can be assimilated quickly. Others can only be assimilated in the course of a long development, or a prolonged contemplation. A symbol has both rational and irrational elements. It combines the conscious and unconscious, both on the inner and outer levels, and all of these are held together as an original and natural unity, prior to mental analysis or commentary. Symbols facilitate the communication of the unconscious to the conscious part of our human microcosm. A symbol suggests, hints, stimulates. Consciousness is thereby awakened, and must use its faculties to assimilate the content of the symbol. To the extent that this is accomplished, the archetype acts with greater or lesser power upon the feelings, intuitions and sensations to bring about change. When consciousness takes a step forward into greater understanding, freedom or clarity, an important inner work has been accomplished.

Runes are powerful tools in this process because they do more than merely refer to archetypes. In the very structure of their iconography, they *are* archetypal. For example, the right side of an occult icon is distinguished from the left side, and both are distinguished from the centre by principles of polarity in relationship to the bindu point of maximum gravity. The right side is traditionally positive in polarity, or masculine, and the left side is negative, or feminine. The centre is the focus of power, representing the inmost, the sacred. Vertical lines move from earth to heaven and back again while horizontal lines represent experience within the eartly time-space continuum. The triangle is a symbol for fire from the very earliest times, because its inherent structure expresses the inner realities of the fire element. The earth element is well expressed by a four-sided square, or if we were thinking in three dimensions, by a cube. Archetypal symbols actually embody the realities to which they refer, just as the rhythms and sounds of good poetry invoke the living energies of consciousness which they describe.

The process of widening that takes place when human consciousness comes face to face with that which transcends all its categories of thought and understanding in an unpredictable fashion is sometimes called empowerment or initiation. As instruments of awakening and enrichment, archetypes have played an important role from the earliest times. In initiation and divination, as well as in myths, rituals, philosophy and cosmology from the dawn of recorded history archetypes have carried us forward in our quest for Truth.

CHAPTER 6

Runelore

> A few can climb to an unperishing sun,
> Or live on the edges of the mystic moon
> And channel to earth-mind the wizard ray.
> The heroes and the demigods are few
> To whom the close immortal voices speak
> And to their acts the heavenly clan are near.
> Few are the silences in which Truth is heard,
> Unveiling the timeless utterances in her deeps,
> Few are the splendid moments of the seers.
> Heaven's call is rare, rarer the heart that heeds;
> The doors of light are sealed to common mind
> And earth's needs nail to earth the human mass,
> Only in an uplifting hour of stress
> Men answer to the touch of greater things...
>
> – Sri Aurobindo, *Savitri*, Book XI, Canto 1

Runes are images, some might say 'archetypal' images. In divination, an image or icon speaks its own meaning in answer to the questions we may have, relative to any given situation. Any given rune or archetype usually comprises a set of related meanings that constitute a field of energy and consciousness. The more structured our thinking is, the more difficult it may be for us to learn the language of symbols and have direct experience of the teaching that they convey.

Occasionally, when we practice divination with runes, it is the inner, unspoken question which is addressed by the runes, rather than the apparent question which our conscious mind entertains. The answers, which in Primal Runes are understood to come from the Goddess, have to get through to us on some level deeper than mere intellect, because they are meant to speak to the intuitive, holistic side of our being. In this process, our usual logic may be overshadowed by the numinous guidance from above, and this is something for which we may be unprepared. Sometimes, we are meant to assimilate the energy or consciousness of several images without completely understanding what they signify. Insight into the full meaning of a reading may not come at the time the runes are cast, it sometimes comes much later. But it goes without saying that when our intelligence is open, alert and unstructured, we are likely to benefit as much as possible from any given reading.

When I use the word "energy", I mean the quality of consciousness and the force which is operative at any given moment of time which allows us to experience a particular reality. Our energy-level establishes the kinds of experiences to which we have access. For example, if we are tired we may also be irritable and unsympathetic, but when we are well rested, we may feel buoyant and cheerful. Usually, we do not notice the quality of the energy, but rather the reactions in ourselves that it makes possible. We recognize our own emotions, our behaviour and the quality of our vitality, and from this we infer what the energy might be. But we have a capacity, largely undeveloped, to experience energy and consciousness more directly than that. It is not only through feelings, attitudes and impressions that we gather indications of what energy is present. Persons involved with oriental martial arts or healing often develop this sense of *chi*, and in ancient languages such as Sanskrit there is a considerable vocabulary for articulating the different phases of both energy and consciousness. Again, it is one thing to discuss energy but quite another to be able to activate it in others. For the most part, energy remains an intellectual concept for most westerners, rather than a living experience.

The Primal Runes signify states of energy and consciousness, and when we work with them we become more aware of these constituents of our human microcosm. Initially, the forces designated by the runes seem to transcend what we know ourselves to be, but once they become alive and real for their user, they act like a catalyst. The Primal Runes awaken various ranges of energy and consciousness so that the limited personality and ego are attuned to, and ultimately infused by, the archetypal realities of the macrocosm. This is what ancient tradition often referred to as bringing about 'the marriage of heaven and earth', and it is a major step toward the attainment of the universal consciosness, also sometimes called the 'cosmic initiation'.

The ranges of energy and consciousness associated with runic archetypes are often impersonal, sometimes nonrational, and frequently mythic or dreamlike in the way they impinge on human awareness. If we wish to embrace these wider ranges of the cosmic reality, or penetrate the lunar revelation which is so important for earth, we must become sensitized to flows of feeling and intuitive attunement that we may not initially be able to articulate or understand. In time, archetypal realities become part of one's own direct experience, and one grows into the wisdom, peace and wideness of being which they communicate.

Only when the logical intellect is counterbalanced by the intuitive and creative side of our being is it likely to preserve a disposition of openness to the depth and mystery of rune-lore. The French have a very good word for this. One who is receptive to the guidance being given can be called "*disponible*". When we seek greater understanding than we can derive from the runes which are before us, we always have the option of drawing more runes or doing additional castings to refine our understanding of the message that we are receiving.

What is discouraged in this tradition is to ask the same question twice, hoping for a more favourable response the second time round. At that point we tend to get readings which reflect our own incorrectness of approach. When our attitude to the divine and the Archetypes is respectful and open-minded, we experience a supportive, helpful presence. However, when we depart from 'right relationship' to the inner sources that we are consulting, we will soon find ourselves set adrift. Skepticism, doubt, disrespect, ill-will, mockery, frivolity, and indifference are all contrary to what is meant by 'right relationship'. These may be present at the conscious or at the unconscious level. Their presence in any degree will tend to mitigate the effectiveness of divination. The inner help will evaporate when we depart from the Way. Indeed, we may have to lose this sustaining and guiding presence before we become aware of its value and miss it. Only then will we re-awaken a sincere need and begin to re-establish the right attitude.

If we correct our outlook and resume a disposition which honours the sacredness of the process, the guiding light gradually returns. The coming and going of higher help on an invisible level, which although not verifiable by the five senses can nonetheless be felt and intuited, gradually educates us about the importance and the nature of 'right relation' to the archetypes in the field of divination. This applies not only when using the Primal Runes, but in many or most other kinds of divination, including Tarot.

In *The Philosophy of the I Ching*, Carol Anthony writes:

> Contemplation is the effort to see, to bring into conscious focus the connections between our external experience and its origins in the image world. If we understand the underlying image, we understand the thing. We see it (in a flash) in its cosmic placement, or hierarchy, and in its relationship to other things. This need to see, to solve a particular problem, exists as a sort of *coan*, or Cosmic Puzzle. It is our nature to solve these puzzles, for through coming into contact with the Creative, we learn about our spiritual nature and the meaning of life. *Coans* are part of the inner growth process by which we bring into being our spiritual existence. ... The problem is inherently cosmic in nature, requiring that we come into the proper relationship with the Creative to obtain its solution. (p 124)

In time, when we are aligned to divine providence and attain access to the divine forces, we are able to accomplish inner change by drawing down celestial powers. Grace becomes the 'doer' of the inner work of transformation in our microcosm. In the West, coming into a steady relation with higher help is sometimes called living in a state of grace, but in the Far East, the same process might be referred to as attaining 'the Tao'. The Primal Runes teach their user to develop intuitive attunement to these invisible, higher forms of energy and consciousness, however we name or understand them, and whatever our cultural background or previous mental conditioning.

Eventually, if we practice consistently and in the right spirit, we become affiliated to the guiding light of the Divine itself. Then, it is possible to complete the work of bringing our microcosm to a state of wholeness and balance. At this point, The Field becomes The Fullness. Each person who undertakes this inner work in a spirit of sincerity based on openness, respect and trust will find that the Primal Runes are a wellspring of inestimable help and support.

One interesting aspect of rune-lore is that the themes associated with any given image or archetype evolve and develop over time, becoming more complex, rich and meaningful. In this world we live in, consciousness is ever evolving, and the core meaning of a symbol cannot signify precisely the same scope of meaning for us today as it did for the earliest Europeans at the end of the stone age. For one thing, our world has become wired for instantaneous communication, and we have seen a coming together of spiritual and religious traditions from all parts of the world. We can draw on traditions of shamanism from many cultures and geographic regions. We also have easy access to excellent historical records of the philosophers and occultists of the past from all parts of the world. Their writings and thoughts about divination, cosmology and symbolism are readily available in modern libraries and book stores, making information that was formerly hard to find quite easy to access. As a tool for research, the Internet gives us wonderful time-saving advantages never before known. Our modern understanding of any given symbol draws on a variety of sources, whereas the ancients would mostly have studied only their own local tradition, apart from some exceptional individuals like Pythagoras or Plutarch who traveled widely.

Students of spirituality and magic are quite used to looking for universal patterns that pull together very diverse sources of information. The best books in these fields furnish rich overlays of correspondence drawn from many cultures and historical eras. For example, Joseph Campbell's books on mythology synthesize quite diverse sources into recognizable patterns. In this he was building on work done earlier in Frazer's *The Golden Bough* and he undoubtedly read Robert Graves' *The White Goddess*. We cannot guess what a wealth of material has been lost to us in the destruction of the great libraries of Mesopotamia, Alexandria and

Rome. It is possible that good study resources for divination and magic may have been more accessible than we know in ancient times, at least in certain cities and for certain people. What is certain, however, is that today we can all study and compare the spirituality and mythology of ancient China, India, Mesopotamia, Egypt, Greece and Meso-America to develop a rich synthetic overview of the meanings of important archetypes. All of this must feed into any modern application of the Primal Runes, if they are to be a tool of relevance, fully applicable to the complex conditions of life in the twenty-first century.

What, then, are the Primal Runes, in essence? The Primal Runes constitute a revelation of the Lunar Law, the main outlines of which are summarized in a separate chapter. To discern a system of divination in the sacred symbols of Old Europe, a combination of intuition, logic, and a good grasp of tradition are requisite. Since we have little direct evidence about how the peoples of Old Europe saw themselves and their world, we must infer from the available sources, some of which are archaeological, and some of which come from later periods of history. The mythology and cosmology of the ancient Near East and Greece, and even Egypt are very helpful as windows into an earlier era which lacks written records. We know that the Indo-Europeans incorporated many elements of previous culture and belief into their own world view when they conquered and absorbed the peoples of Old Europe. Their myths and legends show this quite clearly. The following considerations were brought to bear while studying and writing on the Runes to find ways in which they could be applied to divination:

1) The meanings of the Primal Runes, whatever they might have been to the people who first devised them, must still be able to speak to us in our own time. When a very ancient rune is dusted off and used for divination in modern times, it can not be solely a question of what the given image might have meant to people living seven thousand years ago. It is important to know how the image has evolved over time, and what is the fullness of its current meaning. True archetypes (which the Primal Runes certainly are) are timeless, but what we see in them depends on our own perspective, which includes our cultural and historic placement

and our individual mental conditioning. Meaning accumulates and is enriched with the passage of time.

2) The pattern of lunar time was centrally significant as a primary revelation of ancient Goddess-wisdom. From this, and from certain symbols themselves, we know that four stages of the lunar cycle were of particular importance: the New Moon, the First Quarter, the Full Moon and the Last Quarter. One ancient symbol in particular, a cross inside a circle, is found from the earliest times, and is interpreted as an image of lunar time.

3) The Four Sacred Elements are another important foundation of ancient tradition. Each of the four lunar months can be associated with a phase of energy described by Earth, Water, Air and Fire. In the Primal Runes, the New Moon and two or three days (runes) on either side are assigned to Earth, for a total of six; the First Quarter and two or three days (runes) on either side are assigned to Fire; the Full Moon and two or three days (runes) on either side are assigned to Air, and the Last Quarter, with two or three days (runes) on either side are assigned to Water.

4) Certain runes correspond to the four Turning Points, namely Thunder, Grace, Lake and Mountain. These relate to the Fifth Sacred Element, which is called Ether. Ether is a term (like "soul" or "spirit") which is used in many different ways by different writers at different times. I am using it to mean the plane of reality which lies beyond the Four Sacred Elements. Ether is not exactly pure spirit, but leads beyond mind and connects human consciousness to Pure Spirit. Ether is not mind or the mental plane (to which Air corresponds), and it is not emotion or the astral plane (to which Water corresponds); nor is it Fire (will and vitality). The Ether runes are drawn from symbols involving the sound "A" (as in Father). There are four of them, placed roughly equidistant between the runes of the Four Sacred Elements in the Lunar Cycle, with a further two Ether-runes positioned in the centre to designate Primal Light and Primal Dark, for a total of six. In the unfolding of the Lunar Cycle, the Turning Points and their runes are special times of spiritual opening. For example, Mountain rune signifies consciousness turning inward; Thunder rune signifies consciousness turning outward, and the Grace rune

signifies consciousness turning upward. The Lake rune is a movement of consciousness from the individual to the collective, or consciousness transcending the small ego.

5) The Cypriot Syllabary was a primary source to reference the sounds that were used by the ancients, the sounds that correspond to the various rune-symbols. Thus, from the many signs and symbols (close to 250) which we have so far discovered in the culture of Old Europe, (sometimes called the Vinca Script) a subset corresponding to the Cypriot Syllabary became especially relevant as the only source which could tell us what sounds the ancients would have matched to the various signs. As we have arranged these runes, in accordance with ancient tradition, Earth energy corresponds to the sound "U" as in "BLUE"; Fire energy is expressed in the sound "I" as in "MY"; Air energy is expressed by "E" as in "GREY"; and Water energy is expressed in the sound "O" as in "GO". The sound "A" as in "FATHER" corresponds to Ether. In several cases, rune symbols were taken directly from the Old Europe script because the iconography was a more exact replication of the meaning. Examples of this include Fire, Lake, Field, Water and Fullness.

6) The 28 stages of meaning coded in the Lunar Cycle are well attested in astrology, mythology and cosmology, and they arise as archetypes in other traditional systems of divination as well. In essence, The Lunar Cycle has been understood from the earliest times as an unfolding story of a possibility (for example, the possibility of *apotheosis* that can be attained by a hero) that comes into being from celestial sources, is born into the material world of earthly limitation, is nurtured and developed to mature expression, tested, sacrificed, interred and reborn after three days of lunar darkness. The twenty-eight days of the lunar month are divided into four groups corresponding to the four Sacred Elements. Seven runic symbols from the Cypriot Syllabary (and in some cases the Old Europe Vinca Script on which it is based) constitute the Earth week, seven constitute the Fire week, and so on. There is a correspondence between the iconography of the symbol and the meaning which it expresses in this system. A "Turning Point" rune with Ether-energy is found at the mid-point of each lunar week. These four runes, as well as Primal Light, Primal Dark and Source are

associated with the sound "A", which represents a creative energy of a higher order corresponding to the ranges of meaning associated with the concept of Ether. This brings the total from 28 to 31 runes in all.

7) The 8 trigrams of I Ching were very useful as stages of revealed meaning equivalent to 8 phases of the Lunar Law. For example the strongly yang trigram called "The Creative" corresponds to the rune called Fullness, which is the position of the Full Moon. The strongly Yin trigram called "The Receptive" corresponds to the rune known as "The Field", which is in the New Moon position. The trigram "Fire" gives excellent background meaning to the rune "Fire" in the place of the First Quarter Moon, and the trigram "Water" has overtones of meaning that correspond to the rune placement of the Water-rune in the place of the Waning Quarter Moon. The Trigram for "Thunder" supplies levels of meaning to the rune called "Thunder", centrally placed between the New Moon and the First Quarter. The Trigram "Lake" helps to understand the rune called "Lake", midway between runes "Fullness" and "Water". The trigram "Wood-Wind" comments on the rune called "Grace", halfway between Fire and Fullness, while the trigram "Mountain" supplies substantial meaning to the rune called "Mountain" at the midpoint between runes "Water" and "Field". The meanings of these trigrams in these positions correspond very closely to the story being told by the rising and waning light of the moon at these phases of its lunar-month cycle. In this way, traditional meanings for 8 positions out of 28 were settled. They correspond very well to the lunar unfoldment, and are based on very sound cosmological principles.

8) The Primal Runes are arranged in circular fashion, with the New Moon (The Field) at the bottom, and the Full Moon (Fullness) at the Pinnacle. Three runes of cosmic meaning are located in the centre of the lunar circle: Source, Primal Light and Primal Dark. Art and symbols from the Goddess tradition are often circular in nature, because roundness seems to be a pattern native to the feminine and motherly energies of creation. The Mother's symbol (from Sri Aurobindo's *Integral Yoga*) is one such universal symbol in which four petals fill the central region, and twelve petals occupy the outer area (see Fig: 3, page 37). The Lunar cycle

is one of birth, growth, maturity, waning, death and rebirth, and the complete journey is made once every lunar month (a period settled by convention at 28 days).

The Primal Runes are in some ways similar to the FUTHARK runes, but there are differences as well. Whatever symbols one uses in divination, and whatever historic or cosmic underpinnings they may have, much depends on the integrity, skill and creativity of the practitioner. Sound principles of cosmology and symbolism validate a wide variety of workable systems of magic, but in the end a given tool is only as good as its user.

The Primal Runes are tools for exploring consciousness. Any level of consciousness that we experience is quite cohesive and compelling as long as we are centred within its dimension. But when we move to a finer or more subtle range of vibrations, we attune to an expanded reality. Within our human microcosm, we contain many levels of being, each with its own manifestations of form, colour and energy, and in consciousness we can move from one plane to another. The clashes and intensities of the lower levels give way to harmony and refinement as we move into more luminous realms. However, if we become plugged in to one kind or one level of experience, we may be prevented from going beyond it.

Our access to different sheaths of possible experience seems to depend on the level of energy that animates us, its purity, fineness and harmony. In the lower ranges, our perceptions are constricted. Here, we need intensity in order to manifest our will, and this intensity is often engendered by crisis or challenge. Some people only feel fully alive when they are intensified by the challenges they face, and they would find life quite insipid if it were not filled with turmoil. Their growth is served, at this level, by the need to struggle for survival, to define their personal rights and living-space, to gratify various desires, and to defend what they believe they 'possess' against 'outsiders'. When human energy and consciousness are refined, the human microcosm can begin to interact with reality in a different range of issues. At this time, the harmony of the whole, not its fragmentation, becomes the dominant reality, and the interrelation, not conflict, of individuals assumes prime importance. Humans of undeveloped consciousness experience life in intensely personal terms, since their primary need is to *develop an ego*; more evolved individuals generate a very different, nonpersonal, viewpoint on life and its goal, where the need to widen one's perspective or transcend the ego becomes imperative.

Runes are by definition archetypal. As they are used to go deeper or higher in awareness, the user's awareness becomes less verbal, less linear, less rational, more experiential and more intuitive. Experiences which depend on language and linear thought can only serve to configure the ego, not to transcend it. Time and inner growth are needed to explore other dimensions of reality. Eventually, one discovers ways of interacting with the Primal levels of archetypal reality. When we experience more subtle states of being, we enter the matrix from which the archetypal forces and forms arise. The archetypes may be considered as energy-dynamics, or universal states through which we pass, and where sometimes we linger, in the awakening process. They may seem to vary in form or in content depending on the personal perspective, the individual's mental conditioning or the cultural and religious factors at work, but they are in essence universal. When we enter the transformational process in depth, we will have spontaneous and recurring experiences with symbols, and possibly with archetypal beings. Our dreams and visions are likely to bring such experiences to us repeatedly as we push through and beyond the boundaries of various energy-fields which we are exploring.

Although the levels of reality that we enter are in essence impersonal and unconditional, we tend to pull them down into our own very relative terms of reference so that we can process the content of our experiences in terms which we find relevant. Certain symbols are familiar to us, and we habitually use what is familiar to come to terms with what is new. Analysis opens for us a way to accept and embrace what we experience in the world of dreams. Sometimes, we gain a new perspective and are able to adjust our life to a more expanded zone of awareness. When this results in a commitment to living life in a deeper, more caring way, we have truly grown. But simply translating our dreams and visions into the terms of our mental conditioning does little to expand our consciousness. Rather it brings the magic down and grounds it in our habitual un-awareness. Most often, we try to 'interpret' a dream by analyzing its content. However, when we identify with the content of the dream, we become fixated on one level of awareness only.

Runes are multi-leveled concentrations of meaning. The Primal Runes work on at least five levels: earth-energy, which is practical and grounded; fire-energy, which is dynamic and creative; air-energy, which is intellectual and expansive; water energy, which is intuitive and emotional, and finally ether-energy, which moves from mind toward spirit. It is widely believed that the ancient Egyptian hieroglyphs could be read on three levels of meaning, from the mundane to the esoteric. Only the temple initiates understood the most arcane levels of meaning, and they would have trained for years to acquire this mastery. The Primal Runes are a tool of great subtlety and complexity which can be used with considerable precision to look deeply into almost any level of energy and consciousness, but as with all such tools of knowledge, the result depends altogether on the skill of the user. If you want to master their use, you must try to find or establish the right balance between mind and heart, and bring to the fore your ability to open up your awareness on successively higher levels. The runes reward those who are diligent, respectful and clear in their intent.

Dreams can reflect many levels of consciousness, but we tend to interpret their symbolism within the limited terms of reference of what we already know. If we can surrender the need to know and to explain the content of our dreams, we may be able to experience different states of Being, different worlds of reality, and thereby attune to new ranges of possibility. A dream is not necessarily meant to support or interpret or refine our very personal sense of limited self. It may be an invitation to fly in a wide, unconditional realm of being, where the categories of mind are jettisoned altogether, a state not unlike pure contemplation. As with dreams, so with Runes.

Both dreams and runes engender experiences that expand our awareness beyond its ordinary boundaries, and this expansion is their real content. They do not necessarily imply any need to realize a goal, or attain an intellectual comprehension, or achieve an articulation. How we open and unfold the ranges of experience that we encounter with rune and dream archetypes is up to us, but it is better to handle it as a ticket into new realms of reality and resist the temptation to process it in terms of what is old and fixed in our mental conditioning. The ways in which we allow ourselves to experience reality create the wideness or restriction with which we bring ourselves into being. What we know is simply a mirror of who we inwardly are. If what we see is a very solid, dense and clearcut world, we are very likely living within the confines of our previous mental conditioning. Where we allow ourselves to be transparent to something that eludes or transcends our understanding, what the mystics call the 'cloud of unknowing' carries us into new realms of consciousness. If our compulsion to judge, explain, understand, analyze and define every element of our experience is foremost, then the wonder, bliss, magic and mystery of life will be lost altogether.

Runes, archetypes and mystical experiences have this in common: they are all invitations to a wider life. The *way in which we know ourselves to be real* is re-enforced and empowered by us every time we exercise consciousness along its vectors. If we can move beyond the need to accumulate information, we may evolve a new kind of mind which can experience new energies of consciousness that had formerly been hidden. When we can evoke and enter these new realms of experience, our inner transformation takes wings.

One of the best ways to facilitate this inner unfolding of awareness is to contemplate the foundations of the ancient wisdom. The image of the 'Tree of Life' has served to express and integrate humanity's evolving cosmic vision from time immemorial. In the most ancient reaches of the Western mystery tradition, we find the belief that the gods fashioned humans in the symbolic or spiritual image of the tree. A tree nourishes itself by reaching upward (aspiring) to the light and air of heaven. But its roots reach deep into the breast of Mother Earth, and she supplies it with material substance and form. Thus a tree is a hybrid child linking heaven and earth. The branching blood vessels and nervous system of humans resembles nothing so much as the branches and twigs of a tree. Beyond this, science has confirmed an overwhelmingly identical DNA structure between humans and trees; we share far more in common than we have differences. Your body is a material expression of the cosmic myth. In your unconscious parts, you have roots in the collective unconscious and the dark, atavistic memories of planet earth; in your outer earthly life, like the trunk of the tree, you are a pillar leading beyond fixity upward toward infinity, and in the uppermost reaches of your consciousness you are an antenna that aspires to reach divine light and love in the air and the ether of heaven, and incarnate them in your life.

What the runes are archetypically, you personify in the structure and essence of your being. You exist for the same purpose that the cosmos serves in them. You and they came into existence to unite the heavenly and earthly streams of reality so that celestial potential may achieve physical expression. To manifest the invisible is magic. Runes are magical, living, archetypal powers, a gift of the gods, to enable humanity to achieve the divinely destined manifestation. You have and you *are* the same magic as that which the Primal Runes express in fixed form.

Before the magic of the ancient symbols can be released and directed, the runes must be integrated into the understanding, the energy-fields, and even the physical cellular consciousness of the user. For this purpose, you might want to look at the chapter entitled 'Using The Runes', in particular the discussion on meditation. Edred Thorsson, in *The Nine Doors of Midgard*, offers this insight:

> The runes are "cosmic mysteries," and thus it would seem that they have existence in the objective universe, which indeed they do. However, they are more particularly the principles of consciousness, its framework or structure. And here is the key concept: Since the runes are an objective structure of consciousness it is precisely in that realm (of consciousness) that the runes are most accessible to us. Woden gave us the runes in latent forms - but we must emulate his primal act of rune-winning to make them real for ourselves. Therefore, the runes are subjective patterns that are reflections of objective principles or forms which must be made real by the will or consciousness of the runester. The reality of the runes is to be found in the essence of the gifts of Woden (of which the runes are a road map). Their reality is demonstrated by the very

ability of the runester to be the artificer of his or her own reality; this is part of the essence of "magic". (page 45)

The Primal Runes (in contrast to the Viking or Teutonic Runes) are a revelation of the Great Mother through her epiphany, The Moon. They are not passed on to us by a patriarchal, Aryan father-figure such as Woden. They are continuously mediated in the phases of the Moon from the most ancient times to the present moment. The self-revelation of the Moon continues to this day, and the archetypal energies of its dark and light phases are universally acknowledge, but perhaps most fully articulated in astrology. The Moon mediates the light of spirit (symbolized by the Sun) and transmits it into the time-space continuum of earth. The Tree of Life grows by assimilating this heavenly nourishment and anchoring it in the dark soil of the planet; currently the human microcosm, your physical form and mine, is the most evolved fruit of the primal Tree of Life. Moon measures. To measure is the root meaning of the Aryan root word 'man' (pronounced mun) which is the syllable from which we derive the English word "Moon". By measuring and dispensing the solar light, the lunar revelation slowly enriches the sap of wisdom in the tree of life, and distils the nectar of future bliss in its budding blossoms.

The Primal Runes are gifts of the Great Mother; they are realities inherent in the very fibre of our being, as real as the magic of moonlight, as timeless as the tides. But to awaken this ancient magic and master it, the forms of the Primal Runes, their sounds of power, and their energies must be studied, known and internalized. This apprenticeship, leading to mastery of the ancient powers, is discussed in greater detail in a later chapter, *Using The Runes*. At this time, we have discussed the foundational 'runelore' sufficiently that you may be ready to leap ahead and begin to explore how the runes may be used in actual practice.

CHAPTER 7

Ancient Powers

A rune is a sign that embodies power. It is firstly a visual symbol, secondly a sound, thirdly a meaning related to a cosmology and fourthly an esoteric tool which can be used in a variety of ways, one of which is divination.

We have seen how the most ancient runes of the West come from the culture of Old Europe, and date from a period of several thousand years between 7,000 and 1,500 BC. Many of the signs used in the so-called Old Europe script were etched on cave walls, or on stones or bones in Paleolithic times, and quite a few of them seem to have been in continuous use from the stone age up to the time of the successive waves of Aryan invasions, at which time the Danube Basin, Greece, Anatolia and much of Europe was subjugated by patriarchal warriors.

The Myth of the Goddess by Anne Baring and Jules Cashford does an excellent job of tracing the continuity of goddess symbols from Paleolithic times right up to the age of the Neolithic revolution when the first towns sprang up. It corroborates Marija Gimbutas's research and shows that from Malta to the British Isles and from France eastward to the Ural Mountains up to and during the Indo-European invasions a widespread culture of the goddess flourished. The symbols this culture used as expressions of her powers are found engraved on tools, pots and statues as well as spinning whorls and at least one stone used for divination. These symbols have been called the earliest form of writing in existence, and may be our most direct link to the power and wisdom of the Great Goddess.

For as long as the Great Goddess has been worshipped, the

Moon has been her principal symbol. It waxes for a period of fourteen days from the New to the Full Moon. Then, it wanes. This cycle of growing and fading light seems to have been the first human measure of time. Indeed, the root word for Moon in many languages is related to the idea of measure. A month is a moon-measure of time. Ten lunar months constitute the gestation period of a human fetus.

The phases of the moon were ancient and timeless elements of a sacred cycle of birth, growth, maturity, decline, death and rebirth. The female reproductive cycle, the ocean tides and the living habits of many creatures still reflect this waxing and waning pattern of 28 days. The waxing phase of the Moon is broken down into two units of seven days each, a time period which we designate as a week. Each of the seven days of the week is sacred to a heavenly body. Monday is the Moon's day; Sunday the Sun's day; Saturday Saturn's day, and so on. Four units of 7 days comprise a total of 28 days which is one lunar cycle. The number 28 would seem to correspond to one complete primal cycle in the goddess domain. Thus, 28 units of meaning would seem to be an alphabet of what The Goddess has to say to those who can discern or discover her meaning. We know that the symbols of the Old Europe script were used as part of a sacred system of ritual and divination in the ages when The Goddess reigned supreme, so it is only natural to derive from 28 of the most meaningful signs a set of 'Primal Runes'.

In choosing which runes to use, the Cypriot Syllabary proved indispensable, because of all the remaining scripts, it gave indications of what sounds might have corresponded to the signs which were in use in Old Europe, particularly those of the Vinca provenance which are some of the best known. Of the 55 extant signs in this syllabary, a subset of four vowels and 24 syllables has been chosen, for a total of 28.

The most ancient inscriptions of Cyprus are not alphabetic, and cannot be read, but dating as they do from at least 1500 BC, they are considered to be of great importance. The signs used were non-Greek, and seem closely related to Linear A and Linear B, which were used in Crete and Mycenae. This Cypro-Minoan script was adopted by Greek settlers who colonized Cyprus in the 12th century BC. They used it to express words in their own language. The inscriptions which have come down to us from that early period are for the most part short dedicatory and funerary passages, but there are a few longer, historical texts from the 5th century BC. The use of this script continued well into Classical times when the Greek alphabet had become well established on the mainland. Inscriptions with identical messages in the two scripts have made it possible to determine sounds for each of the Cypro-Minoan symbols. After the conquests of Alexander the Great, Greek culture became dominant and the script fell into disuse.

Most of the signs in the Cypriot Script are identical to those of Old Europe, and others are clearly derivative. In considering how these signs might embody a system of ancient wisdom and divination, several considerations were of importance. The iconography and the acoustic resonance of the symbols had to relate to a cosmology, the most obvious being the phases of the lunar cycle. In magic of all ages, visual form and sound were both important, and the Cypriot Syllabary certainly supplied correlative sounds for many of the Old Europe symbols.

The esoteric tradition of Hermes Trismegistus (also called the Hermetic Tradition) is centrally important to the evolution Gnostic spirituality in the West. From this tradition we have authoritative sources for determining the occult powers of various symbols, vowel-sounds, and syllabic sounds. The Hermetic corpus is a collection of texts which summarize the kinds of cosmology, magical philosophy and occult practice that were prevalent in the Hellenistic Age and the late Roman Empire, but they look back in time at least to the age of Pythagoras, the Chaldeans and Egypt of the pharaohs. The esoteric tradition in the West is steeped in Hermetic lore; its influence is all-pervasive and it is one important window on still earlier phases of occult history when the influence of The Goddess prevailed.

The twenty-eight stages of the lunar cycle may be summarized as follows:

1) At the time of the New Moon, a fresh spiritual possibility is transmitted from the Sun to the Moon and thence radiated into the atmosphere of the earth. The consciousness of humanity can nurse this seed-possibility into manifestation. The starting point of the lunar journey is **The Field**. It is a condition of receptivity, passivity and darkness, ready to receive the creative seed.

2) Seeding is the second phase. Into The Field comes a germ of creative life which will grow and flourish if it is nurtured. For a long period of time, this seed develops in a protective womb.

3) Gestation is thus the third phase. The final form of the developing possibility is still unclear, but at this stage, steady growth takes place inside a protective, sheltered environment.

4) Emergence is the fifth phase. The young possibility develops itself to the point where it assumes a self-recognizing identity and a unique destiny.

5) Thunder is the fourth phase. At this point, the form of the new possibility becomes distinct and self-conscious. It begins to define its distinctness and separativity, possibly by a dramatic breakthrough.

6) Growth is the sixth phase. This is the beginning of an extended learning curve in which the new possibility takes in all it will need to thrive as a unique expression of its inner essence.

7) Challenge is the seventh phase. The moon has moved through one quarter of its journey and the unfolding form has reached a definitive point where something important will happen.

8) Fire is the phase of the Moon known as the first quarter. There is an initiation or awakening of sorts which sets the course for the future. There is a conscious awareness of what the quest is about and how to realize it. A definitive step forward is taken and the initial possibility is confirmed.

9) Choice is the stage where all experience is assessed in light of the central goal as the young possibility finds its way forward to fulfillment. Choices about how to use time, whom to befriend, what to study and how to progress are centrally important at this time.

10) Karma is action and its inevitable result. Karma begins to accumulate as focused activity is undertaken to realize the goal, to manifest the possibility. The karmic residues of our choices and actions become part of the Field that we work on and transform as we grow toward liberation.

11) Creativity develops as the only possible way of achieving the desired result and meeting the unpredictable challenges.

12) Grace is the image of a bolt of energy and light descending from the heights. The inner alchemy of consciousness can be accomplished under this sign.

13) Love comes to the fore as the only way to achieve wholeness and happiness.

14) Courage is needed to translate love into action, to give it expression and to risk being different from the collective conditioning.

15) Fullness is the Full Moon. It is the opposite of The Field. Light and power are at their maximum as the seed which was sown at the beginning of the cycle reaches its complete unfoldment. From this point on, the light begins to wane. The Field has become the Knower, and further progress will be a process of self-transcendence. This means that all previous victories and lessons must be lived in a spirit of letting go and opening up.

16) Descent is a downpouring of the great light. The fullness of the moon is still very strong, and the capacity to see deeply is to the fore.

17) Wisdom grows out of insight. The application of our knowledge in harmonious, selfless action is only possible to the degree that we are letting go of ego.

18) Mastery comes from the experience of serving others with wisdom and surrender to the divine guidance. Mastery is wisdom lived to the fullest according to the inner guidance, which has become steady.

19) Lake is the image of a lake where many waters congregate and blend. In this stage of experience, there is satisfaction, fullness and pleasure in a collective or communal setting.

20) Transmission is the seeding of the possibility in the world at large so that it will continue on when the first light-bearer has left the stage. At this stage it is the fostering of light in others which has top priority, since the personal goals have been largely achieved.

21) Dreamweaver Here the inner gifts and their expression reach their fullness. One is favoured by the muses and attains inspired visions such as a seer-poet or bard might have.

22) Water is a turning point. The image is one of a torrent of water pouring through a rocky chasm, and there is difficulty and challenge at hand. We are at the beginning of the fourth stage of the lunar cycle. The Waning Moon has reached a point where there is more darkness than light, and the darkness is increasing as the light diminishes. It is a time of surrender and return to the Unknowable.

23) Crisis is a time of testing when we accept to enter into the darkness, acting on pure faith, for the sake of a greater light at the end of the tunnel.

24) Sacrifice is the acceptance of loss or diminution for the sake of a greater good.

25) The Knot is the time when a central difficulty must be unknotted. In the mystical tradition this relates to the transcendence of ego, or dying to self.

26) Mountain stands for stillness, perseverance and introversion. It is a contemplative sign, and one of great strength.

27) Transformation is the beginning of a new phase of existence. The embodied form begins to metamorphose into a new level of wholeness and harmony.

28) Merging is unification of the part with the whole, the individual with the Ground of Being, the wave-form with its matrix. It is also the loss or transcendence of the separate self, and in this sense a death. Thus we are back at the starting point and the cycle begins again. Into the emptiness of the void, a new seed can be sown. When complete emptiness is reached, a new beginning takes place and the cycle is renewed.

Three special runes are found at the centre of the lunar circle:

29) Primal Light is the power of consciousness that comes from the divine word at the beginning of creation.

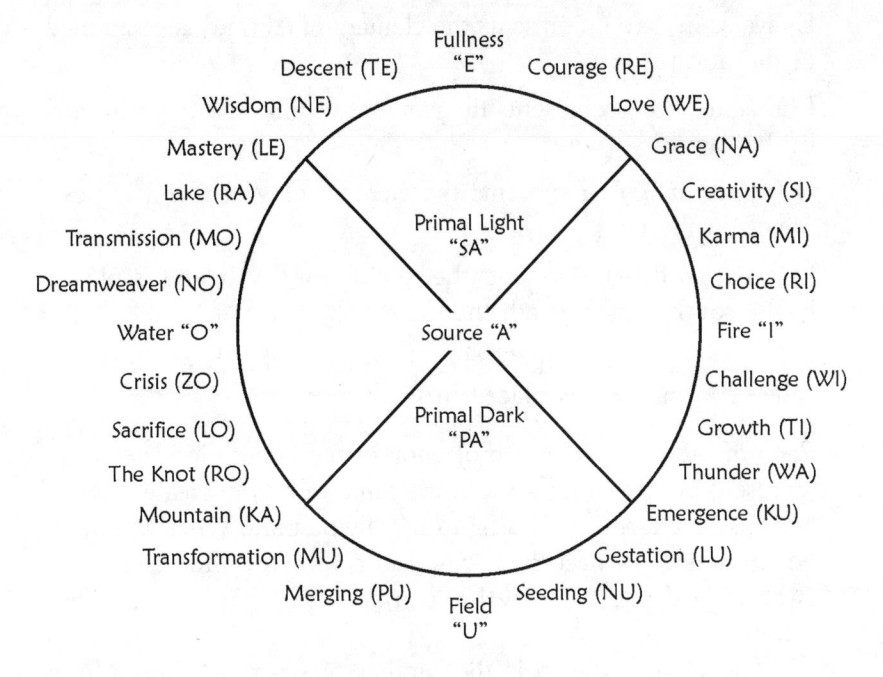

Fig. 4: The Primal Runes Cycle

Around the circle (clockwise from top):
- Fullness "E"
- Courage (RE)
- Love (WE)
- Grace (NA)
- Creativity (SI)
- Karma (MI)
- Choice (RI)
- Fire "I"
- Challenge (WI)
- Growth (TI)
- Thunder (WA)
- Emergence (KU)
- Gestation (LU)
- Seeding (NU)
- Field "U"
- Merging (PU)
- Transformation (MU)
- Mountain (KA)
- The Knot (RO)
- Sacrifice (LO)
- Crisis (ZO)
- Water "O"
- Dreamweaver (NO)
- Transmission (MO)
- Lake (RA)
- Mastery (LE)
- Wisdom (NE)
- Descent (TE)

Center: Primal Light "SA", Source "A", Primal Dark "PA"

30) Primal Dark is the structuring and crystallizing process that takes place as the light manifests as the various planes of creation. The earth's physical matter is the most dense and inert of these. It is also inchoate chaos.

31) Source is THAT which manifests, but is itself beyond all forms and qualities.

Figure 4 shows the complete cycle of the Primal Runes. A rune is not only a sign (visible) which expresses a power (invisible); it is also a sound (audible) and that can embody and project a power. The vowel sounds are the life and soul of words. Each of the vowel sounds resonates with a particular set of divine aspects. While consonants give words their bodies, vowels put soul into them. They are to language what life and consciousness are to existence. In the esoteric tradition we are following here, the vowels are assigned the following meanings:

E (aye as in "say") represents the element of Air and is positioned in the north.

I (ai as in "eye") represents the element of Fire and is positioned in the east.

O (oh as in "go") represents the element of Water and is positioned in the west.

U (oo as in flute) represents the element of Earth, and is placed in the south. It is beneath the skies of heaven (Air).

A (ah as in Father) represents the element of Ether, sometimes called Akasha, and is placed in the centre.

Each of these powers is a projection of the Great Goddess. They represent her dynamic work in the three worlds to create, enliven and dissolve forms according to her divine plan. When a human being aspires to become a co-creator with the Goddess, there awakens a desire to know her workings and participate in her action.

The Goddess, who is the Mother of Creation, moves from her formless aspect as the Supreme Self into manifestation, becoming the primal powers of earth, water, fire and air. She is eternally present beyond her creation, but she becomes the inner power by which creation manifests and she is there in all things as their essence.

The vowel sound of "E" represents Mother Air. She is calm and wide. She embodies all understanding, all wisdom. Her compassion is inexhaustible, her sovereign majesty is supreme. She is there in the wideness above our thinking minds. She floods our consciousness with largeness, might and vast knowing. She is eternally at peace. But within that stillness, she is all wise, all knowing, all seeing. Her will is unalterable, and her vision infallible. The Truth is her sole concern, and knowledge is her gift to those whom she blesses. Her compassion is humanity's greatest opportunity to progress.

The vowel sound of "I" expresses Fire, the Mother of force and strength. Her intensity is irresistible, her will is all-conquering. She is swift to act and her power is victorious. Terrible is she to those who cherish ignorance. Stern is she to those who deal in falsehood. Her warrior spirit never shrinks from the struggle of life, for she is indomitable. She feeds the aspirations of our hearts as they climb like bright flames to her lofty height. She carries us upward, she speeds the way with her passionate love. When the Mother of Fire intervenes, all obstacles are dissolved in an instant. She is vehement and strong, her will is full of luminous speed. Those who are strong and noble do not fear her blows, for each blow is a blessing in disguise. Her conquering might is for those who are brave and true; She carries them to the highest planes of inspiration.

The vowel sound of "O" expresses Water, the Mother of the Waters, the Moon Mother, queen of beauty and harmony. Her magic is irresistible. She charms our hearts and opens them to the bliss of the Divine. She enchants us and causes joy to swell in our souls. She brings rapture and tenderness, love and devotion. She plunges the soul in delight and refines our lives in all ways until we possess the secret of her endless joy. Those who love harmony and beauty are close to her in spirit. They are never tempted by what is ugly or gross. She draws all hearts to the Divine by her powers of love and beauty. She discovers the rhythms and measures by which perfection takes form on earth. She offers us the highest bliss and all things common are made wonderful by her grace.

The vowel sound of "U" represents Mother Earth. She labours tirelessly to bring all things to wholeness and perfection. She is patient and her work is never finished. She guides, organizes and carries forward the work of creation in matter. How detailed and endless is her work, how slow and patient her effort, how persistent and flawless her spirit! She knows each detail of creation and she sees all that must be done to build up the heavenly kingdom on earth and bring it to completion. Nothing is too small for her attention and there is nothing she does not mould and shape. Through her, by her work, all things attain their true form and their final perfection. She suffers our shortcomings through long ages, for she is kind and patient. Persistently, tirelessly she labours on until the great work is complete.

The vowel sound of "A" represents Spirit. The Divine Presence moves from what we call heaven into physical manifestation on the plane of reality we call Earth. The centre is often pictured as the '*axix mundi*', the 'tree of life' or the pillar which connects the higher and lower realities.

The Goddess is One. The names we give Her represent Her aspects. They describe Her ways of working. The names and titles of the Goddess represent avenues of approach by means of which our limited human consciousness can approach Her divine fullness. In the ancient tradition, there were no exclusive walls between the various forms and titles of The Goddess. She was present in all names and forms as the One and singular Source of creation. In ancient times, names of gods and goddesses were secret, and none more so than that of the Great Goddess. Because of its great sanctity, the secret word occurs very rarely in surviving texts - in fact it is found only twice, once in Plato, and once in Apollonius. Plato refers to **EVOUIA**, as life, meaning the Source of Life. The Greeks of Plato's time would have understood *life* to include not only all biological living things; but also things of light, such as flames; the stars, and the moon, so they believed her to be the whole universe, a living universe. This single word which combines all the vowels and their powers is a true name of the Great Goddess, insofar as speech can render it.

CHAPTER 8

Rune Profiles

The Primal Runes are archetypes, which means they are cosmic realities in the inner world. When their energy and consciousness impinges on our world, we are affected on several levels of our being. Our physical bodies and practical life are affected (earth); our vital energy and willpower are affected (fire); our intelligence and thinking capacity is affected (air); our emotions and intitive feelings are affected (water); and our higher ranges of sensitivity (ether) are affected. Therefore the runes' action can be described on all these levels. The way to determine what level the rune's energy affects most is to draw a second rune. That rune will be one of the five families; it will be either an earth, a fire, an air, a water or an ether rune. That is the section you should read, under the heading: Spiritual Meanings for Divination. The mundane level of meaning is noted in a less detailed manner.

In general, a reversed rune indicates that the energies are working in a way contrary to normal. Either the archetypal energies are diminished, or they are present but working in a contrary, adverse, or negative fashion. From the spiritual point of view, of course, every challenge is an opportunity. However, the simple, mundane reality of reversed runes is that they represent some sort of difficulty.

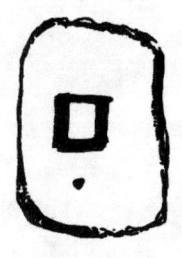

The Field

The Archetype

The Field represents Earth, an energy which is quintessentially *"yin"*. This sign symbolizes receptivity, nourishment, latent potential, darkness, emptiness, the unmanifest, passivity, inertia, the womb. The image of a field ready to be ploughed and planted is intended to convey all of the above. The icon of the Field Rune shows us a plot of land. It is black, fertile earth sectioned off from the land around it. This is the field of possibilities which the soul comes to till, the centrally important work that it embraces when it incarnates. To find one's chosen field and work it fruitfully is the central purpose of life. The soul incarnates into a physical world precisely because it needs a field to work in order to manifest its latent divine potential.

The earliest and possibly the most profound teaching about The Field is to be found in Chapter Thirteen of the *Bhagavad Gita*. Here Sri Krishna teaches Arjuna the distinction between "The Field" and the "Knower of the Field".

In the widest sense, the field in which the soul labours includes whatever has name and form. The term "field" takes in pretty much everything that consciousness can come to "know". Thus mind, energy and matter are all fields of forces which can be discerned, worked and mastered. Spirit, specifically the individualized spirit which we call soul, is the "knower" of this field of phenomena. When the soul brings the mind, the vitality and the physical body into alignment with the spirit, or the cosmic will, then perfect work can be done and the soul's highest ideals can be manifested.

An anecdote from Hinduism illustrates how the concept of The Field is traditionally understood. A holy man is asked what work he does. His reply is: "I am a farmer". When the questioner is surprised, he adds, "This body of mine is my field. I sow good thoughts and actions and in my body I reap the results."

From this, we can easily see how the archetype of "The Field" leads directly to an inquiry concerning the concept of "Seeding", and from there to a mastery of the laws of karma. For as the Buddha said: "All that we are is the result of what we have thought; it is founded on our thoughts; it is made of our thoughts." Seeding, Mastery and Karma are also Primal Runes.

Standard Meanings for Divination
Upright

Earth: Home, hearth and family; a legacy or inheritance; posessions; resources and sources of profit.

Fire: A call to hard work; a thing that needs working on (applied will).

Air: A clearly defined concept, ready to be actualized physically; defining boundaries and ownership intellectually.

Water: A feeling of being at home; to be in one's castle; one's roots, ancestors, earth-connections, racial memory, dharma.

Ether: An inner imperative or empowerment to give physical expression; the power to actualize, concretize, achieve manifestation.

Reversed

Earth: An empty, unprofitable resource, a worthless inheritance.

Fire: Loss, reversal, disinheritance.

Air: Much effort for little gain; a worthless project or flawed concept; a plan that can never be achieved.

Water: Disappointment; overturned dreams.

Ether: A chimera; an unreal or misleading initiative; a potential waste of time.

Spiritual Meanings for Divination
Earth: The Great Work

The Field is the work which is given to each one, the totality of vibrations constituting one's inner and outer makeup. Everything which has been assembled by the soul for manifestation is its "Field" of endeavour. The totality of substance which we call ourselves, from the most material to the highest spiritual, is a field of work. It is there at our disposal for us to develop as fully as we can. This field of action is always there; it cannot be taken away until the moment of death. This is what has been given to us by the universe as our very own work, a hidden project to be carried out night and day, in dreaming and in waking, from the moment we come into the world until we leave, and even beyond the grave. Many people refuse to 'take up the cross' and do the work, but this is a choice of limitation. The inner life begins with a decision to take up the labour, and learn to work upon the field so as to bring it to order and perfection. Many choose rather to try and save the world, forgetting that one can do nothing for others unless one has attained sufficient mastery to do it for oneself. All outer difficulties begin as inner imperfections, either in the field I call myself, or in my neighbour's field. But the moment I see defects in the other, I may be sure that they are also within my own being, and this is the place to begin. When one has changed a defect in oneself, one may have some hope of changing it in another, but not before.

Fire: Claiming One's Will

One only becomes a true individual when one claims one's willpower and applies it to the work demanded by the field one has been given. Until then, one's whims, fancies, desires and aversions create an impression that one is exercising personal will and choice, but in fact one is only being buffeted by the universal forces. The so-called 'pleasures of ignorance' continue to be of absorbing interest, and self-indulgence based on ego continues to be the way one exercises one's "freedom" until one claims the central will and applies it to the work given. The Field is the work given. Only when one begins to work the field does one tap the character and potential of the soul, which is the matrix of one's higher identity and destiny. Then only does one become empowered by That which transcends the limitations of desire, ego and mind. To freely and joyfully choose the work which must be done in the field which has been given is to reclaim one's central will, which had been covered over by the obscurities of worldliness. This is one of the most important steps in the long journey to enlightenment. In the *Bhagavad Gita*, Krishna added one more piece of wise advice: 'Far better to embrace one's own dharma, however unglorious, than to act out the dharma of another, however lofty.' The true inner work is mostly done behind the veil, where we are not recognized or applauded; and the true motive is to be an honest worker whose work is free from any hankering for recognition or glory. Yet those who choose this destiny ultimately claim their willpower, their souls' blessings and their true individuality, along with the peace, light and delight which come from approaching enlightenment.

Air: Establishing Control

Just by virtue of living in the world, the human microcosm is bathed in all kinds of energies, the luminous and the dark, harmonious and chaotic, heavy and light, peaceful and stressful. Everyone's consciousness should act as a filter, allowing an individual to receive only what he or she wants. Ideally, we should be able to think what we want to think and feel what we choose to feel, and not allow thoughts and feelings to arise within us without authorization. However, unless and until one organizes the mental and emotional bodies and establishes clarity, one may have very little control over what is thought and felt. It is sometimes necessary to see our actions, or experience their unpleasant consequences before we realize the implications of what we think and feel. If we wish to clarify our inner world, we must become aware of feelings or attitudes which are negative in nature, and see whether or not we have sufficient self control to reject what we find unsuitable. To establish inner self control means that we cultivate and encourage what we find harmonious and beautiful, and we reject and avoid what we find destructive or limiting. In fact, this is the central purpose of having a physical existence, we learn to control a wide range of vibrations which represent our own particular field of work. In time, we become aware of the divine plan, and we cultivate energies which conform to it, and let go of the rest. Most people do not take up the work implied by their given field. They may do a little of the work, do it halfheartedly, or under duress, but very few do it well, or consciously. Then, among those who do take up this centrally important work, relatively few do it with the knowledge of how it should be done. There is a long and rigorous training involved to master even one aspect of our field, for example thought-control. The most auspicious conditions for the work are: good guidance, a habit of self-discipline from childhood on, a cheerful nature, infinite patience, humility, absolute impartiality, and a growing dependence on Grace.

Water: The Vision

We are each given a field to work, and a task to do, and for each of us the challenge is different. The field that we have been given, the totality of what constitutes our inner and outer nature, must be ordered from the inmost to the outermost. We have a range of vibrations placed at our disposal to work upon as fully as we can, a field of action which is our very own from the time we are born. This mass of energies is there waiting to be transformed, but the key to the work is vision, an inner vision of who we are, what we are meant to achieve, and how we may manifest our dream in this lifetime. To find the work we were born to do, we must discover our hidden soul, and discern its blueprint for our life. For this, we must search out the vision that will reveal to us our true being and our life's work.

It is like walking late at night across a dark field. We know that there is a spring on our land, but we do not know where it is. We know that if we can find the waters of this spring, we will be able to grow many things in our field. The night is dark and noiseless, and as we walk we see only the dark earth at our feet. Then, some way ahead, we glimpse a sheet of water. It is hardly visible at first, just a bit of water on the surface of the earth, dark and obscure. Then, as we watch, the clouds part and a ray of moonlight comes down and lights up the surface of the water. We see its extent, and know that it can nurture all the dreams we have for making our field productive. In this way, if we really wish to achieve something important in life, the secret possibilities of our being will appear and present themselves to our understanding at some point in time. We will have a convincing vision of the true qualities of our inner potential, the divine possibilities with which we are gifted, and what we are really meant to make of our life and our field.

Ether: The Truth of The Field

The words of The Mother give us a picture of the secret nature of The Field:

> The universe is an objectivisation of the Supreme, as if He had objectified himself outside of himself in order to see himself, to live himself, to know himself, and so that there might be an existence and a consciousness capable of recognizing him as the origin and uniting consciously with him to manifest him in the becoming. There is no other reason for the universe. The earth is a kind of symbolic crystallization of the universal life, a reduction, a concentration, so that the work of evolution may be easier to do and follow. And if we see the history of the earth, we can understand why the universe was created. It is the Supreme growing aware of himself in an eternal Becoming; the goal is the union of the creation with the Creator, a union that is conscious, willing and free in the manifestation.
>
> That is the secret of Nature. Nature is the executive Force; it is She who does the work. And She takes up this creation, which appears to be totally inconscient but which contains the Supreme Consciousness and sole Reality and She works so that all this can develop, become self-aware and realise itself fully. But She does not show it from the very beginning. It develops gradually, and this is why at the start it is a secret which will be unveiled as it nears the end. Man has reached a point in the evolution high enough for this secret to be unveiled and for what was done in an apparent inconscience to be done consciously, willingly, and therefore much more rapidly and in the joy of realisation. ... Man is beginning to know what the supreme origin wants of him and is collaborating in carrying it out. Nature wants the creation to become conscious of being the creator himself in an objectivisation, that is to say, there is no difference between the creator and the creation, and the goal is a conscious and realised union. That is the secret of Nature. (*Collected Works*, Vol. 9, (Questions & Answers) pgs. 321-2)

Coming from a soul who had fully realized the consciousness of the Divine Mother, these words are a profound revelation of the pattern-of-the-whole within which our own field, our human microcosm, emerges. The field where our energies are to be expended is a part of this larger picture. The seeming unimportance of our mundane life is actually a precious detail in a glorious divine unfolding. Each small part of creation contains the pattern of the whole; each grain of sand reflects the cosmos; each human body and each human life is a note in a great symphony. When we see that all things are thus bound together in wholeness, we will appreciate that the field we have been given is divinely important in the wide scheme of things, and the work we have been assigned is a vital link in an infinite chain of being. At that point we have the eyes to see and the heart to feel, and the soul to breathe inspiration into the work that has been granted us to accomplish.

SEEDING

The Archetype

A human figure stands beside a curve which represents a wave of energy. The Seeding image includes concepts such as insemination, fertilisation, making a beginning, laying down patterns for future possibilities, sowing karmic obligations, implanting of energies that will yield future results, dispersing one's energies randomly, sowing wild oats, making the investment or doing the work from which a future harvest will result. It builds on the prior reality of a Field which will receive the seed, and it prepares for Gestation, which will bring the seeds into growth.

In the Age of the Goddess, the Mother's power and presence and magic were perceived in all manner of physical, earthly processes, but especially in those having to do with fertility and birth.

RUNE PROFILES: SEEDING

The millennia prior to the Aryan invasions were like a golden or silver age, compared with the violence that came later. Fields, orchards and cattle-herds may well have been held in common, or seen to be the property of The Goddess, and human workers likely saw themselves as her servants, labouring to serve her processes of enrichment and fecundity. The poetry of early Sumeria gives us a sense of this primal relation to the land and its seeding. Samuel Kramer gives us this translation of an early Sumerian paean to nature:

> "The great Earth-crust was resplendent,
> its surface was jewel-green,
> The wide earth – its surface was covered
> with precious metals and lapis-lazuli,
> It was adorned with diorite, nir-stone,
> carnelian and antimony,
> The Earth was arrayed luxuriantly in plants
> and herbs, its presence was majestic,
> The holy Earth, the pure Earth,
> beautiful herself for holy Heaven,
> Heaven, the noble god,
> inserted his sex into the wide Earth,
> Let flow the semen of the heroes,
> Trees and Reed, into her womb.
> The Earthly Orb, the trusty cow,
> was impregnated with the good semen of Heaven."
> – From *The Poetry Of Sumer* (1979) pp. 29-30

Although Sumerian culture was not identical to the culture of Old Europe, its early history had a very similar orientation to the Great Mother, and its early poetry is a good reflection of the attitude of the peoples of Old Europe to the archetype of Seeding. From this passage, we can see that seeding was part of the relationship between Heaven and Earth. It was a cosmic process in which humans participated ritualistically. We see also that seeding was something noble, high and pure, with no sense of sin being attached to sexuality. This contrasts greatly with later Manichean teachings which found their way into Christianity and into the writings of the church father St. Augustine in particular.

Standard Meanings for Divination
Upright

Earth: Reproduction, mating; sexual activity; bonding; fertility.

Fire: Forces of life growing, or being given a chance to grow; to initiate something.

Air: New ideas coming into the mind; fresh intellectual possibilities and horizons.

Water: Getting started; a new beginning; new feelings and emotions.

Ether: A spiritual renewal; a spiritual initiative; new life from on high.

Reversed

Earth: Rape; sexual perversion; pornography; bondage; illicit sex; abortion, or aborted action.

Fire: A false start; a weak beginning.

Air: A peverse mental influence starting to manifest; twisted ideas.

Water: New temptations; new influences of a negative nature.

Ether: Counterfeit spirituality; an influence which seems spiritual, but is not; you are being co-opted by questionable influences.

Spiritual Meanings for Divination
Earth: Problematic Seeding

The "Seeding" Rune tells of new energies being sown into a field which can nourish them. In this case, the reference is to karmic seeds that we sow by our use of consciousness. Our actions, whether in the world of thought, emotion, intent or physical exertion, have consequences which manifest over time by an inevitable law. "As you sow, so you reap"; karmic seeds ripen and create future possibilities or limitations. When any kind of seed is cultivated by repetition of thought, intentionality or outer action, it will bear fruit. The knowledge of seeding, how it is done, and how a particular kind of result can accrue, is part of our karmic education.

Those who are wise see what fruits derive from the different kinds of seeds that they plant, whether consciously or unconsciously. From observing this karmic pattern, one can discern and distinguish what seeds are profitable to plant from those that are best avoided. Knowing what should be avoided and what kind of action should be favoured is very important if one wishes to follow the path of wisdom through to the very end.

Fire: Seeding versus Transmission

Whereas the rune "Transmission" is a conscious passing on of the fruits of wisdom to others, as a mentor does, seeding is often an unconscious involvement in the law of karma. Seeds of future dilemma are frequently sown in oblivion, without the benefit of foresight as to their consequences. But it is necessary to gather all kinds of varied experiences in order to understand and master the energies involved. From this point of view, it is all learning experience which can bring valuable lessons.

Air: Beneficial Seeding

Seeding can be also be an activity consciously undertaken for the purposes of self-development. Just as rain-clouds are seeded to induce rain, so the latent potential in our energy-fields can be seeded with affirmations or prayers or mantras. When we repeat a thought or action over and over, we seed consciousness with patterns that will later bring us results. Rightly directed endeavour is a profitable kind of seeding that helps us to achieve our full potential. Spiritual practices of all kinds can be considered as 'seeding' activities but, like careful farming practices they depend on patient, regular and dedicated cultivation. Erratic, unfocused and scattered practice rarely brings about a suitable result.

Water: Seeding The Imagination

If you have a good imagination, it can be used to build up the potential for your future attainments. Build up a clear image of what you desire, complete in all its details. Build it like a work of art, a painting, or a sculpture, well formed, detailed and clear. Make it real and living for you in your inner vision and feelings. If you do this, and then give it enough time, you will see that the formulation will be achieved. It may take days, weeks, months or years, but it is sure to be realized.

Ether: The Hidden Seedbed

Everything in the universe tends towards manifestation, but some things do not achieve it. Many undesirable human energies are repressed and suppressed, and many people have the idea that unwanted elements can be abolished by this method. However, beyond the physical plane is the subconscious plane, and unless a desire or negative energy is transcended altogether, the seed of its energy, prevented from manifesting in the material world, is driven down and settles into the subconscious mind. There it waits, ready to rise up and reveal itself when conditions permit. Unwanted energies which have been concealed for years may rush up and make themselves known, taking people quite by surprise. If we want to see the repressed elements of our being which are still alive, it helps greatly to examine our dreams. The deeper, uncontrolled instincts which are still alive in the subconscious take on a life of their own in our dreams, and can be detected, and even changed if we go deep enough.

Gestation

The Archetype

The Gestation Rune shows a cup or cauldron sheltered in a cave. The inverted U was the symbol of the Sumerian Goddess Ki (or Ninhursag), and it symbolized a birthplace, womb, cow pen or sheepfold, a place where new life came into being and was sheltered through its early, tender stages. It is a Goddess symbol and expresses the inner life of the womb, the power that prepares the fetus for birth. The upturned cup is a cauldron-image, or a crucible where inner transformation takes place. The Gestation rune is an image of being sequestered, protected, sheltered, nurtured, fostered, guarded, cared for and given time to grow. It is a situation of dependence, or interdependence such as that of a child in the womb. The capacity for self-willed activity apart from the protective environment is just beginning to develop. It is a situation of being mentored, parented, guided, supervised, sustained and shielded from outer interference until a later date when one is more self-sufficient. The small cup or cauldron is a crucible where good things can happen when the time is ready, but the process is not yet ripe. It is a work in progress, an incomplete possibility. The influence of the environment on the individual is very strong, and at this stage benign and necessary. At this stage, good things are being fostered in this interdependent relationship. However, the time of gestation will come to an end and the individual will be separated from the matrix at some point in the future. If one has nurtured seeds of light within, these seeds will bring enrichment at some future time.

One very good source for this archetype is the Dictaion cave of Crete where Zeus was born. It is a massive structure with hanging stalactites, and many figures of gods and bulls have been found there. This was the cave-womb of the mountain mother where the divine child was nurtured. From time to time the divine infant would be brought forth for the renewal of the people, held up by his mother for veneration. However, the final and complete Emergence (the next rune) of the young god takes place only when he has grown into his divine nature and learns to be true to his divinity in the outer world of darkness and ignorance. In *The Great Mother*, Erich Neumann supplies several valuable insights concerning the womb-temple:

> Just as the temple is a late development of the cave, and hence a symbol of the Great Goddess as house and shelter, so the temple gate is the entrance into the goddess; it is her womb, and the innumerable entrance and threshold rites of mankind are an expression of this numinous feminine place. The enclosure, the gate, and the pillars of the temple are symbols of the Great Mother... The dolmen is also a sacral house; by extension it becomes the temple and the "sacred Precinct" in general. The earliest sacred precinct of the primordial age was probably that in which

the woman gave girth. It is the place where the Great Goddess rules and from which – as still in the late feminine mysteries – all males are excluded. ... Thus the primitive fence enclosing the female place of childbearing became a sign for the sacred precinct in general, and the process of birth becomes a prototype for the process of rebirth, of "higher" birth into the heavens as a star or immortal (pgs. 158 – 159)

In the Gestation rune, we are placed in the inner sanctuary of the goddess-cave, or temple. It is a place of silence, stillness, recollection and sanctity. The time of birth, or rebirth is fast approaching. Like the 'Prisoner' card in Tarot, we have been placed in a region of boundaries and limitation so that we can brood on our inner self-form, and achieve wholeness as a prelude to being reborn.

Standard Meanings for Divination
Upright

Earth: Security; womblike conditions; health issues.

Fire: Slow development; gestation.

Air: Cloister; sanctuary.

Water: Safety and protection; nurture assured.

Ether: The protection of the Mother; enveloped in security from on high.

Reversed

Earth: Security threatened; sources of supply disrupted.

Fire: Development arrested.

Air: Protection withdrawn; open to attack.

Water: Vulnerability; exposure.

Ether: The possibilities are wide open; you are unprotected.

Spiritual Meanings for Divination
Earth: Limitation

All forms of achievement require the focusing of energy and intent. In other words, to accomplish a specific goal, it is necessary to limit and concentrate the available resources. Gestation is a time when fixed limits are in place, and these may be beneficial for the development of some future possibility. It could reflect a situation where there is immaturity or weakness which is being sheltered and protected. Or it could be a voluntary choice which an individual might make, to step back from outer involvement and find a sanctuary or retreat in order to re-organize and consolidate. In Tarot, the four of swords is rather like this. We see a figure reclining in a chapel and taking rest. Desirable limits help greatly in the achievement of specific goals. Protected environments are essential for tender, young and growing offspring. The need for protection may refer to a person, or to his or her plans, ideals, dreams, future potential, or any other seed-possibility which requires an undisturbed period of time in which to gestate and gather strength. Limits which are beyond our control are sometimes a providential blessing.

Fire: The Process

There is a reason why the small cup or cauldron is being sheltered. It contains something precious which is not yet ready to be exposed in the outer world. We are reminded of alchemy and the successive heatings and purifications which are necessary to transmute base metal into gold. Our body is a field of experience where we labour to incarnate our highest dreams and ideals. Alchemical symbolism is often understood in terms of inner, spiritual work which a seeker does in the microcosm of his or her physically incarnate being. The end result, or gold, is the purified consciousness which can unite with the Divine. If there is no interference from the outside, the alchemical transmutation will be able to proceed until the work is complete – hence the need for gestation. The Gestation Rune can be seen as a time for nurturing the soul's development and turning inward to regroup and focus on what is essential. It may be a hint that we should, like the Hermit in Tarot, look for some solitude and silence in our life. If we can pay attention to our inner world, we may become more aware of the process by which we are being given a special opportunity to grow and develop and thus to realize our highest potential.

Air: Nurture

The Gestation rune in its airy aspect counsels us to nurture our ideals. In the world of mind, some thoughts are tinged with the glory of celestial possibilities. We can only attract these and develop them if we are finely attuned, if our mental substance is refined and clarified. The reading we do, the poetry we write, the fineness of our aesthetic sensibility, the clarity and order and discipline of our reasoning processes, - all these are a part of what we need to attract and nurture heavenly thought-seeds. If we plant such seeds and tend them, in time we will have a vision of higher integration. We will be able to contribute something to the coming together of heaven and earth in the area of our specialized knowledge. Therefore, treasure and nurture the divinely beautiful and supremely inspired jewels that shine from time to time in the firmament of the mind. They will begin to glow like stars and become part of a pattern, which will unfold into a spiritual destiny. In this way you give birth to the universe of higher possibilities and incarnate them in the mental domains of the earth consciousness.

Water: The Womb

The first and original gestation is the nine months in the watery matrix of the womb. This is the state of paradise before any challenges or corruption, the undivided unity between the soul-child and the divine mother. So closely united are the unborn child and the mother in whose womb gestation is taking place that mother and child are aware of each other continuously on many levels of consciousness. This total attunement is a picture of spiritual oneness and unconditional self-giving. Without being aware of it, the child is incorporated into the life of the mother; and without thinking or choosing, the life of the mother sustains that of the child. The two are one. The mother knows that a difficult passage lies ahead, a separation of the oneness into duality, a birth with blood and pain. The child is oblivious of the fact. But in order for paradise to manifest in the outer world, the soul must experience separation from the primal matrix and learn to make oneness with the Divine Mother a living reality in a fully conscious human independence. All of this is inherent in the meaning of the Gestation rune in its watery aspect.

Ether: The Child

The child of the heart must be nurtured, protected, treasured and lovingly attended to if it is to achieve its destiny. In the inner world, this *psychic being*, an emanation of the soul, is silently waiting to be called to life. In the inner world, when undeveloped, it may manifest in the form of a spark or of a small flame. Or one may see and experience the consciousness of the child in the heart as a being with human form. Each time you open the heart and attune your attention to spirit, a bit of inner life is given to this soul-child. This is spiritual nurture. This is how the gestation of the child in the heart takes place. In the ancient myths and legends, often times we find tales in which the divine child was reared by the goddess in a remote cave until he (it could also be she) attained the fullness of his powers. For example, Zeus was raised by Rhea in the high mountains of Crete. These mythic images are symbolic of the mystical experience we can have if we nurture and develop the child in the heart. A divinely beautiful being grows inside us and its luminous presence links us to the eternal Beloved. If you choose the ether level of the Gestation rune, then it would be wise to consider your relation to the child in your heart. Consider how you can nurture this infant possibility to unfold into its full potential.

EMERGENCE

The Archetype

The image of the Emergence Rune shows a chevron opening upward, cradled in the top section of an "X"-symbol. That which was hidden becomes apparent, possibly arising out of a crisis. The seed which was planted underground pushes through to the surface and experiences the light. From a slow and steady push upward into sunshine and warmth, a young, sprouting plant emerges into daylight. We see the birth and the early phase of a new possibility that will unfold in time. This rune signifies newness, innocence and vulnerability when consciousness is free of fixations and obsessions. It is a time when an emerging possibility has yet to be confirmed. Something which has been obscured becomes visible. A birth takes place, or a new project is launched. There is innate innocence and freedom from mental and social conditioning.

All over the world people have given the New Moon special significance. When the slender silver crescent would first appear from the darkness, there would be joyous celebrations, because what had died was now reborn and the light was still there to nourish the world below. If the Moon dies and then comes to life again within three days, so will the human who has passed into the other life attain rebirth. The emergence of the young Moon is a promise of moisture and sustenance to come. There are an extraordinary number of different ways in which the arrival of the New Moon is celebrated around the world, but the central, awesome event is the moment when the newly born light is first sighted after the days of darkness. Traditionally, the New Moon and the Full Moon were considered auspicious times for marriage, birthgiving, divination, and fostering dreams and relationships.

In the most general sense, this archetype (Emergence), signifies that which has been lost or obscured is restored to its primal freshness and newness. A new cycle of growth and life begins.

Standard Meanings for Divination

Upright

Earth: A birth, progeny; a release; an opportunity.

Fire: A liberation; an achievement (positive).

Air: A revelation; a disclosure; new information.

Water: A new development (positive); an opening; good feelings.

Ether: An achievement; a victory; a new possibility for good.

Reversed

Earth: A death; a suppression.

Fire: Containment; delay; prevention.
Air: Denial; negation.
Water: Repression; energies are capped; deflation.
Ether: A spiritual abortion; being stifled within.

Spiritual Meanings for Divination
Earth: Immaturity
When we are learning about ourselves and our environment in an early phase of self-development, the inferior and superior aspects of our character are mixed up and disorganized. We have no awareness of who we are in the inner world, or how to do the inner work of self development which will be necessary to realize our full potential. This is a time before inner unfoldment of potential. In this state of immaturity, a condition of 'blissful ignorance' may prevail, and yet there is not a lot of blame to be assigned because there is a lack of experience. A certain amount of youthful folly is forgivable, and should not be judged too harshly. At the same time, sound patterns of discipline can be laid down for the future because the unstructured consciousness can easily be guided and shaped. The best attitude that can be taken in one who is immature is eagerness to learn and modesty. With steady perseverance, growth and learning will come, and the latent potential will be revealed.

Fire: Receptivity
At the time of emergence, the consciousness is open and receptive. The intellect is still undeveloped, and the intuitions are not yet clouded over by education and social conditioning. Frequently in life, the training we receive causes the intellect to take the lead, and in time it takes over and sets our program and determines our responses to life. If this happens, we lose our intuitive capacities. The unfixed quality present at the time of Emergence is in need of shaping. It is necessary to find one's way forward in life. Yet, if the intellect presumes to take command of the personality, a future imbalance can occur and a separation from higher forms of inner guidance can result.

Air: Shine

At the birth of a holy being, sometimes a star would shine in the skies. And sometimes at the passing of a great soul, a new star would appear. The great and holy souls shine like stars in the inner world, and sometimes their light also touches and changes the lives of others who cross their path on earth. The emergence of a star in the sky is a momentous event. It is cosmically symbolic of the soul's choice to shine its beauty and harmony into the earth atmosphere in unconditional self-giving. In this way, the soul becomes an instrument of divine compassion, and a channel for grace. Emergence is an early phase of the lunar unfolding, but on the higher levels it can be a time of immense spiritual significance. Let the star of grace and hope shine in your life, and become identified with its action. Then become what you have attuned to and let the divine be the doer of your life. This is the message of the Emergence rune in the sacred element of Air.

Water: Flow

In the mythology of India, Lord Shiva released the Ganges to flow down from the mountains and bless the lowlands. The Emergence rune sometimes points to an unblocking of the floodgates or barriers that have withheld the waters of life and consciousness. It is a divine act of power and grace to have the impediments removed so that the purifying and life-giving waters can flow again. If you receive the energy of the Emergence rune in its watery phase, it points to the possibility of such an unblocking. You may meditate with the water element to feel how it can flow through you and wash away any impurities or blockages and thus allow the emergence of new possibilities that have not yet manifested.

Ether: Pentecost

Spirit emerges from its heavenly abode and manifests as a light and power that reveal celestial possibilities on earth. The story of how flames of light appeared above the heads of the apostles is an image of the emergence of spirit, referred to in Christian theology as the "Holy Spirit" or "Holy Ghost". This is a very special act of grace, equivalent to a 'confirmation' of spiritual possibilities, or in the older mystery school tradition, an initiation. What seems to emerge from a higher domain was and is latent within our own microcosm, but the initiation or act of compassion from on high seems to be needed for its emergence. Sometimes, in the Christian tradition, the descent of a dove, or in the Andean tradition, the arrival of a hummingbird, is taken by would-be initiates as sign of immanent divine emergence. But the mythic or symbolic forms are not as important as the awareness that some divine possibility which has not yet manifested is ready to come to the fore. Our choice and conscious attunement is vitally important at this time if we are to permanently establish this reality in our lives.

Thunder

The Archetype

The Rune "Thunder" shows an upward moving force striking at the space between two chevrons. There is a sense of impact and intersecting waves of energy. A static situation is shaken into activity. There is a similar trigram in the *I Ching* which is termed "Thunder", and it pictures a shaking force that comes up from below the surface of the earth. In Tarot, The Tower is similarly an image of shaking, but it is a big, solid castle rampart that gets blasted. However the Rune "Thunder" comes at the beginning of a lunar cycle, which means that it is not so much a matter of breaking down old, fixed structures as it is a question of awakening latent potential. The situation calls for a good shake or a bolt of force to scatter inertia and galvanize latent energy. Like a sonic boom, the wave of energy comes and strikes the outer surface of the recipient. The recipient may be the mind, or energy-field of an individual, or it may be a situation involving several individuals. If we trace the previous runes, "Field", "Seeding" and "Gestation", the action of arousal, signified by "Thunder", can be seen as the necessary stimulus which breaks open the protective covers of the latent possibility and sets the stage for "Emergence" into a bigger field of activity. It may precipitate a movement from the inner to the outer, from the passive to the active, from the quiet to the dynamic, or from the seed to the sprout which pokes its head above the earth and begins to feed on sunshine.

Standard Meanings for Divination

Upright

Earth: A shakeup; an upheaval; a new opportunity.

Fire: Enter the unpexpected; an internal revolution; opening a new way.

Air: A change of mind; new and important developments.

Water: Powerful forces for change are at work; emotional upheaval (potentially positive if handled wisely).

Ether: An intense event that brings about changes; catalyst for change; the power to act decisively.

Reversed

Earth: Destructive forces at work; adverse changes; disruption.

Fire: To go forward in the same way brings adversity.

Air: Your way of thinking will be challenged, opposed or discredited; disruption.

Water: Resistance (on the part of the querent) to the coming change; pressure to change creates stress.

Ether: "A bolt from the blue"; a disruptive catalyst; a spiritual challenge.

Spiritual Meanings for Divination

Earth: The Will to Progress

Thunder energy moves upward from below the surface of the earth. It represents a will for progress, the willingness to cheerfully let go of everything that impedes progress, to set aside whatever constrains our forward momentum. This is a movement towards a better tomorrow. When this energy is in full surge, it is much easier to be unburdened of old habits, limitations, knots and contractions of energy. There is always an exceptional hour or day when conditions are especially auspicious for a revolution, and this revolution proceeds from an inner impetus whose nature is Thunder. If we are aware of the special time when major change is possible, miracles can be accomplished.

Fire: Fire in the Earth

When a volcano erupts, we have an example of the thunderous power of the fire that lives in the core of the earth. There is also a fire that lives in the earthly temple of the human body. Eruption of heat from within, as in anger, rage, or violence is a distortion of the Thunder power. Its destructive force can obliterate the subtle attunements of spiritual energy and consciousness built up in weeks of aspiration. The true Thunder power is an inner shaking from the depths that makes room for a new insight or energy that is expansive and productive. Never confuse the irruption of ego with that of the inner, creative and spiritual flame of the soul's will. When the fiery will for progress shakes us from within, it will bear fruit in an opportunity or challenge by means of which we can progress.

Air: Shaking the Foundation

Air is the world of mind and thought. Thunder energy shakes from within. Thus the Thunder rune in the Air application refers to a shaking up of thought structures, a testing or breaking down of some basic assumptions which might have been in need of replacement. Many of the things we take for granted are elements of mental conditioning that we uncritically inherit from family, education or society. Although these ways of thinking may be sound in the sphere of worldly practicality, for the life of the ego, or in accommodating the worldly ignorance, they may be impediments to the spiritual illumination of the mind. Therefore, a shakeup of mental conditioning is a blessing in disguise. Do not rationalize or defend what has been dislodged. See in what way a change or re-assessment can open you to greater light in the mind.

Water: Ripples

When water is stirred up from below, it becomes clouded, and ripples appear on the surface. The accumulated sediment at the bottom of a pond clouds the water. It takes time for it to settle down and become clear again. If the emotions are clouded, it is not a good time to take decisions. Wait for clarity. Call in the peace and stillness, let the ripples disappear from the agitated mind. Then see what might have changed and discern how best to act.

Ether: Mandate

The ether represents our lifeline of connectedness to spirit. If the Thunder rune is active on the etheric level, it means that a charge of energy and consciousness has come to us from some deeper plane of our being. This is likely to be an inner shakeup which dislodges some things to make room for others which are more spiritually promising. Because it originates on one of the higher planes of being, it may be quite subtle in nature, and it could take time to discern its full meaning and impact. The inner guide gives us, from time to time, a powerful mandate for inner change. If we accept and act upon this impulsion, we can fully realize its blessing and benefit from it to the utmost. If, however, our attention is distracted by outer concerns, or by the agitation of the mind and emotions, we may miss the opportunity. Look within to the deeper levels to see what the change is and how it can unfold as a change for the better. Do not lament or cling to elements of the past which are ready to change. See the opportunity and be ready to move with it.

GROWTH

The Archetype

The rune for Growth is an upward pointing arrow. Energy is rising and development is taking place. There is a reaching upward and outward to go beyond previous limits and boundaries. There is increase of substance and mobility. Augmentation, building up of life energy, gain, magnification and expansion are all indicated by this sign. Because the arrow points upward, it moves toward the sky, or heavenly region, which signifies a growth of consciousness as well as everything already mentioned. This is a sign of male energy. It has phallic overtones. The dynamic upward push is full of life energy and inner intensity. It may be seen as the growing tip of the young tree, thrusting toward the sky, full of growth hormones, or it may be seen as the spear which stands erect and ready to serve, with aggressive possibilities not too far away.

Standard Meanings for Divination
Upright

Earth: Increase; improvement; progress; positive energy.

Fire: Uplift; amelioration; righteous action; growth.

Air: To champion a cause; promote an idea; get behind a new way of thinking.

Water: Commitment; loyalty; firm intent; emotionally resolved.

Ether: You receive sanction to proceed; a go-ahead indication from above.

Reversed

Earth: Loss, decline, decay.

Fire: Unrighteous, or destructive action; an adverse will; diminishing energy.

Air: Lack of commitment; intellectual resistance; condemnation.

Water: Opposition (emotional); resistance; negativity.

Ether: A contrary oracle; a decision against.

Spiritual Meanings for Divination
Earth: Integral Aspiration

Aspiration is the inner urge to grow in consciousness, to attain wholeness and fullness of being. It is a thing which can be developed, enhanced, augmented. One may come into life with a relatively modest aspiration and then develop it until the inner urge for growth becomes overwhelming, the central need of the entire being. Directed will is largely important in this process, but so also is heart-opening. In time, if one is sincere, the aspiration becomes continuous. If a spiritual seeker is still at the stage where conscious aspiration is an on-again, off-again thing, there is much room for development.

One may have aspiration in the mind, which means that one desires knowledge, reasoning-power, understanding, the capacity of verbal self-expression, or clear and numerous insights. All facets of the mind may be developed and offered to the service of the soul's will, and when this is effected, the mental aspiration becomes complete. If one can observe one's thoughts, control the thoughts and then master the thoughts, one can attain mental mastery. A purified mind does not allow wrong thoughts, and is a considerable addition to the integral aspiration. At the level of energy, or vitality, there may be an aspiration for balance, freedom from emotional attachment, calm, goodwill, or for power. If one wishes one's vital nature to become free of all worldly pushes and pulls so that it may be fully consecrated to the Divine Plan, then one's vital aspiration can be considered sincere. The physical body may also feel a need to develop itself, to become stronger, more resilient, more devoted and disciplined. When one's aspiration for physical wellbeing and good health is based on dedication to the Divine, then the body's contribution to integral aspiration can come into effective play. At the core of the being, there is an intense devotion and urge to be united with the Peace, Light, Delight and Love of the Source, to give oneself totally to the Transcendental Reality and merge and become one with It.

Fire: Self Giving

Growth of consciousness comes from self-giving. This consecrated dedication of oneself must become effective on all levels of the being if it is to bear fruit in a final transformation of life from earthly to heavenly reality. The mind, the vital energy and the physical body all have a role to play, and a contribution to make if one wishes to achieve integral aspiration. The whole significance of life acquires new depth and momentum when these various parts of the being are aligned with the soul and its plan. Lasting happiness, strength and fullness of being come only when there is a sincere and complete self giving to the soul and its divine mandate.

Air: The Mental Ego

A very large part of our growth as human beings is mind-development, and as the mind develops, so does the ego. When the ego appears and begins to take a dominant position in the individual's life, it becomes possible to complete the necessary work which is required before one can become a truly individualized entity. Previously, there was no central will or identity, one was simply a collection of everything that one's group manifested, with very little original input. The ego develops in order to make possible the formation of a fully independent and individualized human entity, and this is a considerable achievement in the evolution of consciousness on earth. Unfortunately, in the course of developing, the mind and ego are often filled with social conditioning and religious notions that limit spontaneity and hamper their scope of will. If one takes on all the conditioning that comes from parents, society, education and religion, one may develop a narrow and restricted mental ego, crammed with notions of correctness, sin, social approval and punishment; or one may become quite selfish, calculating and contracted. The unconscious and spontaneous purity which we inherit from nature is inevitably buried when the ego becomes dominant, but this is only a passage to something larger, not a permanent situation. The soul eventually begins to aspire for a new kind of inner freedom based on alignment with the Divine Will and Presence. At this time, the mental ego must acknowledge and surrender to the soul's guidance. Its resistance creates suffering, and sometimes disease. Our precious individuality must learn to merge with THAT which transcends it.

Water: Growth in Relationship

All growth occurs in the context of relationship, and relationships can be of three kinds. Firstly, we have our relationship to our own inner self. Then, we have a relationship to the world and its life forms, including other human beings. Lastly, we have a relationship to the Divine. The mastery of right relationship works itself out along all of these vectors. When we are growing in consciousness, everything that happens has a special value and can contribute to our progress in self-awareness. Behind all our encounters a process is at work, and according to our power of insight and observation, as well as our sincerity of aspiration, we can discern what meaning and opportunity is afforded us by such experiences.

Ether: Reversal

In the spiritual life, when you stop going forward and upward, you begin to sink back. When you wish to take rest and settle for some lesser satisfaction, a substitute for the spiritual aspiration that nourishes your inner growth, you commence the process of decline. Growth is always a forward momentum to greater ranges of consciousness and fuller measures of expression. Inertia, discouragement, the desire to take rest, and sometimes just plain boredom can slow us down, and if we sink into slothful habits, they can spell an end to our development. Higher help comes to those who call and struggle. True rest comes when we learn how to deepen and widen our awareness into the universal consciousness. Naturally, the development and application of steady discipline is a great support to the process of inner and outer growth. By focusing our awareness on our central goal, and applying our best efforts to its realization, we expedite the day when it will finally become a living reality.

Challenge

The Archetype

The symbol for Challenge has two opposing chevrons and a small vertical line between and above them. The small vertical line would be caught between these clashing forces if could not rise above them, which it seems to be doing. Challenge requires us to become resourceful, insightful and skilful. With this rune, there is an experience of stressful energy, energy derived either from external influences or from internal habit, possibly from compulsive or impulsive behaviour. There may be unruly thoughts and emotions, volatility, passion or some other form of conflicted energy at work, presenting a need to resolve conflicts and differences by establishing a higher harmony. When energies, philosophies or wills clash, one must try to find resolution. A time of testing and trial is often seen as adversity, but it also contains an opportunity. Disruption, stress and opposition demand a solution, but in seeking resolution we must be true to our deepest instincts and not just try to find "peace at all costs."

Standard Meanings for Divination

Upright

Earth: You face a difficulty; you are being opposed.
Fire: Attempt reconciliation; balance both sides.
Air: Diplomacy needed; move carefully.
Water: You are "caught in the middle".
Ether: Try to balance both sides; look for the blessing in the challenge.

Reversed

Earth: You lack the resources to change the situation; the problem is too big.

Fire: You are not free to maneuvre; conflict; aggression.

Air: Reconciliation unlikely; conflict; psychological problem.

Water: You are overwhelmed by the problem; you face relentless pressures.

Ether: It will be difficult to get out from under this situation; some very heavy inner forces are working against you.

Spiritual Meanings for Divination
Earth: A Will for Progress

The Challenge rune presents us with a situation in which progress may be impeded if we do not face the difficulties that lie before us. Whatever hampers our advance must be recognized and transcended. Of course, it is indispensable to have full faith in ourselves and the cause for which we are struggling, but we must also recognize the need to adapt as circumstances require and to be freed of old reactions, habits and opinions. Only thus do we claim the freedom to shape a better future. It is a tremendous privilege to be given an opportunity to make oneself or the world more harmonious and beautiful so that it can reflect a divine reality. Giving way to discouragement, pessimism and despair never helps, because however challenging outer circumstances are, there is a choice or an action which can be a positive contribution. One who has faith can face all adversities without fear.

Challenge is related to ego. Who is challenged? Always, it is the separate self that is challenged, the small self, the concept of self that exists in the mind. The agenda of the ego is wrapped up in its own preferences, its desire to experience pleasure and to avoid suffering. It gives the ego pleasure to form attachments, to entertain the idea that things or people in the outer world can become its belongings, that it can manipulate and exercise power over them. The ego wants to hold on to its possessions and it judges people and the experiences that come its way according to their effects on its agenda of self-aggrandizement. Its comparisons, opinions, likes and dislikes, strategies and activities are all self-serving, and this is its key limitation. One who lives in the ego is trapped in an endless series of desires, some of which can be satisfied, and many of which cannot. The thoughts and beliefs of the mind support the notion that life is all about the struggle to find satisfaction in the terms which the separate ego proposes, but living this way only creates further bondage to the inherent ignorance of the ego-bound intellect. Yet, there *is* a way to escape. One must challenge this conditioning and bring the mind into the light of the Spirit, the Higher Self. The Challenge rune can be seen, from one perspective, as an indication that the time has come to face and transcend ignorance, and open the mind to a greater light than the ego can provide. One of the tools which the mind calls upon to maintain its domination is the power of fear. When we challenge the ego, the mind will evoke a series of fears to raise doubt about what might happen if we alter our habits. These fears can also be challenged; in fact, the Challenge rune empowers us to tackle everything that may limit our spiritual progress.

Fire: The Challenge of Integration

Often, a challenge which confronts us in the outer world is an exterior image of something that needs to be worked out by harmonizing various parts of our own inner being. A human being is comprised of many levels of energy and consciousness. It takes time to become aware of the constituents which make up our microcosm, and then we must learn to harmonize, and finally master them. When we place one part of our being in the light, there are others that remain still unchanged, and these areas of darkness to not surrender until they are acknowledge, accepted, offered and finally mastered. Little by little, these intransigent parts of our being make their presence felt, undermine the harmony which we are working to develop, and call out for integration. When an outer problem or challenge arises, it often points to an underlying factor within us which has come up for transformation or alignment to the soul-purpose. Unification is a lifelong work. As long as one part of us pulls in one direction, and another part pulls the opposite way, we will face challenges which require ever deeper levels of integration. Only when we establish a deep bonding between the mind, the vital, the physical and the soul can the work be considered complete.

Air: Challenging the Mind

The mind can be a good servant, but it makes a very bad master. Having worked very hard to train and educate the mind, it is not easy to accept that we have only completed one phase, and not even the most important, of a very long journey. Mind and ego are obverse and reverse of the same coin. To become an individualized human being, it is necessary to develop a good mind and a sound understanding of what human life is all about. Yet when we want to go beyond the limits of mind and ego, it becomes necessary to transform and illumine the intellect. It takes time and effort to develop the ability to reason, but reason is a wonderful tool for bringing order to our impulses, passions, whims and desires. When we are at the mercy of our vital cravings, we definitely need the ordering capacity of a clear mind. Still, when we have developed our intelligence and reason and established harmony in the emotions, the only way we can proceed further is to illumine and purify the mind. Reason is then seen to be not a resting place but a stepping stone to something higher. Mystical truth is not attainable by logic and analysis. Wisdom cannot be achieved by accumulating information. Only when we begin to rely on the spiritual heart, the soul, and divine grace can we bring the light of divine truth into the mind. Once illumined, the intellect can support the further evolution of consciousness toward full enlightenment, but it must first surrender to the Divine Will. This means that ego will have to take the back seat. To replace ego by surrender to the divine is the greatest challenge one can imagine.

Water: Outer and Inner Challenges

Most people are completely preoccupied with their outer lives. Their consciousness is focused on the things they are doing, the people they know, their job, money, family and the kind of entertainment they prefer. Life can be filled to the brim and kept very busy with the activities that we invent or accede to. Sleeping, eating, working, socializing, having fun,- lifetimes can be spent in such a fashion.

From this kind of outer life and the experiences it can give us, we develop an individualized personality and an ego. To complete this development is one phase of the work which the soul must accomplish before it can proceed further in its evolution. To be a 'younger soul' means to be completely pre-occupied with all that the outer life entails, and it is widely imagined to be what a "normal" human life is all about.

At some point, the consciousness of the individual deepens sufficiently to become aware of the inner life. At this time, the soul and its aspiration is felt, and the purpose and direction of life take on a new quality. One gives less importance to the superficialities of the outer life, and pays more attention to the question : "Who am I? and What is the purpose of living?" When one becomes more interested in the Source of life than in the variety of its outer manifestation, more interested in the goal of the soul than in the success of the ego, one begins to withdraw energy from the outer surfaces and concentrate it in the inner depths. This shift from the outer to the inner is a reversal of attention and energy, and it undermines the validity of much of what we have identified with in the past. The ego, the mind, the education and the social conditioning that have previously played important roles may now seem somehow shallow and incomplete. We hear the rhythm of a different drummer, and we feel the call to pursue happiness in a new way.

Ether: Challenge is Opportunity

Our human tendency is to see stress, difficulty and uncertainty as something undesirable. We do not like to be destabilized in any way. We cling to our preferred notions of 'the good life' and base our decisions on previous experience. However, if we wish to evolve beyond what we currently have and are, it is necessary to dismantle and re-assemble the constituents of our existence and attain a new balance on a higher level of harmony and peace.

Challenge immediately focuses us on the need for change. It has been said that when we are reluctant to follow the light, suffering becomes the teacher. Challenge is a hint that suffering may be headed our way unless we make adjustments. It is a diagnosis of difficulty. The difficulty frequently seems to be something in our outer life – a problematic relationship, a heath issue, a financial dilemma. But when we look closely, we see that the outer challenges are usually symptoms of an inner attitude, disposition or point of view that we harbour and cherish within our own mind. Once we change this way of seeing and being, the difficulty can turn out to be an opportunity, or even a blessing in disguise. Who suffers? Only the ego. The *way* in which suffering approaches us is very interesting since it reveals how we are identifying with ego, the small self which separates itself from the pattern of the whole. When we can see the true difficulty and its roots in our own attitude, the next challenge is to let go. That being done, the outer problem may vanish altogether.

FIRE

The Archetype

This rune stands for radiance, brightness, the light-giving aspect of fire, sunrise, the dawn of consciousness, intellectual enhancement, the creative impulse, warmth, illumination (as yet incomplete), learning, and growth in clarity and power. In the *I Ching*, the trigram for Fire points out that it must cling to its fuel, which is its source of strength. Thus the idea of holding firmly to a base of supply and nourishment is also part of the image's meaning. However, the Fire Archetype is often understood as creative and spiritual energy, focused willpower, enthusiasm, initiative, bold endeavour, zeal and striving. Bold action is favoured by this sign, and vigorous application of energy whether mental or physical is also fully supported.

Standard Meanings for Divination

Upright

Earth: Power to make changes; potential which can be manifested physically.

Fire: Clearly directed will; focused motivation; good communications.
Air: Good order; a balanced approach; light in the mind.
Water: A creative possibility; creative energies in the heart centre.
Ether: The urge toward transcendence; ascension; a higher light coming into the situation; energies favourable to success.

Reversed

Earth: Suspension of action.
Fire: Will not actively expressed; power is blocked.
Air: Preoccupations cause delay; inner clarity is obscured.
Water: Feelings clouded; intuition blocked; creative energy stifled.
Ether: Conditions for progress negated; higher guidance blocked.

Spiritual Meanings for Divination
Earth: Higher Energy

We are taught that our energy comes from the food we eat and the air we breathe. To some degree, we know also that the level of energy we can sustain is related to our psychological health. Spiritual energy is something that we may not be familiar with. It is received from above, not from below, and it links us to the Source of creation. When we aspire to connect with it, when we have sufficient trust, faith and wideness to identify with it, the experience of being infused with the fire from above can become our very own. We have all at some point or another felt lifted up above our ordinary boundaries and limits into something lighter, loftier and sweeter. The force that makes this uplift possible is spiritual fire. From such experiences, temporary though they are, we see that we can enter the flow of something much bigger than our limited human preoccupations. If we ever taste the fullness and power and enlivening quality of this higher energy, we could wish that it was a permanent part of our experience, and then we would begin to ask how we might cultivate it and make it our own. At this point, we enter the domain of spiritual aspiration, which is itself a child of the fire.

The higher energy is infinite, but we must know how to receive it, identify with it, and merge in its source. First one becomes aware of the higher energies, under what conditions they enter into the being, and how they are spent and lost. Then, one identifies the way to call up such energies and maintain contact with them through intention, affirmation, inner will, or whatever method is most suitable. There are many kinds of energy to which we can be attuned, and we must master many levels of consciousness in order to receive them. It is easy to waste what we are given. Only when we work for the higher energies do we learn to value and sustain them.

Eventually, the fire which awakened our aspiration at the beginning of our spiritual journey will bear fruit. We will learn to sustain our contact with the power and presence of the inner light. Fire is light, will, energy and consciousness, a living reality that transports our consciousness beyond the realm of words and thinking into a direct experience of higher life.

Fire: The Fire of Spiritual Will

Some people have awakened within themselves a will for self-discovery and spiritual realization, while others have not. Some seekers have placed this aspiration for light and truth at the centre of their lives, but most have not. When this will for progress is alive in the heart, and present in all that one says or does, it can be said that the inner fire has been lit. Some have achieved this without being able to explain the process or even recognize it. They feel attracted to the Divine without any mental notion of what it is, or any philosophical explanation of what calls them to self-transcendence. Usually, however, a conscious aspiration is needed if one wants to make the inner flame burn bright and strong. This requires the development and application of will. Spiritual will burns like a fire in the heart and purifies all parts of the being. Any defect that stands in the way of progress can be taken and tossed into this fire. At certain stages of meditation, one can actually see and feel the spiritual flame in the heart, in fact the ancient seers of India gave it a name Agni. Whenever something arises which blocks the way forward, it can be offered to the transforming fire, and the way will be cleared.

Air: Fire from Above

Physical fire is an expression on this earth-plane of a force that can be found on many other planes of reality. In different traditions, these planes are described with different terms, but one of the more common designations refers to the etheric, astral, mental, buddhic and atmic planes. In each of the inner worlds, that force which we call 'Fire', which is designated by the Fire Rune, expresses itself differently. When we experience it in our own inner microcosm, Fire's most distinctive manifestations include intensity, brilliance, power, light of understanding, uplifting momentum and motivating enthusiasm. In the material world, this essential force manifests as physical flame. This too has its own distinctively fiery characteristics such as giving off light, purifying, consuming, separating (ore from dross), breaking down, and heating. Flame turns poison to purity. Its heat and light enter into matter, consume it, devour it and rebuild it to a higher order of perfection.

In the Indian spiritual tradition, the spiritual fire is called Agni. Agni manifests as willpower, knowledge, revelation, the capacity to see the future, and as the fiery intensity which is capable of transforming earthly creation into something more divinely perfect. As Agni purifies and burns away the dross of human nature, the hidden forms of divinity (or inner Godheads) are revealed, and when the fire completes its work, the full force of revelation comes to the fore and human consciousness takes on the qualities of a seer or a sage. Unconsciousness, inertia, dullness, ill-will, laziness and ignorance imprison Agni. He outshines them all when his transformative power is invoked. To identify with Agni and his work is to open oneself to the highest possibilities that life can afford. On the subconscious level, Agni is instinct; in the conscious intellect, he is understanding; in the purified intellect, he is illumination, and in the transformed and perfected human being, he is spiritual realization.

Water: The Work of Fire

In the Gestation rune, we saw the image of a cauldron under the arc of a protective covering. In the Fire rune, a flame has been lit and the watery contents of the alchemical cauldron have been heated. The refiner's fire can change the raw material of human nature into something pure and beautiful. Perhaps for many lifetimes, we have struggled and laboured to create a fully individualized human nature. However imperfect, obscure or limited the result, it is an important achievement. If we have this attainment, we have gone beyond the protective matrix of Gestation, and we have a cauldron that is ready to receive the transformative force of Fire. The contents of the cauldron must now be offered to Fire. By its action, what the cauldron contains will be transformed into something of unearthly perfection. At last, when the transmuted material has reached a high degree of purity, it is taken up and subsumed into the fiery spirit and becomes merged in the fullness of heaven. Then, the work of fire is complete. The ego-based individuality becomes a divine personality able to act in the world as an instrument of the divine guidance and the divine will. Under the influence of the Fire rune, a beginning can be made in this process. But the completion of the work will require many further stages of experience and the contributing energies of other runes, each in the appointed time.

Ether: Seek The Dawn

The world is unconscious and covered over with the darkness of ignorance. The Gods are asleep. They await the hour when light will begin to penetrate the darkness and create a space for them to enter the earth atmosphere and begin their work. The fire forges earthly forms. It awakens life and desire in these forms. Then, it awakens mind and the light of inner understanding. Next, it fosters the spirit of adventure and the aspiration for heaven. Finally comes the spiritual dawn, a time when dreams and aspirations can be realized. At this stage, the fire from above can effect an alchemical transformation of human life and release the varied elements of our being into the blissful current of divine liberation.

The manifestation of will is made possible by Agni, for he *is* the spiritual will. Agni reveals the divine by means of the sacrifice. Through the power of sacrifice, the spiritual dawn is hastened, and the hour of God approaches when all things dreamed and invoked can be realized and manifested. Through the power of sacrifice (and sacrifice is also a Primal Rune) the spiritual seeker can awaken the flame of aspiration, intensify it, bring his or her human capacities to their highest expression, pour all elements of the being into the transforming fire and finally emerge like the phoenix. divinely transformed. Agni, the god of fire, leads the sacrifice and keeps it incorrupt through the long journey out of darkness and into the dawn. The flame of spiritual awakening seeks this dawn when the soul's dreams can be realized.

CHOICE

The Archetype

The runic symbol for Choice is made up of three short vertical lines and one line that joins them. The upward thrust of the three lines is truncated by the horizontal line, but they become part of one unified glyph. Choice means focusing intention and attention on what is significant. The many possibilities must connect to the one principle which unifies them and is worthy of a supreme effort. To exercise choice with a focused will along the lines of our inspiration is the most favourable level of this rune, but whether or not we align with our soul's plan, we are always faced with the need to choose, and our destiny arises from the choices we make.

> Life is a perpetual choice between truth and falsehood, light and darkness, progress and regression, the ascent towards the heights or a fall into the abyss. It is for each one to choose freely.
> – The Mother, *The Collected Works*, Ch.14, p.29.

To some extent, the Choice rune cuts against the grain of our previous conditioning. We have been taught that progress comes from the manipulation and exploitation of resources outside and around us, such as nature, other people, and the social, political and economic systems of our culture. We have also been conditioned to believe that the power of thinking is what makes us superior in all the world, and that analytical thinking is the best way to plan our strategies for dominance. In the West, religious conditioning has often equated pleasure with evil and concluded that desire was something to repress. Physical life was considered a vale of tears, a place of moral testing, something to endure, not to enjoy, a place of reparation for sin and preparation for the otherworldly blessings of heaven. Trained to see the feminine energy as a source of temptation and Nature as primal chaos, the patriarchal male psyche contracted into its moral codes as the only sure pathway to salvation.

The Choice rune opens a possibility to exercise a different option in an expanded range of possible options. If we can bring the power of the heart to the fore, and align with the light of the spirit, a whole new set of possibilities comes into play in which *choice*, not strategic thinking, or the scriptures of theology, becomes centrally important. The thinking mind directs us to make choices that satisfy the ego and its wish for superiority, but the spiritual heart influences us to choose the harmony of wholeness. Perhaps for much of our life we have acted according to our mental conditioning and following the example of others. This is, after all, the approved way to win acceptance. We have indulged the ego, exercised the power of the mind, acted according to our desires, struggled for self-aggrandizement, and as a result tasted the limitations of selfishness, greed, callousness, intolerance, impatience and restlessness. The Choice rune suggests a new possibility. If the power of choosing moves from the mind and ego into the domain of the spiritual heart, we connect with our real power, the power of oneness with all life. Everything we are, and everything we have assembled around us, comes from exercising choice; moreover, choice and karma are inextricably linked in an endless causal chain. If we can learn to choose from a deeper level of our awareness, we can give birth to a new quality of life and a new way of experiencing the depth of its beauty. The Choice rune invites us to explore and experience that possibility.

Standard Meanings for Divination
Upright
Earth: A turning point; decisions of importance.

Fire: You have several options; there is no obvious best way.

Air: You need to study the situation, and to discern your way by considering various options.

Water: Use your intuition and follow your heart as you weigh what is right for you.

Ether: Try to choose as your higher guidance suggests; surrender your choice to a higher source of direction.

Reversed

Earth: What you need to know is unavailable to you.

Fire: You are moving ahead unwisely.

Air: Your discernment is questionable; there is confusion in the situation.

Water: Appearances are deceptive; you face a dilemma.

Ether: There is no clear resolution; your inner guidance is disrupted.

Spiritual Meanings for Divination
Earth: Taking Up the Work

Only when consciousness is liberated from the pulls and pushes of desire and attachment can we transcend our animal nature. This is an inner work that must be taken up and attended to tirelessly and sincerely, and it is the central choice that faces us from the moment spiritual aspiration is awakened. The heart and the soul are under the influence of divine Light and Love, but for the other parts of the being to surrender to this higher influence, a lengthy and demanding inner discipline must be embraced. If we simply repress desires and sit on them, they will rest in the subconscious regions of the mind and vital and then at some point when we are vulnerable, they will rise up and cause turmoil.

The first thing to recognize is that desire chains a person to his or her weakness and ignorance. These desires are not, as generally supposed, personal to the one who experiences them; they are waves of energy that pass from person to person. Human beings are washed in these waves, but do not create them. Most people are caught and tossed about by the surges of desire because they do not discriminate higher from lower energies, and because they have not developed a focused will that favours Truth over falsehood. Self indulgence is the normal disposition for most human beings, and this opens the door to many undesirable energies such as envy, depression, laziness, hatred or even violence. Although desire is not an intrinsic part of our true nature, it does have the power to invade and deform the parts of our being that are receptive to its influence. The mind's obscurities and doubts create a favourable ground for this to happen; in fact the mind and vital together often oppose the choice of the heart and soul and an inner conflict arises between aspiration and desire. In this matter each one must choose which part of the being to follow, and from the choice follows the destiny.

Fire: Choose Discipline

Only when there is aspiration for a more perfect life does one realize one's full potential. If there is a strong intention to master the lower nature and to transcend desires, it becomes indispensable to take up some discipline of inner transformation. Any form of practice which is suited to one's character and disposition can be of value, but it is necessary to actually practice our chosen discipline sincerely, consistently and patiently. When we choose a life of inner discipline, we move more directly toward our higher goals. In fact, no significant achievement is possible without establishing priorities and focusing the necessary time and energy to attain them. Everyone who ever realized something remarkable has understood this law and put it into practice. In the beginning, it may not be possible to bring order and harmony to one's entire life, but one can at least begin with a small decision and establish it as a regular habit.

One excellent practice, for example, is to set aside time for meditation on a daily basis. This decision to meditate can be supported by spiritual reading, or by associating with people who have similar interests. Souls who share common ideals discover a bond of inner unity and their mutual sharing reinforces the transformational work they have taken up. The foremost friend is the teacher who by an act of unconditional love offers assistance to become established in a life of spiritual discipline. Whenever we experience this selfless love, we are inwardly opened and widened to the action of divine grace. Once we can live in a state of grace, we begin to attract auspicious conditions for making inner progress. To choose a life of discipline is to take a giant stride toward the reign of grace. However, the first step toward any goal is to see with clarity what must be done, and for this we must feed the Fire within, and the light it gives, and apply it to the choices that are before us.

Air: Avoidance

One way that the inner light can be sustained and intensified is by letting go of whatever limits or darkens the inner light of consciousness. Every false idea to which we pay attention has the ability to undermine our central will to be aligned with our higher Self. There are disintegrating influences that will foster inner disorder should we be so unwise as to give them a place in our mind. Seemingly harmless ideas or associations are poor nourishment if we want to sustain a high level of energy and consciousness. When we doubt, criticize, or label, we are dealing with unhealthy energy. When we prevaricate, make excuses for our trivial thoughts, words or actions, or indulge our petty preferences, we become attuned to a contracted consciousness. Because such things seem harmless, the unwise man (or woman) indulges them, and by habituating himself to what is dangerous, he becomes vulnerable. Through unconscious association, we can become attuned to hidden trouble; we can give inferior energies a place in some part of our being because we are self-indulgent. We must recognize the energies that touch us or seize our attention for what they are, and when we are faced with a lure, a delusion, a half-truth, a cover-up, a rationalization or any other falsity, we need to take a step back. The wise one does not judge the evil in others. Rather he sees and rejects even the small deviations from Truth that occur within himself, and by so doing he sustains the central choice to find and follow the divine guidance that whispers from within.

Water: Cultivate Intuition

Intuition is the sense that we have as to whether something feels right or wrong. It is not the same as conscience. It is like an early warning system which can alert us to the approach of some thought or situation that is incompatible with our ideals. Again, it can recognize and give assent to what is good and acceptable. Once we let objectionable things enter our consciousness, once we rationalize and cover over our intuitive sensitivity, we can easily lose touch with this delicate inner guidance. When intuition is interrupted by the mind and vital, which always prefer their own agenda, we have entered the danger zone. Intuitive knowledge is not emotionally reactive, it is balanced in tone, even when alerting us to danger and cautioning us to be still. When intuition prompts us to accept or to reject something, the movement may be so subtle and deep that we can easily miss it. But it is a flawless indicator of where our true nature wants to take us.

To live by the guidance of our spiritual heart is to remain open to inspiration and grace; to question or challenge this guidance is to generate inner conflict and unease. We are able to listen to intuition by being free of lower impulses and preferences. Stillness and inner receptivity to our inner guidance can be cultivated; by looking inward and listening to our own heartspace, we can learn to recognize the promptings of intuition. This choice is one of the best that we can ever make.

Ether: Take Sides

Within each of us is a superior and an inferior consciousness. The sages of the *I Ching* used to refer to these parts of the being as the "superior man" and the "inferior man". The inferior man works with energies of degeneration, decay and death. Doubt and fear are evident when the inferior man comes to the fore, an inner state which often gives rise to conflict, tension, obstruction, deception, and disharmony. When the superior man is dominated by the inferior man, the central will for wholeness is fragmented. Until such time as we restore order, we are prevented from identifying absolutely with what is good and true. The work of inner transformation demands that we resolve this split and restore our inner world to the influence of our Higher Self. Once we make a choice and decide that we want to bring order and harmony to our inner world, we are challenged to penetrate the deepest levels of our attitudes. It is from this profound level that human beings choose either to follow the light, or to indulge, and thereby empower, the darkness. By choosing a fundamentally wholesome course in life, we set in place a central will for harmony, openness, goodness and trust. This single choice to live in the light of Truth predetermines many other, subsequent choices. Because we have decided to follow the light, to live in the light and ultimately to surrender to the light, the darkness automatically recedes. The superior goal can only be attained by the superior part of our being. The "inferior man" uses inferior means and acts from self-serving motives. The "superior man" pays attention to the quality of his motives and conduct and places the emphasis on moment-to-moment integrity. He feels that the goal will take care of itself if he honours the Truth in the eternal Now. To take sides and identify with the "superior man" is to exercise the power of choice in the fullest measure. It prepares, and in large measure determines, our future experiences with the runic archetypes of Karma, Grace, Love, Courage and Fullness.

KARMA

The Archetype

The rune for Karma resembles the letter "M" placed over a horizontal line. We have the image of an up and down movement contrasted with a steady, horizontal plane which acts as a foundation. The up and down pattern represents the swings of fortune experienced by the superficial consciousness of the lower self, the pulls and pushes, desires, joys and disappointments of the ego-bound human self. The steady line beneath all of this represents the inner being, the true Self which abides in the continuous peace of the Source. The rune suggests a need to seek balance as one faces and transforms all kinds of ingrained patterns. Only through consistently sustained practice can we foster favourable qualities of thought and character. Self development enables an individual to untie the inner knots that limit or bind.

It is not only a matter of facing one's mistakes, because not all karma involves retribution and payback; it is more a matter of learning to live harmoniously in balance with nature and with the spiritual laws of the universe.

The process of inner transformation brings about a sharpening and a deepening of perceptions. As we grow in awareness, we develop the capacity to alter limiting patterns of thought and behaviour. Slowly, we rise above the pull of the past and pay off its debts. The concept of karma is sometimes associated with notions of fate and inevitability. However, this rune teaches us to firstly to recognize the reality of how karma works, and secondly to undertake the challenge of inner transformation to clear away negative debts and to sow seeds for a better future. The Seeding rune is an early experience of generating karma where the full implications of one's thoughts and actions are not grasped. The Karma rune, however, draws attention to the laws that govern causality and tells us about the need to take responsibility for our future even as we study the processes by which deeds ripen and bear fruit.

Standard Meanings for Divination

Upright

Earth: Ups and downs; mixed results; variable fortunes; justice.

Fire: You can do better than you have been doing; more will and creativity needed; you need more focus.

Air: Innate wisdom and strength need a more steady expression; discern your core motives.

Water: Inconsistent expression (or manifestation) of core values; your heart is not centred.

Ether: You are reaping what you have sown; this situation is karmic in origin.

Reversed

Earth: You labour under conditions of inevitability.

Fire: Struggle is vain; karmic patterns prevail.

Air: Your thinking is being conditioned by circumstances.

Water: Emotional karma needs to be examined; your heart needs a higher source of guidance.

Ether: You can do better than you are; centre yourself and strive for higher discernment and help.

Spiritual Meanings for Divination
Earth: Neutrality

Frequently what we see in other people is not their excellent and soulful qualities but their very human deficiencies and failings. We often need to make an effort to believe in the redeeming elements in others when their worst qualities are glaringly obvious. One way in which karma works is: "As you judge, so you shall be judged". A judgement hurts the one who pronounces at least as much as it limits the person judged. In the act of judging, energy which would otherwise flow and develop into many latent, positive possibilities becomes fixed and crystallized according to the notion we have fixed in our mind. Such a judgement becomes at times a limiting, self-fulfilling prophecy. To believe in the good that is inside others, and encourage it, is more beneficial than to pronounce on their obvious deficiencies which are so easy to see and enumerate. If we find it impossible to appreciate the excellence of another person, at least we can disengage from our negative judgements about him or her and cultivate a neutral attitude. In this way, we remain open to the potential goodness that is there, but not yet in evidence, and according to the laws of karma, "as you sow, so shall you reap". Since relationship is a two-way street, we are likely, reciprocally, to be spared some of the karmic reckoning that our faults might otherwise attract.

Fire: Willful Indulgence

One who has not seen or understood the limiting nature of karma can to some extent be excused for not taking up the means of nullifying it. But there are others who know enough to make changes in their lives, but who still persist in the old ways that harm themselves and others. "Well," they say, "that is human nature; what can you expect?" The folly of people like this can be called 'willful indulgence'. They have the means to recognize and even to change their weaknesses and problems but they rationalize and justify their behaviour in order to prolong the association with various attachments and pleasures. Saint Augustine of Hippo was in this boat when he was a young man just awakening to his spiritual side. He prayed: "Lord, grant me purity, but not yet!" Somehow, the self-conscious insincerity of this petition makes us smile, but it is a perfect example of what many people do to delay applying the medicine which might change their lives for the better.

Part of human nature likes to continue on doing what it finds pleasurable. In other words, it is worth putting up with the negative consequences of passion in order to continue enjoying the pleasure. The vital cravings and the mental prevarications come together and assert that human nature must be indulged, or else life would be no fun at all. Camels chew thorns even though it makes their mouths bleed, and some very intelligent people smoke cigarettes knowing full well that it increases their chances of developing cancer. For some people, the spiritual life is put on hold, since it is inherently contradictory to take up a discipline whose sole purpose is to change human nature while clinging to its obvious indulgences. Many people look for relief from their symptomatic disorders without any sincere desire to address the underlying cause of suffering itself and be done with bondage for good. For these, the relentless law of karma is unavoidable.

Air: Ego and Surrender

Karma is a construction of the ego. It arises when ego pursues its own self-serving motives in thought and action. When ego abdicates its pride of place and is replaced by a higher and more spiritual guidance, karma comes to an end. Before ego can generously efface itself, it must be developed, refined and nourished with an abundance of learning experiences. When ego becomes ripe and one attains an insight into the ego's relation to desire, suffering and karma, then it is possible to begin the work of transcending ego. We all have certain faults which we express time and again in a seemingly endless round of repetitions. These can be traced back to one theme: *me* and *mine*. If the ego can come to terms with its own inherent limitations and open itself to a higher power, then liberation from limiting karma can proceed much more quickly than it otherwise would. This is the path of surrender. When one turns to the Divine Grace, it can nullify the consequences of karma, but for this one must have reached a point of sincerity where the fault is not repeated. If, instead of endlessly repeating the negative vibration, we can erase it, then the past may be completely purified. This requires a very sincere prayer or aspiration, which is something for which many people may not be ready for. If we have not awakened aspiration, if we are not completely candid and sincere, if we have not developed our willpower, then there is still much work to be done before we can change our karma.

Water: Desire

The shape of our karma comes from the story of our relationship with desire. Desire makes us feel that we are incomplete and causes us to feel that we need to possess something beyond what we already have in order to be satisfied. Yet, once the object of desire is attained, we lose interest in it, and we turn out to be, in fact, *not* happier than before. We have all, no doubt, had the proof of this truth in our own experience. The Buddha has said that there is more joy in overcoming a desire than in satisfying it. Each victory over desire is a triumph over ignorance. We can each experience for ourselves the happiness that comes from lightening our load of karmic involvement by mastering even one desire.

The restless need to possess something, and the anguished sense of being separated from the object of desire are two forms of what the Buddha called suffering. He taught that suffering comes to an end only when desire itself is extinguished. In this way also, he might have added, karma comes to an end. But karma has subtle roots in our attitudes and intentions. Often, our consciousness is shaped and charactized not so much by the things we say and do as by the underlying attitudes and dispositions that make it possible to behave unwisely in the first place. Therefore, the Buddha stressed the need for insight into the nature of desire and its mastery. This teaching is critically important for everyone who comes face to face with the relentless action of karma and feels trapped in a limiting round of actions and reactions born of ignorance.

We came to earth to rise above the pulls and pushes of desire and attain oneness with the Source. Since this Divinity is at the core of creation, and is indeed *the essence of our own being*, we really lack nothing at all and need not look outside ourselves for happiness. If we discover that our deepest need and our ultimate reason for living is to unite with the bliss of our own Higher Self, then desire and its shadow, karma, will lose their power. This is a giant step on the road to liberation.

Ether: Unlearning

When we are at the evolutionary stage of developing a fully individualized human personality, the ego is a most valuable asset, but when we want to go beyond the limitations of our imperfect humanity and enter into the universal consciousness, ego becomes a liability. Many things that are good at a certain phase of development become impediments to progress at a later stage. Whatever helps the consciousness to widen and unfold its full potential may be called 'good', from the spiritual point of view. Thus, challenge, difficulty, suffering, opportunities for selfless service and the blows of karma can all in their own way, and at the right time, help the pilgrim soul to grow and deepen. Only the moralistic human mind conceives of an absolute good which is identical at all times and in all places for all people. Frequently, individuals who think like this are only too happy to convert 'sinners' to their own belief system or impose their so-called truth where it does not fit. They often have no notion that something "good" becomes a liability and a burden when the timing is not right, or when it is out of place.

Ego, so necessary in the early stages of the soul's development, becomes a constriction as our consciousness widens. For the ego, self-aggrandizement and strategy are always present in subtle or obvious forms, for the ego's underlying motive is to build walls against fear by acquiring power. The power may be financial, intellectual, moral, social, political or some other variant, but the result of the ego's relentless drive for acquisition is always to strengthen the small self. Karma is undone only when we choose to unlearn and release this contraction (masquerading as acquisition and aggrandizement) and open the heart and mind to an eternal Truth that far transcends philosophies, theologies and belief systems.

Creativity

The Archetype

The rune for Creativity shows a horizontal line, and above it a second horizontal line which has become an upward-pointing arrow, like the "Growth" rune. It suggests, symbolically, that one has made use of the earthly milieu to kindle the fire of creativity and begin manifesting the brightness of consciousness. Creativity is in essence magical power. It may be gathered, concentrated, transmitted or dissipated, but it emanates unceasingly from the higher regions and settles its blessings on one who is receptive to the Muse (the Mother in her nine creative aspects). Creativity enhances our talents, abilities, potentials, inspirations, motivation, imagination, and spontaneity. Fertility, force and sexual energy are undoubtedly present in the creative impulse, but the power of Eros needs to be channeled into productive lines of endeavour. It can, for example be used to extend our senses to encompass the invisible worlds that surround us, beyond the boundaries of the five senses. Under the sign of the Creativity rune, we have the opportunity to attain a close working relationship to what *I Ching* calls The Creative, or in runic language, The Fullness, which is the revelatory power of the infinite consciousness. Any of the creative arts may serve to open us to this end.

Standard Meanings for Divination

Upright

Earth: The situation calls for creative thinking; be innovative and original.

Fire: Your creativity is strong at present, so honour it.

Air: Think creatively; open your mind to a higher order of harmony and beauty.

Water: Feel your way to a new kind of expression; intuit a creative response to the opportunity before you.

Ether: Go your own way; dare to be different; rise above convention.

Reversed

Earth: Do not innovate at this time.

Fire: You are deficient in creativity at this time.

Air: You are pulling things down; watch out for your ego; pull your mind out of the rut.

Water: Do not tamper with the process or you will spoil things; elevate your feelings and sharpen your intuition.

Ether: You are performing far below your potential; you have disconnected from the muses.

Spiritual Meanings for Divination

Earth: Innocence

When the intellectual mind plays too obtrusive a role, creativity is blocked. Finding the right balance and maintaining openness to inspiration is a learning process, the end result of which might be called 'innocence'. When we cultivate the disposition of openness in a conscious way, doubt and fear are kept at bay, and we have the resilient perseverance to keep on trying until we feel comfortable with the result that emerges – much like a child learning to walk. Innocence is preserved when we avoid comparing our progress with that of others, when we forego the expectation of reward as compensation for our endeavour, and when we establish humility as our fundamental attitude in relation to divine fullness. When we have innocence, we forego strategic calculation, and we are not overly enamoured of the fruits of our labour. The state which Zen calls 'no mind' means to be free of the interference of intellect (when it is not needed) and to regain the freshness and purity of the original or natural mind, which in I Ching is called "Tao Mind". In this return to innocence, openness and trust are preserved in the face of developments that might dismay others, because by keeping our disposition like that of a child, we attract the help of the forces of inspiration. The creative aspect of the divine is often pictured as being female; indeed, the nine Muses were personifications of the divine Mother's creative dynamism. To have an enriched relation with the creative power of The Fullness, nothing works as well as the innocence of a child. However, it is not a mask we put on for the sake of some result, it is the natural way our heart responds to the compassion of infinite supply. It is a recognition of the true relation of the microcosm to the macrocosm, the human part to the divine whole, and the wonder of participating in the Mother's own self-revelation.

Fire: Formations

A formation is an expression of energy-in-form that moves toward actualization. Magic is essentially the power to manifest intention on the physical level, and creativity is similarly a capacity to give expression to the dreams and visions that uplift and inspire us. When we nurture and affirm and meditate on our aspirations, we put into them an energy which is sure to bring about what we believe. There may be delays and obstacles; the earth may not be ready for the creative vision you bring down, but your persistence and your faith will be able to breath such life into your imaginative formation that it will eventually take birth and find a place in the outer world. The mind is a channel in this process, not an originator, and not the real doer. The formations which have most value for our own progress and that of others come from above. They come as intuitions, dreams, visions, prophecies, moments of grace and promptings of inner guidance. One must have great purity to bring these energies through without introducing any distortion, great trust in the wisdom of the divine Grace, and an immense willingness to give time, energy and effort in service to this unfolding possibility. When we add ardour, faith and trust in the divine Grace to the dynamics of creativity, the results can be beyond our wildest imagination. Or, to put it another way, we can see the highest imaginings with which we have been blessed taking shape as earthly realities within our own life. Formations become manifested realities according to certain inner laws, and if we fulfil the conditions, the results are inevitable.

Air: Higher Imagination

The power of imagination opens many doors for progress and is worthy of cultivation. Artists, poets and other creative people are constantly becoming aware of inner realities and giving them expression so that they may be shared with others. The power of expression must be equal to the grandeur of the inner vision if there is not to be distortion, and it is rare to have a truly balanced genius equally adept at envisioning and expressing a high creative possibility. The quality of a creative vision is related to the height, purity and intensity of its energy and consciousness. The great souls who come to earth have this inner work to accomplish: they give form and expression to powerful visions that change the world for the better. Imagination opens the way to realisation. In fact, what we call imagination is an ability to go beyond the domain of things already realized and into the realm of things yet to be manifested, thence to express and eventually to actualize the high possibilities that can shape the future. What is seen and then powerfully uttered becomes seeded into the earth atmosphere where it begins to move towards full manifestation. Although imagination is denigrated and rational logic is exalted in much of our modern educational training, the truth is that imagination holds the key to a better future. As a student at school, one may not be encouraged to develop imagination or to use it constructively, but the soul and the heart will always nurture the inner capacity to dream and to envision a richer and more beautiful existence than that which we have inherited from the past. Therefore, when the outer schooling is complete, or even well before one graduates, it is not uncommon for aspiring souls to be drawn inward to the inner teacher and to be initiated from within into the mysteries of the creative imagination. The outer world and our academic teachers may be altogether unaware of how the inner teaching communicates itself from the soul to the mind, but if we experience ourselves being called and gifted from above, it is something to treasure and honour.

The soul comes to earth to accomplish something unique and wonderful, not merely to be fitted into the outworn patterns of the past. Therefore, even if we are not appreciated or understood, the inner unfoldment of all our creative gifts, and in particular the development of our higher imagination, is something absolutely indispensable not only to our personal progress, but to the world at large.

Water: Devotion

If we wish to maintain our contact with divine creativity, we have to learn something about devotion. When we have this quality, we are able to nurture and give birth to the dreams and visions that arise from deep within the space of the inspired heart. When a hen has laid her eggs, she stays with them and is in close contact until they are finally hatched. In the same way, a writer, poet, artist or musician must nurture the seeds of the creative inspirations that come his or her way. These germs of creative possibility must be brooded over, cared for, fostered and finally birthed into perfect form within the limits of what is possible in the three dimensional physics of planet earth. Inspired ideas can come at any time of the day or night, and sometimes at the least opportune moment. They must be attended to from the instant they register their arrival, much like the mother must turn to her baby when it cries. If we do not watch carefully and listen attentively, the inspirations will pass by, never to return. The Muses offer their creative light to the souls who will nurture and care for their gifts and tend to them lovingly until such time as the birth into form is complete. This process of continuous caring is called devotion. The devotion of a true artist or poet is not essentially different from the mystic's loving attention to the approach of the Divine Beloved in the chamber of the heart. Both the artist and the mystic care enough to give themselves totally to an inner labour of love. In this they become co-creators of the divine revelation on earth.

Ether: The Path of Beauty

The cultivation of beauty can be a path to spiritual realization. Through the development of aesthetic sensibility, one effects a refinement of consciousness that eventually lifts the mind and heart above the clamor and darkness of worldly turmoil. One of the best ways to outgrow the darker instincts, passions and desires is to cultivate the love of beauty, and become a channel for its expression. In time, with persistence, we become that which we contemplate. Pure beauty is an aspect of the Divine Reality. The love of the Divine as beauty is a pathway to spiritual attainment because the beauty-aspect of the Supreme Reality can take up our entire enthusiasm and fill the mind and the will with an overwhelming zeal to express and realize the best that has been seen and felt. Artists and creative people in general know how to give themselves completely to what they love, and this is something they have in common with the mystics, saints and liberated souls. Their innate sense of harmony, the care they give to their craft, the unconditional commitment they have to their relation with the Muse – these are all spiritual dispositions, and they bear fruit in a deepening and an elevation of consciousness. If you are called to the path of beauty, you will not be permitted to remain a dilettante or a dabbler. You will become fully dedicated to the goddess of divine harmony, and you will become her voice, her channel and her living embodiment on earth.

Grace

The Archetype

The runic symbol for Grace is the image of a pillar descending down from the heaven-plane into the void. It does not seem to connect with the earth plane (there is no horizontal line beneath the vertical one), as does the rune for love. Grace comes down unconditionally from the heights as a pure gift. It is an action of the heavenly plane directed downward into earthly consciousness. This rune signifies a possibility of opening the consciousness in attunement to subtle energies. It means also that higher planes of awareness can be touched and assimilated to bring about lasting change. This change can be on one or several levels of the being.

An *integral* transformation would include the subconscious mind, the conscious mind, the cells of the body, the vital energy, the emotions and the ego.

Standard Meanings for Divination
Upright
Earth: Invoke higher help; the divine guidance will be there if you ask.

Fire: Focus your will and intent on the higher help that is available; put your energy into connecting with higher help.

Air: Your thinking is receptive to a higher light; try to open your mind to your inner guidance.

Water: Try to intuit the providential forces which are at work, and align with them.

Ether: The divine action is at work; become its channel; make peace with heaven.

Reversed
Earth: You are on the wrong course.

Fire: You are willfully courting misfortune if you persevere.

Air: Be humble; admit that your course is without heavenly sanction.

Water: Your hearg's balance and harmony have been compromised; try to open your heart to grace once again.

Ether: A spiritual misfortune awaits you if you cannot change; heaven's displeasure should cause you to reflect.

Spiritual Meanings for Divination
Earth: Resistance
The action of grace is like the wind which blows where it will. The human mind would like to be able to contact grace at will, or to even control it, but this is impossible. At various times in history, religious institutions have come into existence with a view to supporting the spiritual potential of their members. But in time,

the domination of the religious leaders, the narrowing definition of which beliefs are 'acceptable', and the self-interested political dynamics of the organization become a form of interference with the action of grace. At times, an institution may actually oppose the potential of its members because it fears that their insights, revelations or progress may undermine its agenda. Historically, we find many cases where there is a book of divine revelation which is considered the final word of God, and all subsequent revelations are forced to fit into its pattern; worse still, mystical revelation itself becomes suspect and puts one at risk of being punished by a religious Inquisition. We all have our individual forms of resistance to the action of grace, and the intellectual mind is frequently very active in this process. However, the collective mind and the institutional ego generated by dominant groups are more pernicious forms of collective suppression. Religious leaders often sow seeds of fear, promising reprisal for those who follow their inner guidance beyond the boundaries of collective approval. By granting or withholding sanction, religious authorities seek to hijack the process of grace, channeling it into sacraments or rituals and claiming that outside the framework of the approved system, there can be no salvation. To be excommunicated from the body of the faithful is held up as a form of spiritual death. It takes tremendous courage to find and follow one's very own inner guidance in the face of such well organized resistance.

Fire: Cultivation

A long and unobserved inner preparation usually precedes the descent of grace, and even after grace intervenes, there is a need to work hard to keep and develop what has been given. Thus, self-discipline in one form or another is indispensable. Saint Ignatius of Loyola used to say that we should pray as if everything depended on God and work as if everything depended on us. But we may want to consider a subtle amendment of his words of wisdom. The grace can work through us if, as we work, we have the sense that we are instruments of a higher power and presence, and that this higher power is the real doer. The results are not our concern; our only real concern is to be constantly in touch with the inner, guiding light. Thus, although we give ourselves completely to the action of grace, nothing in the end depends on us, and all depends on the Divine Will. If we really believe in the power of grace and want to surrender to its action, we will cultivate this disposition and in the end we will bring it about in living experience.

Grace manifests progressively as we outgrow the influence of ignorance and identify with the Higher Self. Although grace often seems to intervene in a miraculous way, its real effect is to lead us into a constant and living union with the divine. The work we do to prepare and cultivate ourselves is indispensable. Grace acts only in conditions of Light and Truth, and to establish these conditions, we must be sincere, devoted, self-giving, faithful, persevering and humble. To cultivate these qualities is to expedite the full descent of the all-transforming grace.

Air: Thinking

What we think colours what we experience. But all thinking is based on memory, and is heavily conditioned by the ego-structure. As we know, the ego is highly resistant to transformation. The reasoning mind will often paint the process of transformation in frightening colours as a negation of the joys of life, or as vain and prideful aggrandizement of our too-limited humanity. In order to be receptive to grace, the mind must become quiet and settle into a different kind of attunement. Meditation is a great help in finding this space of mental receptivity. Because we participate so fully in what we think and believe, it is important to read the words of truly illumined souls who can speak to us about the inner life from their own direct, lived experience. But even then, all preconceptions, notions, expectations and preferences must be set aside in our own mind if we want to be a pure channel for the action of grace. In periods of silence, when strategic effort and inner struggle have been abandoned, a higher level of mind, the illumined mind, may open up to the guiding light of spirit, leading directly to true realization.

Meditation is not thinking, and contemplation, which is an advanced form of meditation, is even further removed from the filtering or distorting action of the intellect. There is a kind of brooding or reflecting which the spiritual heart can do as it nurtures and gestates the seeds of divine light within, but this is far different from the linear thinking of the rational intellect. Our culture and educational training put great emphasis on the refinement of thinking skills. Most of this training is irrelevant when we begin to learn directly from the inner teacher according to the action of grace. If we cannot let go of our previous training and our social conditioning, we will delay or abort the action of grace. Therefore, let go of thinking activity and open the heart when grace makes its presence felt.

Water: Vanity

In time, one comes to understand that all worldly things, all mental formations, all material efforts are futile if they are not in harmony with the divine plan. When this insight dawns, a tremendous advance is possible and the divine grace will be there to support it. When profound insight dawns, we have an opportunity to give ourselves to the divine light and love and to identify so closely with them as to become their instruments. When the mind and heart open to the spirit, a great victory is achieved in the inner world, and many things become possible that were formerly incapable of realization. Grace makes the divine plan unfold with wonderful speed and harmony, but all the merely human ideas, energies, intentions and means that we employ to substitute for it in the end turn out to be mere vanity. Therefore, whatever has *not* been consecrated to the supreme providence will turn out to be empty and meaningless. Once touched by grace, the heart longs to live constantly in its radiance. Nothing else nourishes us so deeply or fully as that life of our life. In the light of grace, the vanity of worldly things becomes so obvious that a great step forward toward full identification with its action becomes possible. Grace is always there to bless those who have decided to correct themselves.

Ether: Consecration

Full self-giving to the action of grace is the most auspicious of all possible developments in our inner life. If we place our existence in the hands of the divine, it is very important that we do not harbour any expectations for a particular result. When there is a sincere aspiration to love, to serve and to give what one has and what one is to the widest possibilities of life, without asking for anything, then the best that can be will come to pass. When divine guidance becomes the doer behind our choices and actions, we can be said to have reached the threshold of consecration. Consecration means the dedication of mind, body, heart and soul to the Higher Self, and the living out of this commitment every hour and minute of our life. Such a thing becomes possible because of the openings we have cultivated to the action of grace. By many small steps, a long journey is completed, and the soul's homecoming is foreshadowed by our aspiration to make this life one of consecration to Truth.

LOVE

The Archetype

The rune-image for Love is a vertical line or column reaching upward from earth to heaven. The earthly and the heavenly planes of existence are each represented by a short horizontal line, and the two planes are joined by the central axis. This is an image of a higher plane of light and consciousness united to a lower plane of physical manifestation by a vertical pillar. The core idea is uniting, unifying, bonding and connecting. This may imply the human developments of relationship, affection, attraction, intimacy, and sympathy. Yet, in essence, love is a cosmic force, universal in scope, however we may reduce it to our own limited human perspectives and accommodate it to our imperfections. Love unites what has been fragmented, bringing unity out of division. For the human heart, the experience of love is one of the most precious gifts life can offer. There is an opening and widening of consciousness under this sign, a deep and hopefully sincere feeling, possibly involving idealism and commitment, and at the same time a requirement to do the needed work that makes the achievement permanent.

Standard Meanings for Divination
Upright
Earth: You are moving in wholeness and balance.

Fire: Go forward in the matter at hand; heaven and earth are in happy unison.

Air: The situation is highly auspicious; good motives and good intent are present.

Water: Love is favoured, blessed and supported in this situation.

Ether: Your spiritual and earthly affairs are linked in mutual good order.

Reversed
Earth: There is the appearance but not the reality of balance here.

Fire: You have deceived yourself; deception and false appearances are at play here.

Air: You do not recognize the inherent reversal of right order in this situation.

Water: You believe in something that is not as it appears; what looks like real love is not.

Ether: Beware of delusion, ehchantment, enticement and allure; entrapment is a real possibility.

Spiritual Meanings for Divination
Earth: Message
There *is* something worth waking to, worth living for, worth giving oneself to, and that is love. Love comes originally from heaven and enters the darkness of earthly life via the axis mundi, which is the 'tree of life'. It brings a ray of light into the darkness of matter and a hope of finding oneness. Thus, love is a path of return to the Source. Love can be called the 'joy of identity'. The discovery of hidden identity between the microcosm and the

macrocosm is an experience of bliss. When we can discover love in our heart, we have a secret key by means of which we may merge with That which transcends us. The lover and the Beloved ultimately merge, bringing a loss of separativity through absorption into a greater reality. The bliss of this mystical state of oneness is the means by which love draws us into the fullness of the truth of our being. It is the nectar which attracts the bee to the blossom, the beauty which inspires the poet to sing. In bliss, the lover returns to an experience of the eternal Source, crossing all the phases of the sublunar manifestation to finally become the blissful fullness. Through love, the Field becomes the Fullness.

Fire: Alchemical Love

The quality of human experience depends on the quality of the underlying energy, and the kind of energy at work in the human microcosm reflects the quality of consciousness behind it. If we can alter the quality of energy, we can achieve possibilities which are beyond the present spectrum, and nothing refines energy so powerfully as unconditional love. Love takes energies of all kinds and harmonizes them on a wider scale. Love links energies of all kinds to that which is deepest, the soul, and undoes the strategies of the manipulative ego. The heart is the cauldron of alchemical transformation. It is enough to focus awareness in the depth of the spiritual heart and allow stillness and time to effect the transmutation. A higher state of awareness comes to the fore when we do this, and clouds of obscurity dissipate. Gradually, with practice, this transmuting experience becomes natural and even automatic. Emotional issues are placed in the light of the soul and dissolved, but the energy which has been bound in them is released for growth. As time passes, deeper patterns of limitation are raised up and transmuted. We learn to let go of anything and everything that constricts the heart in any way, moving beyond emotional reactivity to acceptance, trust and oneness. Our penchant for analysis, rationalization and mental interpretation is no longer the primary channel for relating to life. We learn to tune in to the energetic forces which underlie the outer appearances of things, and we grip the inner, hidden levers by which energy can be refined.

In the Gestation rune, the cauldron was sequestered in the protective womb, but in the Love rune, the cauldron can be active in the process of alchemical transformation, refining the dross and transmuting the pure gold into the fabled philosopher's stone. In getting from the consciousness represented by the Gestation rune to that of Love, we learn that we must let go of anything that binds or contracts our consciousness or our energy. While not indulging the mind's habit of labelling and judging, we nonetheless learn to recognize and release anger, melancholy, self-importance, excitability, self-righteousness and strategic calculation as inappropriate to the heart's will for unconditional love. Once the heart's deeper harmony is established, new energies become available and the fullness of our potential is released for growth. To choose unconditional love is to surrender emotion, thought and ego and everything else that limits and separates, in favour of wholeness and harmony. Love is the great "yes" to the fullness of life's richness and the transcendence of the boundary-creating ego.

Air: Inhibited Love

All subtle forms of resistance to the celestial power of love prevent love from flowing. Love cannot be possessed, hoarded, measured out, or used strategically for personal satisfaction, because love ceases to be love when any of these motivations or attitudes are attached to it. Any form of negativity, suspicion, alienation, mistrust, judgmental thinking or separativity inhibits and corrupts love. Therefore, for love to flourish, the would-be lover must become a clear channel, like the pillar of the rune-symbol that unites the heavenly plane with the earthly plane. Love cannot abide obstructions to its flow as it seeks to unite all parts of the broken universe into a single, blissful whole.

Although there is a deep need in all humans to taste love, there is also an innate fear of being open and vulnerable. When our ego makes an attempt to secure itself, or consolidate its gains, the pristine flower of love is bruised. The threat of rejection may be cherished as a subconscious fear, causing fluctuations in our willingness to be open and vulnerable. Eventually, we pull to us the things we fear, because this is the only way we can face and conquer them. In this sense, the old saying that 'we hurt the ones we love' sadly comes to be a part of our lived experience. We actually generate the loss of those we love by doubting and judging them.

The highest love is to want what is best for the beloved, without any admixture of selfish motive. This ideal requires that we recognize and transcend the different strategies of 'inhibited love' which the mind and ego propose as a substitute for the vulnerability of unselfish love.

In this regard, it may help to remember that the child in the heart is always vulnerable. This divine child knows the meaning of wonder, spontaneity, joy, enthusiasm, and yes, love. When we can find and identify with this part of our being, we may learn the deep wisdom of tender-heartedness as a way of relating to all life. The paradoxical truth is that each human being who forsakes the towering fortress of the mind to become the tender vulnerability of the heart finds a permanent sanctuary or resting-place on the lap of the Divine Mother's tender compassion. There, in that embrace, there is constant protection. This higher help is what makes it possible to love while being eternally a child of our soul's dreams. This is one of the building blocks for a later stage of attainment which is signified by the rune, "Dreamweaver". In this later stage of development, we are guided by the Muses to sing and celebrate and spread the spirit of inner freedom.

Water: Lesser Love

Sometimes human beings put boundaries and limits on this irresistible power of union which draws us back to the fullness of our being. Whereas divine love is unconditional, a lesser, very human kind of love exists which is a form of bargaining. "I will love you if you love me." We give, but guardedly; we open, but incompletely; we trust, but with hesitation. Our mind persuades us that we are thus protected from pain and abuse, but in fact the "bartering love" is only our mind's way of validating mistrust and self-limitation. "If you do what I want, I shall love you. But if you displease me, then I do not want you." If we practice this kind of conditional bargaining as a substitute for unconditional loving, the power of love will not be able to work its alchemy in the crucible of the heart, and the celestial joy will not find any home in the terrestrial manifestation.

Another way in which we limit love is to consider whether we are loved or not. This is more of the bartering attitude. We give according to the measure in which we receive, but we do not give unconditionally. Only when one can love without the need to receive any form of recompense, without imposing any self-serving conditions, can love become for us a true liberation of the spirit, and a doorway into lasting happiness.

Ether: Re-Directed Love

We are creatures of habit, and even after the heart begins to open, we renew the old borders and patterns and polarities that previous habit has established. When we begin to experience the refinement, widening and exaltation of energy that comes from unconditional love, we are faced with a critical imperative. Either we lift the entire life into this heightened potential, and embrace the new quality of experience, or we revert to the easier, more familiar domains of intensity and continue on in the old ways. To choose to love well and deeply is not an easy slide, because the societal norms that have conditioned us are still wedded to the old patterns of perception, and what passes for common sense reinforces the past.

If the cauldron of alchemical love reminds us of the earlier Gestation rune, the demands of redirected love look forward to the dynamics of the Courage rune. A person who has not tamed the emotions or mastered the desires could be toying with danger if they empowered the will and the psyche to a higher level of energy and thereby inflated the ego. Mixing new wine in old containers is dangerous because the outmoded way is to dissipate love into emotional attachment and become bound by the persons, objects, goals or belief systems that we claim as "our own", (with ego as the possessor). To channel new intensities of energy and consciousness along old pathways is unwise. In any energy-heightening practice, we are challenged to reach a more encompassing consciousness, but when the fear-driven programs return, it brings disruption. We need further maturing to grow through and beyond this experience of recoil and contraction. In time we will learn what it takes to be stabilized in the more refined energy-fields of unconditional love.

It takes months, years and sometimes decades or lifetimes to access and integrate a higher consciousness and to make it permanent. Touched by the beauty and wonder of love, we open the possibility of a new way of life, but to do the actual work of re-ordering all parts of our being in harmony requires fortitude and endurance of the highest order.

COURAGE

The Archetype

The image of this rune is two vertical lines surmounted by a chevron. The symbol seems to point bravely upward, the double lines giving an impression of strength and resolve when compared to the similar symbol for the rune Growth, for example. Under the sign of Courage, one has the opportunity to use the challenges, difficulties and dangers of life to develop strength and firmness, to consolidate the gains of the past and prepare foundations for further growth. The power of this rune suggests that we need to be able to stand firm and to remain confident, holding to what is right and true. This rune suggests alertness, vigilance, strength, a righteous fight or crusade, a persevering and steady mastery, a quiet fortitude and a refusal to be shaken from the path that leads to light. The Courage rune is the archetype of the spiritual warrior.

Standard Meanings for Divination

Upright

Earth: Physical resilience is yours; good health and physical strength are yours; a fast recovery; persevere and be brave.

Fire: Dynamic will power is more than adequate; upright action is favoured; where your strengths lie.

Air: Think boldly; initiative, drive and commanding power are favoured; where to direct initiative.

Water: Strength, courage, virility and manhood are favoured; be forceful and energetic.

Ether: The archetypal force of the warrior consciousness is with you.

Reversed

Earth: Depression; loss and deprivation; low vitality or illness.

Fire: Insufficient will or motivation; failure.

Air: A change which will be unpleasant.

Water: An inadequate emotional response; conflict; missed opportunity.

Ether: An attack; a punishment; a crushing burden.

Spiritual Meanings for Divination
Earth: The Hero

The heroic age saw a change of values from the matriarchal pattern of earlier times. The hero was often a solar figure whose life centred on conflict and mastery. Often he was pitted against some aspect of the lunar goddess culture which he sought to change. For example, Apollo destroyed the great oracular snake Python at the oracle of Delphi, and then seized control of the shrine in his own name. This was considered a typical heroic achievement, although more often the mythic hero is human or semi-divine, a man like Hercules who strives to realize his immortality by battling with adversity and fate. The life of the hero finds him pitted against opposing forces, supported by a heavenly father, or a member of the patriarchal pantheon such as an Olympian God or Goddess, and exercising the violent arts of combat or war to attain some goal. In the past, when humans were growing from the group consciousness into a more fully individuated humanity, this was the strenuous road to becoming a fully self-empowered individual, beyond the control of the tribal taboos, beyond the limits of the matriarchal bond.

Only a truly individualized consciousness can take on the

challenge of the strenuous heroic life and battle bravely for the good cause, drawing on the powers of faith, endurance and courage. In the heroic age, there was a striving to go beyond the group consciousness and realize full individuality and personal freedom, and the archetype for this endeavour is usually a masculine one. The Courage rune may come up when we need to step beyond our social conditioning or the opinions of others and strike out in a way that may not be collectively sanctioned or officially approved in order to be true to our inner guidance. This is never easy, but willingness to take risk often creates an opportunity to develop further courage and to empower the will with higher help from realms unseen. We know that Homer's heroes were constantly supported by the gods and goddesses, and we too have inner guidance and blessings when we dare to go forward on our eternal quest.

Fire: Victory Over Fear

If fear is the denial of our fullest possibilities, its home and resting place is the mind. How easily the mind beguiles itself into thinking that it knows the demands of life and love and can manage all aspects of experience efficiently. Deep down, however, the mind is a coward, because it rests on memory and the past and the limited domain of what is known, resisting the summons of love to venture beyond the small self into uncharted territory where the barriers and walls come down. It is easy to cook up simplistic answers to life's challenges and substitute them for the demands of real growth. It is easy to bury one's head in the sand, to give responsibility for our well-being to healers or priests or magicians, or to stay within the comfortable borders of what has been approved and sanctioned by society. To rely on the mind is to fall back on the supports of the past and to create comfortable rationalizations to sidestep the demands of courage. Whether from excessive concern for security, or a lack of trust in the Divine, or lack of confidence in oneself, the mind becomes expert at explanations and evasions that boil down in the end to one central concession – giving way to fear.

Fear opens inner doors and makes us more vulnerable to that which is feared; in fact, oftentimes fear attracts what is feared.

When we think obsessively about something we fear, we set up an energy which tends to actualize it, and in this way we create self-fulfilling prophecies of doom. The distinction between a "terrorist" and a "freedom fighter" is largely a matter of whether we are seeing through the eyes of fear or not. A strict discipline is needed to cure the mind, vital and body of fear. When we face fear, we shine a light into the depths of our own unconsciousness and ignorance and if we are not willing to face what we find there we usually seek consolation in the mundane realms of what is familiar and comfortable. True courage is the willingness to face *everything* in life whether in the inner or the outer world, whether obvious or hidden, without recoil or hesitation. Only those who can love and trust the Divine will be able to go forward and face whatever life brings, undaunted. Therefore, the Love rune precedes the Courage rune and is its enabler.

Air: Strength

Courage goes hand in hand with strength, and strength has much to do with inner stillness. The sign of true strength is an ability to gather one's energies together and spend them as one wishes while remaining balanced and unperturbed even in the midst of crisis. By being still, we rest in our true source of strength, the connection to the Divine. Whenever there is agitation, it is an indication of some weakness. Restlessness also is a sign that inner strength and courage are not yet complete in their development. Genuine quietude is a great power to have at one's command. Those who have true courage are always calm, it is the weak who are agitated. Only when we discover a deep need for inner calm will we be motivated to practice some of the means by which it can be established. Without mastery of thought, the mind and vital energy together will react in unpredictable ways to a variety of conscious and unconscious fears.

In ordinary mortals, the vital being and the physical body have not placed themselves in the power and presence of the Divine, rather they are tools of the mind and ego. In this condition, they are moved by all the common forces of the cosmos : mental forces, vital energies, emotional pulls and pushes, collective suggestion, individual and collective karma – the list is endless. To be the plaything of such forces is to forfeit all possibility of developing inner strength. Even the failure to have our own way, and to see our preferences indulged, can unsettle the mind and vital sufficiently to make them restless. Once restless, we easily become agitated, and by then a door has been opened to subtler forms of fear, nervousness and anxiety that prevent us from establishing calm in the nervous system or in the energy bodies. Thus, the sages have always taught: if you would be courageous, cultivate strength; if you would grow in strength, learn to be calm and still. One of the centrally important practices leading to equality and equanimity is, of course, the discipline of meditation. But from earlier experience we should have learned that meditation empowered by unconditional love will always be more powerful than mere mental concentration.

Water: Stages of Courage

It takes courage to become an individual, to rise out of the collective consciousness and discover what is true and permanent within one's own being. It takes greater courage to offer that precious individuality to the Divine and embrace a process of continuous widening into the formless spirit. Greater even than these two stages of courage is the courage needed to die completely to self when the Divine accepts our surrender and calls us to the state of absolute oneness with Source. To go forward on the path of life requires dauntless courage, the courage to let go of all we cherish, possess and identify with in order to embrace a still larger and higher identity, the identity of the human with the Divine. Consider then, if you have not already attained this ultimate goal, that whatever level of courage you have been required to develop already, a still higher demand awaits you ahead. The road winds ever upward and the path becomes steeper as it ascends. Therefore, do not give way to the temptation to rest or retire from the struggle of ascension. The stages of courage are passages that gift us with all we need to maintain our momentum and win through to the levels of still greater wideness and blessing. Unfailing courage is synonymous with an absolute trust in Divine Grace.

Ether: The Courage of Vigilance

The hallmark of courage is a willingness to practice vigilance. Because vigilance demands relentless concentration, it challenges our habitual inertia and self-indulgence. It is often in the unseen inner battles against heaviness, obscurity and ignorance that the greatest victories are won. The Mother says:

> To be vigilant is not merely to resist what pulls you downward, but above all to be alert in order not to lose any opportunity to progress, any opportunity to overcome a weakness, to resist a temptation, any opportunity to learn something, to correct something, to master something. If you are vigilant, you can do in a few days what would otherwise take years. If you are vigilant, you change each circumstance of your life, each action, each movement into an occasion for coming nearer the goal. There are two kinds of vigilance, active and passive. The passive vigilance gives you a warning if you are about to make a mistake, if you are making a wrong choice, if you are being weak and allowing yourself to be tempted. The active vigilance seeks an opportunity to progress, seeks to utilise every circumstance to advance more quickly.
>
> – The Mother, *Collected Works*, Vol. 3, pp. 202-3

It is in this sense that any victory of light over darkness, awareness over inconscience, or dynamism over sloth is a victory of courage. Courage is the active will of love, the steady faith of unshaken commitment, the unhesitating "Yes!" to the Fullness of the future.

FULLNESS

The Archetype

The runic symbol for Fullness is a Full Moon radiating light in all directions. Fullness in this instance means the illumination of consciousness from within. What began as a spark or gleam of light with the rune Fire has now become a radiant fullness. This sign signifies fruition, exaltation, heavenly power (called in I Ching: "The Creative"). It can also mean contact with the Higher Self, inner light, spiritual illumination, favourable outcomes, including success and prosperity. It is a highly auspicious sign. It was at the time of the Full Moon that the Buddha attained enlightenment. When the light of spirit shines unobstructedly through the soul, it raises all parts of the being that are receptive to their highest possibility. The soul and the spiritual heart are most attuned to this light, but it is possible for the mind, the vitality and the physical body to develop receptivity as well.

Over the centuries, many societies nurtured in sacred attunement to the Goddess and the Lunar Law have been brought face to face with destruction. Over a period of several millennia before the birth of Christ, the matriarchal cultures of Old Europe were rent asunder by the warrior Aryans, and their peaceful ways were submerged in new forms of patriarchal religion. In the 16th century, the Aztec and Inca empires fell, and then for a period of two centuries or so, one by one, the native tribes of North America were wiped out. As these peoples faced destruction, their elders commended the sacred teachings to secrecy; the portals into the other world were closed down, and the holiest artifacts of sacred tradition were hidden away. From the Native Americans we have a prophecy that when the destruction was greatest, when the earth itself cried out for relief from greed and exploitation, a Revealing Time would come, and the great grandchildren of the destroyers themselves would implement a rebirth of the old ways. That time of revelation is now, and the Primal Runes are a part of it. Along with other teachings from the living library of Mother Earth, the Primal Runes help to bring about renewal of the harmony between heaven and earth. This beauty and harmony of attunement to the Source is the essence of Fullness, and the core meaning of the Fullness rune.

The Fullness referred to by this rune is the fullness of Light, the Light of Consciousness. Sun is spirit; Moon is that within the human microcosm which can mirror spirit and express its law. Always the soul *can* do this, but frequently it is obscured by the mind, vitality and physicality of our raw human nature. In evolved humans, the spiritual heart and the higher mind can reflect the light of spirit; these parts of the being are the first to develop a lasting attunement to the guidance from above, the first to discern what can be used for the evolution of consciousness, and what needs to be released. Moonlight is rich with possibilities for creativity, divination, and higher harmonies of visionary attunement. However, when the receiving medium of human consciousness is impure, the power of the Moon's fullness can energize the fantasies, illusions, deceptions and hallucinations that have not been cleared out from the nether regions of the unconscious. Hospital wards and insane asylums are never as busy as on Full Moon nights, because this energy can feed human weakness just as well as the inspired guidance of the Muse.

Standard Meanings for Divination

Upright

Earth: Material gain; prosperity; reward; recognition.

Fire: Overcoming opposition; victory; wholeness.

Air: Clarity; understanding; perception; enlightenment.

Water: You have what it takes to win; joy; glory; completion; fulfilment.

Ether: A fortunate opportunity; a heaven-sent blessing.

Reversed

Earth: Loss, disappointment.

Fire: Obstacles; eclipse of fortune.

Air: Delay; disruption.

Water: Problems; obscuration; disharmony.

Ether: An ineffective course of action; an inauspicious situation.

Spiritual Meanings for Divination

Earth: The Dog and the Wolf

Frequently, the Tarot card for the Moon portrays a wolf and a dog baying at the Full Moon in the sky above. These images suggest the transformation of unconscious or untamed thoughts, feelings and actions (symbolized by the wolf) into conscious, tamed ones (symbolized by the dog). The Moon is a magical sign, and the rune of lunar Fullness stands for the high tide of magical empowerment. The light and the darkness within human nature, the dog and the wolf, are the given raw material which we inherit at birth as the Field which we are meant to work. But the tapping of vision, creative power and imaginative capacity are possible only when we cultivate and apply these gifts. The Muses, understood by the ancients to be the ninefold creative outpouring of the Moon Goddess, endow humanity with these magical and creative capacities. Yet, the degree to which an individual is connected with this reservoir of power, and the wisdom with which the power is applied, are a matter of personal choice. Nowhere are the stakes higher, for better or worse, than at the time of Fullness, and the Fullness rune draws this to our attention. There is an abundance of light, and if we identify with light we can achieve the very best that our capacity permits. Yet this same light can emphasize the darkness of the obscurities that we have within us and bring *them* into high relief. In a way, this is a blessing in disguise. When things that need resolution and transformation are placed squarely before us, we are able to deal with them.

Fire: Stability

One of the greatest helps in the spiritual life is equality. When this has been developed, it establishes unshakable poise in all parts of the being, making it possible to maintain inner stillness and clear perception even in the most trying circumstances. With equality, we can face the ugly and the beautiful in balanced openness. The differences between what is high and low, flawed and perfect, agreeable and disagreeable, good and bad, do not unsettle one who has equality. It makes possible a correct discernment of what is genuine beneath the surface appearances of things. Lacking equality, the soul is easily shaken by the shocks of life and the discrepancies between appearance and reality. When the Fullness rune comes up, it indicates a time of high energy and special possibility, to be used either for a great leap forward, or to precipitate a stumble into one of the deficiencies of our nature. With equality, we are inwardly steady. Thus our discernment and our judgement are more likely to accord with reality than to flow along the lines of its many possible distortions. Since the lunar energy can play out in so many directions, both harmonious and disruptive, nothing stands us in greater stead than equality when we come to a moment of potential empowerment. At the time of the Full Moon, when the Buddha achieved enlightenment, he touched the earth to have her bear witness that his spirit was clear. All the forces of illusion and temptation had flooded in upon him, and he had withstood them. Beyond the normal interpretation of this gesture, we can see the idea of being grounded in the perfect poise and stability of Mother Earth as the best protection against the riotous and fantastical energies of derangement which are prevalent when the Moon is full. It can be seen as a reminder of the importance of equality when the energies are high and the stakes are fraught with consequence either for great good or for evil.

Air: Duality

The West has inherited a heavy dose of Manichean dualism in its approach to life. The Manichean point of view is that matter represents darkness, ignorance and evil, and human birth is an entry of the soul into a hopeless sea of obscurity for a time of testing until those who are worthy can ascend to heaven. Thus, the forces of good and evil, light and dark are eternally pitted against each other and life on earth is a battleground for the soul. Born in sin, pulled by darkness, the soul must cling to the saviour-god who is in the sky above and pray for redemption.

During the Age of Pisces, a great deal of effort has gone into suppression and repression of the physical body and asceticism and penance have been hailed as the road to salvation. Many of the Christian saints exemplify this philosophy in a striking way. However, as the age of Aquarius dawns, a different way of thinking begins to come to the fore. While many people still believe that they are earthbound, physical beings searching for spiritual experience, more and more people can say: 'I am a spiritual being passing through an earthly experience.' Just as the Moon reflects the Sun, the human microcosm is an embodiment of the spirit, and intrinsically divine. The body is not the embodiment of ignorance, but the instrument for the soul to achieve a great victory over ignorance. Matter is not evil, it is a crystallization of spirit, a canvas on which the soul can create a higher vision. Earth does not exist simply as a springboard to heaven, it is the Field of possibilities and it awaits the descent of heaven for its full transformation. Rejection and repression are not solutions to evil, they are part of the problem. They are part of the ignorant strategy of the mind that breaks the oneness of reality into billions of separate perceptions with names and labels, only to exercise its limiting propensities for separation, judgement and self-aggrandizement. In short, the mind creates duality and then does battle with it in the name of God, religion, or whatever philosophy is current.

The Fullness rune is a critical time because it can bring about a resolution of duality into harmony and oneness, or a worsening of the extremes by which the mind's struggle in duality generates suffering. Much of our religious tradition and our historic mental conditioning are quite useless when we face this moment of truth, but the Fullness rune invites the seeker to see the wholeness of life and its inherent goodness as the underlying reality.

Water: Imagination Fulfilled

The scientific way of thinking tends to downplay the value of imagination. But imagination is an important component of spiritual realization. Whatever we can envision, picture in full detail, aspire for and vivify in the mind's eye can be materialized as a reality in life. If we visualize and energize our fond dreams, they will become realities. How long this takes depends on several factors, not least important of which is our skill at building up a clear and detailed mental picture, our persistence in energizing it, and the favourable or unfavourable conditions of the environment in which we live. The result could come in minutes, hours, days, weeks, months, years, decades or centuries, but the result is sure once the work is done. The water aspect of the Fullness rune indicates the inevitable success which attends all well directed effort to realize worthy dreams. The time when spiritual dreams can be realized is sometimes called the Hour of God. The Fullness rune indicates that the conditions are favourable for the realization of the things we have nurtured in the world of imagination. Beyond this, it counsels us to make good use of imagination and to choose wisely the goals that we wish to manifest.

Ether: Success

The Fullness rune in Ether favours success. But success brings with it an unfavourable possibility. Always the true success is the degree to which we learn, grow and evolve in light. Success sometimes fosters a hardening of the personality into some kind of vanity, pride, arrogance or self-inflation. Apparent success may blind its beneficiary to the veil of coarseness which is settling in over the inner spirit. The inner Truth my find it much more difficult to thrive in conditions of outer success than it does in circumstances of adversity, because suffering is a great teacher of humility, awareness, compassion and gratitude. Outer success can be a defeat for Truth if we do not accept it in the right spirit. Success is a harder ordeal to pass through than misfortune.

> "It is in the hour of success that one must be especially vigilant to rise above oneself."
>
> – The Mother – 15: p.88

Here again, equality is inestimably important, because it is the best guarantee that we can preserve inner balance. Success can take one farther and farther away from the Truth unless the goals have been sanctioned from above, and the results accepted in a spirit of selfless detachment. Most people pour time, energy and care into achieving results and are by no means indifferent to the fruits of their endeavour. The Fullness rune cautions that success has attendant dangers, and the Shadow can easily begin to grow if we ignore them. When success comes your way, consider its role in your ultimate progress, and remain grounded in the peace, light and delight of the soul. All things that cause us to swing up and down with elation and depression must be seen for what they are: occasions to learn and grow. The rose is not without thorns, and the successes are not without risk. Therefore, the favourable energy of the Fullness rune can best be applied in the light of wisdom and mastery, which lie just ahead in the cycle of the lunar law.

Descent

The Archetype

This image is a downward pointing arrow or an upward pointing chevron with a line ascending from earth (actually from the centre of the "V" which is a Goddess symbol) to heaven (or vice versa). The point of the arrow rests on the earth horizon. Thus insight must always interface with its milieu. We may envisage either a descent from higher to lower, as when the light of inspiration enters the field of the mind's understanding, or an ascent from the V-shaped Goddess symbol upward. The rune can be interpreted in either of these ways. The rune indicates that the mind attains power to focus on subtle realities. There is new, penetrating vision into the essence of an issue. We should honour our intuition when we receive this sign, because we have an opportunity to attain a higher vision, a metaphysical insight, a psychic opening or experience, possibly a revelation, inspiration or divine message. The end result of this process should be new understanding. Once celestial energy emerges from behind the veil, we have an opportunity to let go of our mundane preoccupations and our mental conditioning. It is necessary to exert some effort to sustain and expand this contact with celestial power, to learn to preserve and apply this energy according to the principles of wisdom. Transformation must be integral. That is to say, the unification of a human being requires the yoking of Earth (sense awareness), Fire (vitality), Air (intellect) and water (emotion) and bringing them under the direction of the soul.

Standard Meanings for Divination

Upright

Earth: Consider the basics of the situation; focus on fundamentals.

Fire: A dynamic empowerment; your will is catalyzed.

Air: A new understanding; a revelation; a vision; an enlightenment experience.

Water: Try to intuit and follow the higher guidance at work; attune the heart to spiritual influence.

Ether: Turn to higher help, it is present and available to you; become the instrument of a spiritual force.

Reversed

Earth: You have put the cart before the horse.

Fire: You stand against the heavenly mandate.

Air: Your human mind is acting in ignorance.

Water: Your ego and self-will are misdirected.

Ether: You are acting as if you were God; reconsider.

Spiritual Meanings for Divination

Earth: Inner Progress

A heightened consciousness can be brought into one's being at this time, touching not only the inner psyche, but also the very cells of the body. When this happens, new capabilities and sensibilities which have been latent can begin to unfold. The process can be rapid or gradual, and some of the attendant experiences can be either positive or negative. Negativities come to the fore when light moves in to dislodge them; higher states of consciousness always bring a sense of peace, bliss, or wholeness. The longterm results tend to a refinement of awareness. It becomes more difficult to maintain emotional attachments to defined life structures, rigid belief systems, patterns of domination or control, or alignment with people or fixed needs that generate pain. One becomes more aware of the quality of the energy in which one lives, its intensity, wideness, fineness or coarseness, and the rhythmic patterns of return and renewal within which phenomena arise and fade. There is a greater inner capacity to experience and participate in the multi-layered richness of life, not in terms of its outer appearances, but more in the realm of inner dynamics of energy and consciousness. To remain open to these inner dynamics, it is important to cultivate and sustain greater openness, balance, calm, transparency, and flexibility.

Fire: Intention

To change the destiny of the material world, it is necessary to bring down a higher power from above. Every descent of transforming power and vision from on high represents a potential miracle, but the human vessels of reception and diffusion are for the most part insufficiently prepared. The degree to which higher energies can be accessed and a new consciousness established depends largely on one's wellbeing, balance and above all on purity of intention. Important insights may come, but translating them into permanent realization requires sustained effort. There is no substitute for the transformative quality we access when we have direct experiences of higher levels of energy. Our limitation arises from the planes of consciousness in which we habitually reside, in terms of which we define our reality. Thus, when we step into wider, deeper or more luminous realms of awareness, we have illumining insights about the most fundamental questions of life, enabling us to go beyond our normal range of ideas and imagine a better world. Beyond this, we experience a growing commitment to help bring it about. We realize that life is not really concerned with the dilemma of our separativity, but invites us to participate in the collective evolution to a higher consciousness. We begin to think in terms beyond selfish benefit, for the good of the whole. At this time, the quality of our intentionality supports and enables our growth in awareness, and the universe sends us new opportunities to contribute and to progress. When we move beyond a self-absorbed and ego-centred set of concerns, our aspiration widens and we can channel the greater intensities of light to which the Descent rune refers.

Air: Nonverbal Understanding

Much of what passes for wisdom falls into the category of mere verbalizing. The verbal mind likes to deal with well defined ideas, to compare, sort, contrast and analyze them. Yet true understanding does not arise in this manner. In order to know what is behind and beyond the words, one must be in contact with a world that is beyond form. If the mind is silenced, consciousness can rise into the dimension from which inspired ideas descend and have the true understanding of the things to which words refer. True attunement arises in silence, not in verbal noise. The deep teaching in a book yields its richness only when we can read in mental silence. As long as the words of the teaching stimulate the external mind and appeal to the surface understanding, the deeper wisdom does not arise. Traditionally, the teachings of enlightened masters have been communicated in silence. Perfect understanding arises in the seekers when there is inner attunement to the truth that transcends verbal expression. When there is a descent from above of some higher vision, insight, power or possibility, there is often a rush to put it into words. Even in the silence of meditation, the verbal mind is eager to start casting the inner experience in sentences of explanation. But this dilutes and diffuses the transformative power of the higher energy, reducing it to lesser formations with which the ignorant mind feels comfortable. When one can relax into the widness of the higher mind, the fullest possibilities of realization are established. The Descent rune is about raising the understanding above the range of mere words into the nonverbal openness of higher consciousness.

Water: Develop the Insight

The Mother has shared a very valuable insight about the process of descent:

> An idea from a higher domain – if pulled down – organizes itself and is crystallized into a large number of thoughts which can express that idea differently. Then, if you are a writer or a poet or an artist, when you make it come lower down still, you can have all kinds of expressions, extremely varied, around a single little idea coming from very high above. And when you know how to do this, it teaches you to distinguish between the pure idea and the way of expressing it. (*Collected Works*, Vol. 7, pg. 92)

Creative expression follows naturally from the Descent rune's action of bringing down higher insight. Evolution comes about not merely by seeing or saying a higher truth, but by re-organizing the world in light of it. Only when the creative artist is a clear channel can there be transmission of an undiluted vision. What the Mother calls a "pure idea" can best be known by intuitive attunement, and this is more a matter of mysticism than of craftsmanship. To develop and express something beyond the normal range of understanding demands a high order of creative talent, and it takes courage as well. The Nobel laureate, Dr. Eric Kandel has said: "We are who we are in good measure because of what we have learned and what we remember." This is a very good statement of the nature of mental conditioning. The Descent rune opens a door beyond the limits of our conditioning and suggests that we can become channels of a higher, deeper vision of life's possibilities. When we are committed to develop, to express and most of all to live the dreams and visions that descend into our consciousness, the world can evolve to a new level of harmony and beauty.

Ether: Remember Love

Love is the energy that knits together what has been fragmented, and restores wholeness and holiness to everything that has been divided. It is the forces of separation that bring about limitation of consciousness on earth, and they are strongly present in the human mind and vital. Only when there is a direct descent of the Divine Grace, penetrating the depths of matter and the obscurities of life, can a new ascent and return to wholeness be attempted on the part of humanity. The climb from unconsciousness to full awareness and from darkness to light is a slow evolution stretching over millions of years. Here on earth, below the canopy of heaven, we labour to make life into something more luminous and perfect, but only when the higher help descends can a lasting and significant transformation be effected. Every advance that we make, everything for which the proud mind takes so much credit, is based on an insight that has penetrated our darkness from a higher region of wholeness and light, in essence a touch of compassion from above. Divine Love penetrates all things, sustains and directs all life towards a return to the Source. For the most part, the human mind does not perceive or recognize this gradual unfoldment, or its origin. When on rare occasions the active compassion of heaven is recognized, the individualized ego finds it difficult to accept. Human nature experiences the purity and power of any heavenly descent as a disturbance to its equilibrium and a challenge to its inertia and comfort. Only when reduced to the banalities of the mind, or warped to the comfort-level of the vital are the divine realities widely accepted. To accept Truth in its purity, the human consciousness must itself become pure, and it has always been the work of the advanced souls, the saints, sages, seers and liberated souls, to bring about this purification. The human being who would channel something beautiful and perfect into the earth atmosphere must remember that it is a labour of submission to Love, and in all humility the demands of love must be embraced and honoured if the Descent is to be fully realized and established.

WISDOM

The Archetype

The rune for Wisdom is a bolt of lightning centred between two vertical lines which delimit its force in a field with two boundaries. We should envision these two vertical lines as being in a process of outward expansion. The energy from on high radiates outwards and modifies the boundaries of our personal reality. The Wisdom rune heralds a time when our consciousness is becoming more aware, and there is a greater capacity to attune to realities that are formless, ineffable and ungraspable by rational intellect. We have learned that sustaining "true feeling" is a very important means of higher attunement. Wisdom shows us how to expand our consciousness and how to live the knowledge that comes to us. In essence, this wisdom can be thought of as the capacity to live in right relation with the higher guidance that comes to us, without distorting or violating its integrity.

Standard Meanings for Divination
Upright

Earth: You are called to exercise more wisdom than you have been doing.

Fire: Higher guidance is available if you open to it; an insight brings the solution to a need.

Air: Mental strength, virtues and graces; mental illumination.

Water: Your heart's wisdom is called for; listen to your heart.

Ether: A higher, wider and deeper illumination is coming your way.

Reversed

Earth: Your so-called wisdom is folly.

Fire: You think you are wise, but you are not; you are making a mistake.

Air: You have clouded your better judgement; your mind is in darkness.

Water: You are acting silly; try to feel your way into a more sensible course of action.

Ether: Clear up the obscurity in this matter; submit to higher guidance.

Spiritual Meanings for Divination
Earth: The Cloud of Unknowing

Our awareness that we *need* wisdom often arises most acutely when a situation goes awry. When we depart from the Cosmic Order, we experience disharmony, or suffering, and the source of this disharmony must be located if it is to be corrected. It may be that what we are doing or thinking is basically right, but our timing may be wrong. Thus, one important aspect of wisdom is to do or say the right thing *at the right time*. This is one of the challenges that come to us when an opportunity for wisdom is present. From this challenge we have the opportunity to develop a response, and the way we choose to respond will determine whether and how we grow in awareness. The normal response when we face a challenge is to fall back on the mind and its memory for a possible solution. But wisdom asks us to reach out and acknowledge invisible forces that are initially beyond our ken. We naturally begin by attempting to *understand* the invisible processes, perhaps with a subconscious notion that eventually they may be *mastered and controlled*, for the mind's agenda is usually to attain power. But in time, when more wisdom dawns, we learn to participate directly in the flow of reality in an unconditional openness. We learn not to demand intellectual understanding at the outset of a new inner experience; we are willing to learn as a result of submission to something that transcends our grasp. We learn that when we approach life with the attitude of already knowing, it undermines the vulnerability that is a precondition of new learning. We pass through various degrees of maturity in our relationship to this higher mystery; we learn to open more deeply, to trust more implicitly and to suspend judgment based on memories of the limited and conditioned past. In living thus, we come to experience wisdom as a growing relationship with the Great Mystery, an accommodation of the human mind and will to life in what the mystics call the 'cloud of unknowing.'

Fire: Uncritical Wisdom

When we want things to be better, we may begin by inwardly criticizing a situation which we are experiencing, or the individuals involved in it, thus further disturbing our inner equilibrium. Wisdom brings equality, serenity, and inner composure. By focusing only on what is immediately in front of us, we avoid the tendency to observe others with an inner, critical eye, which keeps tensions alive on the subtle level.

> The true love for the Divine is self-giving,
> free of demand, full of submission and surrender.
> It makes no claim, imposes no condition, strikes
> no bargain, indulges in no violences of jealousy or pride
> or anger – for these things are not in its composition.
> – The Mother – *Collected Works*, Vol. 14:p.137

In one sense, wisdom is not different from what The Mother calls "the true love for the Divine", or unconditional self-giving; by way of distinction, it is always other than conditional relationship, several varieties of which are mentioned. In time, experience teaches us that wisdom does not come by reaction, or by indulging the process of reactivity on the emotional or mental level. Wisdom comes by a ripening of insight into a disposition of right relation. In other words, it is a quality of openness and attitude rather than a success strategy. Wisdom does not supply the mind with new tools to manipulate reality, rather it teaches the mind how to overcome its strategies of control altogether, substituting the radiance of the heart's attunement to Truth. We can easily read words like *balance, surrender, trust* and *love*, and imagine we understand. But this is not wisdom. Wisdom is the humility of unknowing which alone qualifies us to absorb and live these realities so that they become the core of our awareness and the quality of our outlook on life.

When we decide to actually live the teaching, as contrasted to thinking about it or discussing it, The Mother teaches that we will need four kinds of strength. Firstly, we will need the strength of absolute sincerity. Then, we will need the strength to set aside our personal preferences and desires. Thirdly, we will need the strength to set aside the noise of the mind and actually listen to the guidance that comes from within. And lastly, we will need the willingness to obey promptly and unhesitatingly when we receive the inner guidance. It is often said that wisdom goes beyond knowledge by implying a capacity to actually live and practice what we know in the mind. The four strengths summarized here are the indispensable constituents of that living.

Air: Emergence of Surrender

Wisdom develops only after we have gathered experience and made choices. Prior to the dawn of wisdom, we have to go through the ups and downs of karma, and learn how to transform this bumpy ride which we call life into something better than what we started with. Until we achieve a consciousness sufficiently clear that we have higher insights to act as guidance, everything we do will inevitably be ego-bound. In the more mature phases of our soul's journey, we attain greater clarity of understanding. With this enhanced mental light, we can notice old habits of indolence or carelessness creeping up on us and take corrective steps before these tendencies go too far. We know our weaknesses, and we know how, where and when to seek help on the inner planes. Wisdom emerges from the mass of half-truths, limitations and conditionings which constitute our undeveloped humanity, which is the Field we were given at the journey's outset.

Maturing through the cycles of the Lunar Law, we learn how to relate correctly to The Fullness, or The Primal Light, allowing "It" to become the doer of our life. When we realize that we cannot, in and of ourselves, accomplish self-realization, we open a doorway which makes it possible to enter a very special state of mind which might be called 'right relation to Source'. We cannot learn the art of transcendental right relation as long as we attempt to force the matter by means of our mental will. What we learn is surrender; we discover that we grow best by not interfering in any way with the spontaneous action of Grace in our lives. Grace, which is indicated in its spiritual essence by the rune Primal Light, and in its experiential blossoming as the rune Fullness, responds most directly to real humility. Humility opens the spiritual heart in such a way as to make possible reliance on Source, which alone has the capacity to be the doer of all things in our life. By recognizing the powerlessness of our clever strategies and special abilities in the spiritual sphere, we take a giant step toward surrender.

Water: Become Conscious Within

When the power of wisdom becomes fully active, we will have learned that there is an empty space deep within our psyche where our thought processes can be seen for what they really are, waves that rise and fall on the surface of a vast ocean of consciousness. When we hold to the essential truth of our being, and step back from riding the ups and downs of karma, we can discern what is valid and positive in the experiences that come our way. Our mind becomes universalized, which is to say we see all forms of experience, both inner and outer, through an attunement to the Cosmic Will. Before we turn energies or ideas into outer realities, we become fully conscious of them and weigh their merit. When our attitudes or choices or intentions are out of harmony with the Cosmic Will, we draw to us the negative consequences of such disharmony. Even if we are not fully consecrated to the light, the need to avoid suffering can act as a powerful motivation for growth, as the Buddha well understood. All of this is implicit in the stage of experience called "Wisdom".

Ether: Oneness

Wisdom is a mature awareness of the unfolding process which the soul has entered into by choosing to be incarnated. It is an unfoldment of light, the light of consciousness, which gradually outshines all the encasements and distortions and layers under which it has been buried. Prior to the action of Grace, or the Descent of insight, we have a vague and imprecise notion of what consciousness might be; what we can grasp is as clear or obscure as the purity of our own reflecting medium, the clarity of our own consciousness. Initially, our notions are foggy and unrealistic, but in time, as we follow the path of self-development, this changes. There comes a time when we are able to contact the Primal Light of consciousness, undistorted by our own ignorance. Then we see that consciousness is infinite. It is the same everywhere, only the distorting action of the mind had divided the reality of oneness into the appearance of the many. The difference and division that had been so dominant in our experience then takes on a different aspect; it appears like the waves on the surface of the ocean – ceaselessly fluid and multiform, but in essence One. The complexity of consciousness and its multidimensional expansion into various planes of manifestation remain apparent, but beyond the appearance of multiplicity is the awareness of oneness. When the awareness of underlying oneness comes to the fore, the great boon of wisdom has been won. It is something to treasure, a promise that life can never be the same again.

Mastery

The Archetype

The rune symbol for Mastery shows the 'lemniscate' image, which we have come to consider to be the symbol for infinity. Mastery is the ability to actualize harmony, to balance opposites and fuse them within the self so that the heart brings together earth and heaven in the dimensions of energy and consciousness. Where there is mastery, one has the power to be centred in Truth. The term "mastery" means the height of accomplishment. This can only be attained when one recovers one's inner freedom. This means getting beyond the pull of old habits, personality and cultural conditioning, and becoming fully responsible for one's ongoing self-development. Power from on high is only given to those who can manage it wisely, within the divine order and balance of life laid down by cosmic law.

Standard Meanings for Divination

Upright

Earth: You have more-than-adequate resources for success.

Fire: You are up to the challenge; your skill will bring success.

Air: What you are doing is correct; eloquence, persuasiveness.

Water: You are at the height of your powers; inner authority; power to rule.

Ether: Onward to victory; magical knowledge; higher help.

Reversed

Earth: You are deficient in what you need for success.

Fire: You are overconfident; pride precedes a fall.

Air: Your ego is deceiving you.

Water: You may be overmastered; if you are faint-hearted, you will falter.

Ether: You may lose; you face domination.

Spiritual Meanings for Divination
Earth: The Nature of Mastery

The power of mastery is not well understood. It does not consist in skill with words, or in convincing explanations. Words may emanate a certain force which has a temporary influence on the mind, but they do not control the movements of the forces of ignorance. The mastery or control of ignorance consists in opposing its vibrations by stronger, higher ones which bring about annulment. One who has mastery accomplishes this simply by his or her presence, without words or arguments. Just by his or her silent presence, or gaze, one who has mastery sends out a vibration of peace, calm and quietude that brings the light of knowledge and purity into the disturbed chaos of ignorance. Only a few exceptional beings have a conscious and organized inner life on the higher levels of awareness, and of these not all mix and circulate in the outer world so that one could meet and benefit from their presence. Although spiritual seekers aspire for mastery, it is the rare soul who has actually attained it. The path to mastery is one of continuous change. In seeking to acquire greater openness, transparency and inner freedom, one is always being shifted and changed by inner forces that act on a very deep level. It is not easy to keep the inner balance when the unfoldment of consciousness is rapid, because mind and memory are useless and ego is an even more serious impediment. One must somehow find the power to continue functioning and facing the challenges that life brings even as the normal reference points are changing. Openness to change is necessary, but it must be balanced by strength, flexibility and wisdom. Wisdom can no longer be the content of past experience. It is the depth of continuous, heart-centred relation to Truth, which goes beyond anything the mind can effect or articulate.

Fire: A Gradual Climb

Learning to serve the higher power and be led by it is a gradual climb to full consciousness. The soul begins its human sojourn in the most menial positions and gradually gathers experiences of all kinds as it learns about life in human form. Slowly the evolving human learns to let go of faulty habits and in time rises to positions of leadership. But the movement from willingness to mastery is long and arduous. The mind and ego, while useful at an early stage of development, can no longer be the interpreters of experience. We come to rely more on the heart, the soul, and the action of Grace. We take life seriously, but not too seriously. Our effort is steady and patient rather, not characterized by fitful bursts of intensity, and reverse swings into despondency and sloth. We try to keep our attitudes correct and to learn the art of right relation which we exercise with our peers, our inferiors and with the divine guidance which we receive from within. We will inevitably experience setbacks, but these we accept as learning experiences, not permanent failures. We want to make the correct impression on other people, but we do not become attached to the impressions we make or fail to make. We let go of our mistakes, learn from our omissions and set aside our regrets. We release ourselves from all vestiges of pride and fear, learning from our shortcomings and adjusting as necessary to be more open to the divine possibilities of our situation. Our resolve to constantly do better is firm. In time, the ill-effects of our mistakes fade away, as we remain true to the inspiration from above. The soul moves steadily toward a condition known as Mastery.

Air: Attainment

When one attains recognition and influence, inner strength and constancy of character are fully tested. When the soul finally attains mastery, or the capacity for spiritual leadership, every thought, word and deed has power and this inner influence flows without conscious effort. The Mastery rune reminds us that it is enough to preserve a constant inner immersion in the flow of Grace and let the divine will work its way. The old techniques of exercising influence are no longer admissible. Calling attention to our ability or position or using clever mental strategies to defend ourselves must be abandoned, along with emotional reactions to the mistakes and misbehavior of others. In earlier stages of development, it was perhaps permissible to defend oneself by argumentation, or to exercise one's legal rights in order to attain a goal. But in the more advanced stages of development, and with increasing spiritual responsibility, this is no longer sanctioned from within. The inner power acts through modesty, and from the viewpoint of the ego one is relatively defenseless. Every time the new way is abandoned, every time the old ways are resurrected, one strays from the path and the light diminishes. There is no room for pretense. The light flows through us as long as we are attuned to it by right attitude, inner purity and openness, but if we pretend that we have special importance, or take comfort from the honours of leadership, we soon find that the divine blessings are inaccessible. We must then repent or continue to dissemble. Everything we earn by perseverance and devotion is a gift, and remembering this helps us to remain humble. Our emptiness, innocence and receptivity are the only qualifications we have for leadership in the spiritual life. In time, as a result of a long climb in experience, we attain Mastery by means of an absolute reliance on the guidance from above.

Water: To Live The Truth

Mastery means to live what one inwardly knows, to live the divine plan of the soul. One embodies the light and shines it on all. Simply by being, one makes a difference in the quality of energy and consciousness of others. Mastery is a stage in life when wisdom has been assimilated, and one has achieved alignment with the divine will. This rune symbolizes harvest time, ripeness, fullness, prosperity, success and attained riches. Whatever field of endeavour one embarked on, under this sign the rewards are reaped. Things are at a peak of bounty, in the sense of yielding fruit. But the question arises: "What next?" It is easy to relax, enjoy life and begin to slide backward. But true mastery is a process of continual self-transcendence. It is by self-giving to THAT which transcends human limitation that ever wider states of consciousness are achieved. The effort to live in right relation to Truth becomes a progressive surrender of the ego, mind, desires and even preferences to the guidance that comes from the Higher Self. The Mastery rune can only be effective when there is no tendency to sink into convivial indolence, rather a will to remain constant in perseverance. Perseverance in self-giving gradually creates a capacity for surrender. Only when surrender of the human to the divine is irreversibly established can full realization dawn, and only then does the risk of backsliding recede. At that time, the action that happens through us originates in a higher guidance; we are conduits for the divine outpouring whose origin is the hidden world of infinite possibility.

Ether: Change

The Mother has said: "To learn how to observe in silence is the source of skillfulness." (4:330) Deep observation brings insight, and this allows us to change and transform what is imperfect into something more divinely beautiful and harmonious. Mastery is the capacity to change hatred into harmony, jealousy into generosity, ignorance into knowledge, darkness into light, falsehood into truth, wickedness into goodness, war into peace, fear into courage, uncertainty into certitude, doubt into faith, confusion into order and defeat into victory. (15:239) The mind always wants to identify issues, differences, points of disagreement and the intellectual content of any dispute. But its ability to bring about lasting change is limited. However, the spiritual heart works in a different way, recognizing energy as it operates on the emotional level, and transmuting this energy into something less crude. Then the feelings of hurt, jealousy and anger can be raised and transformed into peace, oneness and harmony with a widened outlook. A lasting change can be effected by the act of placing awareness in the light of the soul.

When one is pure, one is not touched by evil because it does not exist in oneself. This inner freedom can be attained by cultivating the habit of not noticing evil, not speaking of the evil in others, not perpetuating the vibrations of evil by criticizing or judging it verbally, and thereby never contributing to the spread of evil. One refuses to give ignorance the force of one's attention and the support of one's consciousness. To do this, one must be able to clearly see what is wrong without suffering from this wrong or tolerating it within one's own being. Then, one is no longer shocked or disturbed by it. When ignorance or evil can be seen from a height where its vibration cannot reach, it has no power. When consciousness abides in its own highest height, in the light, in the spirit, the human personality is free, unaffected by so-called evil. Only this kind of mastery can effect lasting change.

However, beyond this degree of attainment, one can also cultivate an awareness of Truth, a vision of the supreme Beauty, Goodness and Harmony that is behind all manifestations in this world. When one sees the divine in all things, the distortions of ugliness and wickedness are perceived to be a thin veneer of falsehood, not fully real. When one has this power of perception, this consciousness of the true vibration, one can bring forward a higher harmony and manifest it in the material world. Thus, distortions and deformations are replaced by a more perfectly ordered creation that resonates the harmony of heaven in the evolving reality of earth. In this way, power to observe in silence a capacity to effect lasting change. This is one of the hallmarks of mastery.

LAKE

The Archetype

The image for the Lake rune resembles a body of water. It is taken from the oldest signs of the Old Europe culture, rather than directly from the Cypriot Syllabary as many other of the Primal Runes are. In the Western tradition, a pool or sacred spring can be thought of as a gateway to another world where insight and communion with nature or the gods can be attained. Still water may provide a mirroring of archetypes as we gaze into its depth. As we become aware of mysteries hidden below the surface, we widen our vision of life's possibilities. The *I Ching* trigram known as "Lake" also comprises many of the same meanings as this rune. In nature, a lake is formed when streams of water flow together into a single body in happy congress. A place of harmony is created, and nourishing waters accumulate there to foster life. There is serenity and happiness for all who assemble. This place stirs up good feelings in the heart. The atmosphere is cheerful, delightful, one of enrichment and good fortune. In such a place, one has pleasing vistas and good company, and there is laughter and happiness. Still waters are places of safety where beauty is added to nearby homes. These images, of course, are metaphors for a state of inner development where harmony and balance have been established to such a degree that the individual becomes a blessing and support to all. Water has always been a symbol of consciousness, and when consciousness has accumulated in abundance, humans can happily evolve into a wider congress with heaven.

Standard Meanings for Divination
Upright

Earth: Rest and enjoyment are indicated; harmony and abundance prevail; a harvest of rewards.

Fire: Reaping of rewards; it all comes together.

Air: Good, open communication; re-unions; enjoyment of life.

Water: good luck; abundance; fulfilment, completion; luxury and pleasure.

Ether: Fortunate meetings; the circle is complete.

Reversed

Earth: Disharmony, disruption, disunity.

Fire: Your rest is over; its time for preventive action.

Air: Superficial appearances of harmony are deceptive.

Water: Things begin to fall apart.

Ether: Impoverishment on many levels; fractious energy.

Spiritual Meanings for Divination
Earth: Blessings Accumulate

Because we have sincerely sought and gratefully received, because we have been conscientious and humble, we have evolved a way of life that can become part of a communal fullness. There is a joy that we experience when we are first touched by the Fullness. There is a greater joy that comes when it takes possession of us. But the greatest joy is to embody and offer everything that Heaven has and is to the aspiring hearts and minds of earthbound humanity. A milestone in our own spiritual journey is achieved when we can see that this could actually come to pass in our own life. The Lake rune is an indication that we are oriented toward this possibility, but that further effort will be needed. The abundant waters of a nurturing lake accumulate drop by drop with each rainfall. In every instance where we choose self-giving over self-indulgence, we are filling up the lake of our future joy. The small steps that we take each day, unknown to any but ourselves, are what eventually bring us to the shores of the Lake. When we arrive at the Lake, solitary effort is joined to a wider circle of collective endeavour.

Fire: Goals

It is not reconciling the interests of competing individuals that creates durable harmony among people, but rather the revelation of their pre-existing oneness. If the unity that underlies common goals can be felt, difficulties can be successfully resolved. Building unity is itself a worthy goal. One who is not seeking any special advantages, but working unselfishly to promote the general wellbeing, reflects the unifying energy of the Lake rune. But if earlier runes such as Love, Grace, Fullness, Descent and Wisdom have been absorbed as life lessons, the individual will not necessarily be goal-oriented in the normal way. The *Bhagavad Gita* teaches that we have the right to work, but not to claim the fruits of our endeavour. The Lake rune is not so much an energy of toil and achievement as an image of harmonious accord which spontaneously nurtures collective harmony and wholeness. There is no need to fix the inner eye on specific goals; they come about in their own time when we simply keep to the path of attunement to Source. When you seek only the kingdom of Heaven, everything else is added on providentially.

Air: Collective Consciousness

Many spiritual paths in the past have focused on the solitary asceticism and discipline required to attain individual salvation or liberation. But only a collective endeavour can bring the reality of heaven down to earth and establish it permanently in the terrestrial atmosphere. Oneness comes about when individuals voluntarily sacrifice their personal agendas for a more important collective goal. Where there is a community of interests, each individual feels himself or herself to be a part of this whole, and each will have a distinctive contribution or quality to add to the collectivity. Human energies join and amplify when gathered around a unity-building principle. What Grace can do individually and inwardly, collective consciousness can replicate, up to a point, by the magic of synergy. We must not carry this idea too far, because there are differences, but it is fair to say that, for example, the solitary practitioner of meditation will usually benefit substantially by joining with others who practice in the same way. Leadership devolves naturally on individuals who are aligned with the inner truth, and who express it with kindness and friendliness. The power of joy, which is at the core of the Lake rune, is a great force for unification. People will struggle through all manner of difficulties and hardships when their hearts are won over by benevolence. In older models of institutional control, the use of force, intimidation, fear and manipulation was not uncommon. But the Lake rune shows a different energy of cohesion based on individual and collective alignment with truth. Only when the soul leads all parts of our being into adherence to the light is one qualified to play a role of leadership in a community.

Water: Collective Aspiration

The Lake rune is a teaching about collective aspiration and the enhancement of possibilities that can take place when unified consciousness is established. Human beings can collectively evoke an energy and consciousness that is finer and more powerful than any individual can summon on his or her own. That is why individual aspiration for inner development often leads a seeker to join with other seekers and to form like-minded groups for practice or study. Under wise guidance, group dynamics can result in intensified energy fields that make possible higher states of consciousness. The collective energy empowers the process which is unfolding in each individual and in some cases helps to bring about a breakthrough to a whole new level of awareness. It is a very special gift and calling to be able to orchestrate a group of individuals into a unified collectivity; but still greater wisdom and maturity is required if the collectivity is to develop and maintain a momentum toward higher levels of attainment. Group projects which have tight deadlines can mobilize a collective effort and motivate people to achieve self-transcendence. This is one example of how groups of people with shared goals bring forward their finest qualities in situations of urgency or crisis, something that often happens when a country is at war. Although the empowerment of group activity is not well understood, it often comes into play. Repeated experience will show that any setting where people achieve unity of purpose will be a situation of heightened energy, but the quality of the energy is more important than the ritual which gets the group there on the mental level. People become integrated to the setting where their energy is enhanced and empowered, or deeply committed to a belief system within which they have experienced growth, but a long maturing is needed to learn the mastery of these states of energy and consciousness independent of the setting or the group or the belief system. Only one who has internalized this is capable of leading groups of spiritual aspirants. It is easy to become addicted to what works, more challenging to master the energies involved and establish the higher consciousness permanently.

Ether: Interdependence

The state of spiritual awakening is not dependent on any outer circumstances in life, yet the attainment of this awakening can be expedited by wise choices of how and where we use our time and energy. The Lake rune in ether asks a seeker to consider the relationship between the individual and the community as a schooling in relationship and experience which is rich with possibilities for growth. One of the key elements of the Lake rune is joy, or bliss. The bliss which arises from profound communion with the Divine exceeds all other kinds of joy in quality and depth. Once we come into relation with this universal and eternal bliss, there is no further need for an outer object, an outer cause, an outer setting or community to find joy. Because divine bliss has no dependence on an outer object, it can be continuous. In whatever outer circumstances we find ourselves, the bliss of self-realization can flow continuously, even through and beyond disease, crisis and death itself. Having found the Source of joy within oneself, nothing else is needed. One who has such attainment becomes a most valuable resource, a true friend, a mentor and guide to all souls who seek the way. There is a subtle radiation of energy and consciousness that moves in silence from those who have it to those who seek it. Thus, by their very presence the awakened souls can be an influence for upliftment and inspiration. One who is continuously in right relation with the Source of bliss becomes a catalyst for others, and often a community of seekers will be attracted to such an individual, like bees to the nectar of fully open blossoms. The awakened consciousness transcends, and thus ultimately disrupts, the boundary-enforcing strategies of the ego-centred consciousness. Limitations are exposed, brought to the fore and challenged when the undeveloped mind and ego are placed in proximity to a spiritually transformative energy. Thus, a continuous will for self-transcendence is indispensable for those who choose such association. The nature of interdependence requires us to be grateful not only for the blessings of spiritual association, but also for the difficulties and challenges that are an inevitable component of collective aspiration.

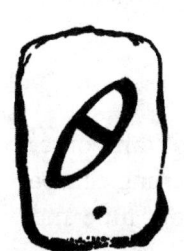

Transmission

The Archetype

The symbol is one of an ellipse divided down the middle into two parts. It resembles a cell beginning to divide into two, so that there is self-replication or passing on of genetic information. The line in the centre of the ellipse is a permeable membrane which allows transference of information and substance from one side to the other. The wholeness and integrity of the cell is not broken, but it has begun to multiply itself by division. This occurs only after it has reached mature and complete development. The rune "Transmission" is concerned with communicating wisdom and inspiration. It includes both mentoring and discipleship, for they are ways of expressing and living sacred relationship. Since themes like diffusion, multiplication, mentorship, replication, service and teaching are present in this symbol, issues of communication, speech and writing often come up when it is drawn. Under this sign, there is a sharing of sacred tradition, a transfer of the living consciousness of Grace and Fullness, Love and Wisdom.

Standard Meanings for Divination

Upright

Earth: Challenges resolved successfully; your intent carries through.

Fire: Use your influence to advantage and you will succeed.

Air: Take care to inform and educate, thouse associated with you.

Water: Give attention to successful communication; differences resolved.

Ether: Distinctions become a unifying factor; the pattern-of-the-whole is clarified.

Reversed

Earth: A challenge remains unresolved.

Fire: Differences remain unresolved.

Air: Unsuccessful communication; you are unconvincing; your influence is inadequate.

Water: Blockage; constriction of flow; impediments need attention.

Ether: Communication disrupted; isolation; misunderstandings.

Spiritual Meanings for Divination
Earth: An Energetic Process

Spiritually developed people radiate the light of consciousness, and this light brings about transformation in those it touches, at least those who are aspiring and receptive. The energies of transformation are radiated, not taught. They cannot be appropriated by rational inquiry, and intellectual habits of learning do not really work very well when this new process of energetic learning is at work. This light is not physically visible, but it can be felt. When touched by this energy, one begins to see and understand and feel in a new way, one has the sense of inner lightening or release. Such an experience widens one's vision of life well beyond the boundaries of intellectualism. This energetic presence of light touches the dark regions of the psyche that resist opening and transformation and these parts of the being may respond with agitation and discomfort. For the most part, however, people become more peaceful when they experience the presence and power of spiritual light. They may even experience a mild euphoria, joy or bliss. Those who are receptive and open have good experiences, while those who are blocked and resistant will likely feel uncomfortable. Light and love bring about oneness. The boundaries between self and others begin to dissolve. The structure of one's personality and ego begin to change in subtle ways that may not be understood. Things that were formerly important may no longer seem meaningful. New areas of interest and involvement develop. The superficial personality with its social skills may seem somehow shallow and empty because one is capable of new ranges of intimacy and affection.

Our most important lessons are not learned by having questions answered by some expert. In the beginning, we do not know how deeper things are learned, but after being touched by the light, we are motivated to seek for further light, and we discover, or are taught from within, the meaning of receptivity. In the Transmission rune, the thin membrane that divides (and unites) the two sides of the ellipse represents the focus of the transmission process. It is an unfolding learning experience in which equilibrium is thrown off balance so that one can discover the way to restore balance, but a *new* balance of heightened energy and intensified consciousness. In this fashion, higher degrees of order are transmitted from those who have it to those who aspire for it.

Fire: Stages of Transmission

A teacher who can effect a direct transmission of higher consciousness is relatively rare. Such a teacher or guru hopes that as many students as possible will recognize the presence of the subtle realities and learn how to enter them by a process of inner identification. According to his or her receptivity and capacity, each seeker can learn to carry a measure of this heightened presence. The act of sharing seems to bring about a deepening of the presence, as does collective practice of meditation. Initially, the teacher or the setting which has helped one to achieve altered states of consciousness will be quite important. This is an essential developmental phase. In time, however, a seeker learns to find the spiritual presence in other ways, and eventually becomes conscious that it is always available from within. It takes a certain maturity to progress to the point where one need not cling to the group or teacher, but need not reject them either. To gracefully accept the means given for progress, and continue to move forward, demands great depth of sensitivity, flexibility, openness.

Some seekers become dependent on the group, or the guru and are incapable of transcending their dependency. Sometimes, such people create pretexts or rationalizations for rejecting what they have come to depend on, as if that would be a solution to their weakness. They become critical of the teacher and disillusioned by that which formerly inspired them; they find flaws in the human personality of the teacher, or disagree with the teaching which had formerly filled their lives with meaning. But rejection is not a solution for attachment. Both are imbalanced and extreme positions. The gift of light, once received, will mature in its own good time. It will reveal the flawed motives which may have motivated seekers to approach a teacher, or the selfishness, self-doubt or ill-will that have been limiting the inner progress. Such flaws must be brought to the surface in order to be healed, but they may provoke rebellion and rejection rather than gratitude and relief. Thus the transmission process is at every stage full of possibilities and pitfalls, opportunities and traps. The Transmission rune points to a process with many stages in which wisdom, maturity and spiritual foundation are all eventually established.

Air: Teachers

The transmission rune is an elliptical sphere with a dividing line in its middle. It is oneness expressing itself in duality. Finding a way to live this experience is an ongoing challenge both for teachers and the seekers who approach them. "A cell," The Mother tells us, "is composed of different radiances, with a wholly luminous centre, and the connection is established between light and light. That is, the will, the central light, acts on the cell by touching the corresponding lights, by an inner contact of the being. Each cell is a world in miniature, corresponding to the whole." (12:345) Something similar to this takes place in the process of spiritual transmission. Traditionally, the guru has been the focus of the transmission process, the luminous centre of radiance. More recently, some highly evolved souls have been teaching meditation, or radiating its power and potential, in a way that encourages students to adapt to the consciousness within the group as a whole rather than fixing on the evolved teacher at its centre. The true teacher wants all his or her students to bring forward the power and presence within their own hearts. But many students replicate their child-parent relationship in their relation to the spiritual teacher. One who is a perpetual child may have an excuse to delay taking responsibility for his or her own development, thus remaining passive and submissive rather than taking the risk to be truly creative. This naturally diminishes the guru-disciple relationship and its richness; but it may also define and restrict the teacher to the narrow parameters of his or her students' expectations. Yet it has often been the approved traditional paradigm, especially in the East.

Humans worship freedom, but fear change. They easily crystallize the relation to the divine into a limiting pattern, a comfortable rut which minimizes challenge and obviates the need to progress. At some point, the teacher is faced with a need to shake things up so that further progress may be possible, and at this time there is always a risk that the comfortable seekers will run away, rather than rise to the challenge. Both teacher and student grow by participating in the process of transmission because their mutual attunement to Source replicates light and anchors its manifestation in the planetary evolution.

Water: A Supra-personal Process

Humans have individualized personalities. Even spiritual teachers still have the fullness of their human individuality as an outer shell through which they manifest the energies (and consciousness) of transformation. Students whose consciousness is still fixed at the level of mind, ego and personality may not be able to intuit what it is in the teacher that abides beyond all these. They may not recognize what it is that gives the teacher his or her radiance, wisdom and magnetic power. They know that they are inspired and elevated in the teacher's presence, but they cannot explain the mystery which is at work. It is a mistake for the student to take the human personality of the teacher as anything more or less than a point of manifestation of the divine consciousness. And it is also a mistake for the student to take his or her own mind, ego or personality as anything more than a vessel whose sole purpose is to become a perfect instrument of the divine.

The human surrenders to the divine in the process of the guru-disciple relationship, but the human is never called upon to surrender to anything or anyone other than the truth of the Supreme Self. If the spiritual teacher can move the seeker forward in this process, then he or she is serving the divine wisely, whether or not the teaching method is understood by the student. Students are not required primarily to understand the inner working of the teacher, but rather to accept and to practice in light of the guidance and with the support of the inner presence. The understanding comes later, when faith and inner deepening have prepared the way. Thus the Transmission rune points not so much to an interpersonal as to a trans-personal process wherein the human in the seeker approaches and opens to the divine in the teacher. The human element is not set aside, but used as an instrument to serve the growth of consciousness. In serving, it develops the capacity for surrender which leads in the end to the fullness of realization.

Ether: Openness

The qualities required for successful transmission are, for the teacher, a degree of inner realization and a willingness to serve, and for the student or seeker a measure of openness, receptivity, obedience, faith, fidelity to practice and sincerity. The teacher must be willing to accept all that the student has or is, the knot of limitation which wants to burst its bounds and flow beyond fixity. The student must be willing to accept the discipline which the teacher requires, and fulfil the rules and obligations of the way. There is no calculation, strategy or self-aggrandizement at work, only a mutual service of the divine possibility, on the teachers part by selfless giving, and on the student's part by progressive opening and self-transcendence. Open-mindedness is a great asset for a would-be student, but open-heartedness is even more important. The sweetness, intimacy, innocence, affection and depth of the master-disciple relation is like no other. Only the heart which opens like a blossom in the sun can feel the loving devotion of the soul's unfolding bliss. Of all the friends, mentors and helpers that one can meet in life, the spiritual teacher occupies a special place unlike any other. The Mother defines openness as follows:

> Openness is the will to receive and to utilise for progress the force and influence; the constant aspiration to remain in touch with the consciousness, the faith that the force and consciousness are always with you, around you, inside you and that you have to let nothing stand in the way of your receiving them. Openness is a release of a consciousness by which it begins to admit into itself the workings of the Divine Light and power.
>
> – The Mother, *Collected Works*, 14:151

> Now, if one is able to consciously unite with one's psychic being, one can always be in this state of receptivity, inner joy, energy, progress, communion with the divine presence. And when one is in communion with That, one sees it everywhere, in everything, and all things take on their true meaning.
>
> – The Mother, *Collected Works*, 8:305

The term "psychic being" means soul-contact. When the student sees the teacher as a point of contact for the relationship to the divine, there is an unparalleled opportunity to transcend ego and intensify the momentum of the spiritual practice.

DREAMWEAVER

The Archetype

The rune for Dreamweaver consists of two crooks back to back and pointing at an upward angle of about 45 degrees. The Dreamweaver image is similar to that of "Courage", but open-ended. The energy is no longer that of struggle for attainment; one has grown into an open channel, a passageway for the rhythms, harmonies, insights and inspirations that come from a higher plane. The attainment may be that of a seer, a visionary, a bard, a poet, an inspired prophet, but whatever its form the higher consciousness is active. The human microcosm which has become a receptive channel for the infinite consciousness can be oriented in many directions, not only up and down; the mind which has touched the infinite consciousness draws imagery and inspiration from many sources.

One who attains the power of The Dreamweaver rune becomes a builder and renewer of life. He knows the magical power of the Word and uses it to bring inspiration, harmony and wholeness into the earth atmosphere. Martin Prechtel describes very well the power of the Word in the shamanic tradition:

> To the shaman, all the places, animals, weather, plants and things outside in the world are also inside of you as your twin, and together everything makes an immense four-dimensional series of concentric cubes: the layers that stretch outside and inside simultaneously to create The House of the World, or World Body. This structure is made by the Builders, certain Owners or Gods with their original sounds and words. These sounds and words become

tangible meaning, made to live as they are spoken. Each God word builds the House of the World by echoing off the other words. These spirit world soundings, when made all at once, form the spiritual song of the world. This combined sound, when it gets here to this world, becomes vibrant and tangible, and grows the world in the form that we see and are. This song is the nervous system of the Universe. When an individual falls ill, something in this World House-Earth Body is being attacked, gnawed away... The shaman assesses the destruction and, after dealing with the cause, begins to rebuild the World House of that person's body by remembering all its parts back to life – by making it echo off the original Flowering Earth, what shamans call the creations, the Big Earth House Temple. He does this by speaking or singing out a sacred map, following a natural order of holy words and magical sounds in a rhythmic roll call. This is a miniature, or echo child, of the Original Big Sounds used by the owners, the Gods, to make the entire World Body we live in.

– *Secrets of the Talking Jaguar*, pp. 278-9

This passage reflects a Mayan, shamanic world-view that differs very little from the cosmology of Old Europe. The Primal Runes are one such collection of sacred sounds as Martin Prechtel refers to, and which, by the way, he learned to apply just as described. The sounds of the Primal Runes outer (utter) the powers inherent in the Lunar Law. These energies flow in sequence through the 28 days of the lunar cycle, which is the primal paradigm of the Great Mother. The Dreamweaver rune refers to the magic of sound and the mastery of the bardic, shamanic lore by which beauty and harmony are restored, and the microcosm and macrocosm are brought back into balance. The Dreamweaver rune conveys the power of inner attunement and vision, as well as the expressive skill of the bard to put this into music and words so that it can change the minds and hearts of the community. The poet, the mystic, the singer, the harpist, the public speaker, the visionary artist and the song-writer are commonly gifted with aspects of the Dreamweaver power.

Standard Meanings for Divination
Upright
Earth: You can materialize or create something true and beautiful at this time; express beauty.

Fire: Use your imagination; explore your creative fantasies; tune in to your dreams and your visions.

Air: An inner journey; a quest; a seeking.

Water: Follow your heartfelt intuition, your ideals; be still and attract inspiration

Ether: Open to the muses; pay attention to the artist inside you; use your powers of magic.

Reversed
Earth: You are closing doors; you are failing to express your creative possibilities; an aborted creative project.

Fire: You are dis-empowering your imaginative, magical potential; beware false prophecies.

Air: Your communication with the creative side of life is interrupted; your mind has closed too many doors.

Water: Your heart is oriented in the wrong direction.

Ether: You have lost contact with the muses; you are not keeping faith with your inspired side.

Spiritual Meanings for Divination
Earth: Expression
For someone who has been carried deeply into a new and higher consciousness, there is often a perceived need to somehow express the energies that have been evoked. If this is the inner feeling that has arisen, it is probably wise to acknowledge it. This comes to the fore as a challenging but fulfilling inner urge to express energies that are essentially formless through some kind of creative endeavour. Poetry, music, painting or dance can integrate various parts of the being with the inner flow of formless

light that has been evoked and provide a training in self-dedication to the inner guidance of the Muse. On the one hand, the forces of Mastery move the seeker's consciousness toward infinity; on the other hand, there is a need to integrate these energies into one's life and stabilise what has been achieved through the process of offering what one has and is to the wider world. It is a painful experience to have to re-direct the awakened and inspired mind back into routine areas of mundane activity with no hope that the inner spirit can 'outer' itself. Here, the purity of intention is supremely important. Whereas many performers are motivated by a desire for fame or wealth, the spiritually creative soul seeks only to open more completely to the inspirational forces of the beyond by becoming their channel, their instrument, a clear voice for what is being inwardly revealed. The world does not afford many opportunities to express higher levels of energy and inspiration, but where there is an inner need and a clear will, it can be done.

Fire: Manifestation

The light which we receive from a higher source is not something to be possessed or hidden, it is meant to be shared. The gift is actually something which flows from heaven to earth; the individual seeker who experiences the action of the Muse is merely the letter carrier. The energies of awakening are meant to be brought to life in the body of earth, not merely in the domain of conceptual theory and abstract philosophy. One who becomes a voice for the energies of inspiration moves to the centre of the circle within which the dialogue between heaven and earth is occurring.

Realization of a higher consciousness is the first stage of heaven's action; manifestation of what has been realized on earth is the second, but equally challenging, requirement if the marriage of heaven and earth is to be consummated. In this sense, the Dreamweaver rune is a calling to play a part in a cosmic event. Many artists are caught up in a highly personal expression of their own emotional and intellectual issues. However, the Dreamweaver consciousness is supra-personal. Only one who has transcended the knots and difficulties of his or her personal life and risen to a higher and freer level of awareness, touching the universal consciousness and experiencing the flow that connects the microcosm and macrocosm, can become a voice of prophetic revelation. The Word can only express its purity and power through a human instrument which has been consecrated and elected for this very special role. Bards and sages are not self-created, although their self-dedication is indispensable. The seer-poet is a 'vessel of election', a creation of sacred forces from above, an instrument of the Muse and a child of Grace. This sacred function was well understood in the age of the Goddess, and oftentimes it was part of the shamanic calling. Then there was no separation of sacred and profane; all of life was sacred. The re-unification of what has been divided and separated is the core of the heavenly mandate for earth, and the essence of what is awakened when the Dreamweaver energy is at work.

The word "manifestation" is used by The Mother in a special sense:

> What I call a "descent" is this: first the consciousness rises in an ascent, you catch the Thing up there, and descend with the consciousness, bringing it down into you. That is an individual event. When this individual event has happened in a way that proves sufficient to create a possibility of a general kind, it is no longer a "descent", it is a "manifestation". What I call a descent is the individual movement, in an individual consciousness. And when it is a new world manifesting in an old world – just as, for comparison, when mind spread upon the earth – I call that a manifestation.
>
> – The Mother, *Collected Works*, 8: 134-5

The Dreamweaver rune in Fire concerns the process of manifestation, just as the earlier Descent rune was about the individual connection to a higher reality.

Air: The Fashioners

The Dreamweaver energy of Air is about manifesting the reality of the fashioners on earth. First, a word concerning the fashioners, as explained by The Mother:

There is an entire world which is the world of the fashioners, where all conceptions are made. And this world is very high, much higher than all the worlds of the mind; and from there these formations, these creations, these types which have been conceived by the fashioners come down and are expressed in physical realisations. And there is always a great distance between the perfection of the idea and what is materialized. Very often the materialised things are like caricatures in comparison with the primal idea. This is what Sri Aurobindo calls the archetype. For many things – the physical and the primal ideas – these archetypes, live in what Sri Aurobindo calls the Overmind. But there is a still higher domain than this where the origins are still purer, and if one reaches this, attains this, one finds the absolutely pure types of what is manifested upon earth. And then it is very interesting to compare, to see to what extent earthly creation is a frightful distortion. And moreover, it is only when one can reach these regions and see the reality of things in their essence that one can work with knowledge to transform them here; otherwise on what can we base our ideals to conceive of a better world, more perfect, more beautiful than the existing one? It can't be on our imagination which is itself something very poor and very material. But if one can enter that consciousness, rise right up to these higher worlds of creation, then with this in one's consciousness one can work at making material things take their real form.

– The Mother, *Collected Works*, 7: 122-3

First comes the ascent to a world of higher reality, then the descent of the consciousness which has been experienced, then the manifestation of this higher reality on earth with the minimum of distortion, according to the possibilities present where the Dreamweaver energy touches down. It is clear that this process goes far beyond the normal artistic procedure of imaginative fancy based on earthly experience. We can understand more clearly why Dreamweaver energy seeks a consciousness which can be a pure channel and why creation in its light is a sacred ritual effecting the unification of celestial and terrestrial reality in their divine Source.

Water: The Priesthood of Beauty

In the physical world, according to The Mother, it is beauty which best expresses the Divine. Beauty is perfection of form, and the material world is a domain where the formless realities of the inner planes seek to manifest in physical expression. If beauty is the best that the Divine can achieve in matter, then one who reveals beauty on earth should be considered as a priest or priestess of the sacred. Beauty puts physical creation into contact with its Source by the harmonious manifestation of perfected forms. To contemplate beauty elevates the soul, and to create beauty on earth is to participate in the heavenly revelation. Many artists have lost sight of art's sacred role, but in ancient times the understanding was very much clearer. In fact, when the Primal Runes came into existence, thousands of years BC, all art was related to the Goddess in one way or another, and form was intimately connected to ritual, the shamanic revelation of the inner worlds to the outer consciousness of awakening humanity. The Primal Runes embody the first thoughts of creation, and the magic of the fashioners. They are building blocks of future possibility based on the foundation archetypes. The priesthood of beauty is a Dreamweaver gift. It comes to those who open their hearts in aspiration to a higher and deeper vision of life's possibilities.

Ether: Culmination

Anyone who can concentrate with any degree of force and persistance can formulate inner currents of magic which will sooner or later achieve manifestation. But there are certain people who have special gifts, or who follow a discipline which has activated inner capacities that allow them to contact the world of the fashioners and tap the creative possibilities which they find there. They can discover the right thought forms, words, rhythms and expressions to clothe and manifest the rarefied and uplifting energies of the archetypes, and bring them into physical form. The Primal Runes refer to this special gift through the Dreamweaver symbol, especially in Ether. This is but one of many possible paths of inner development, but for bringing together realisation and manifestation, it is the ultimate stage to which humans can aspire at this point of our evolutionary development.

It is very likely that anyone who activates this power will take an interest in music, or poetry, or colour, or ritual because these are the traditional means through which the vision of the higher worlds has been expressed. In our own time, cinematography has emerged as an important new art form, and archetypal tales such as *The Lord of the Rings* resonate in the popular imagination with tremendous power. Gifted artists may very well advance the frontiers of popular awareness and tap into the true archetypes without fully understanding the process of spiritual attunement or the wider implications of the work they do. The Dreamweaver rune opens up the gift, but only with time is the talent and capacity and understanding of it fully activated.

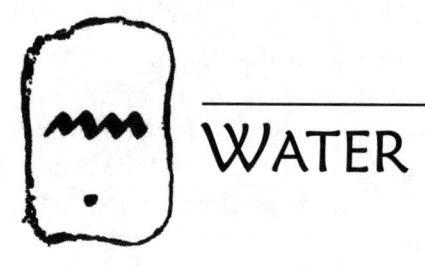

WATER

The Archetype

This symbol is a wavy line, and we find it in use from the very earliest times in many parts of the world. As a symbol, water is rich in associations. For example in the *Tao Te Ching*, we read: "The highest good is like water. Water gives life to the ten thousand things and does not strive. It flows in places men reject and so is like the Tao."(8) Water can flow in narrow channels (as we see in the *I Ching* Trigram) or it can move in vast, oceanic tides. In the former case, the image is one of toiling, labour and danger as water descends rapidly through a narrow channel ("places men reject"). This trigram suggests that one must work within boundaries, while exercising caution and persistence.

Water has always been an agent of purification since it acts to dissolve crystallized formations. In ancient symbolism, as far back as the Vedas of early India, water stands for consciousness. If you tune in to the cosmic forces at the time of the lunar third quarter, you will note that it is a time when consciousness flows into the deep, hidden places of the underground psyche and plunges thence into the depth of the abyss. There can be difficulty and danger when we explore the descending chasm, but this journey to difficult reaches of the inner geography helps us to master and integrate what has been denied and repressed. If the First Quarter Moon represents a 'crisis of action', the Third Quarter is a crisis of consciousness. Facing the eventual dissolution of structures, (the action of water) one must seek for fulfilment in the face of decline. In the order of the runes, Water comes after a high point, but it may bring an experience where the old ways of relating to situations suddenly cease to work. The narrow chasm through which water pours in the Water rune is like the confining laws and ideas of the human mind; they cannot hold the energy of the multidimensional consciousness in their restrictive confines. The rushing water of consciousness may overflow the rigid channels through which it moves at any time as it rushes impetuously forward with its irresistible accumulated energy.

Standard Meanings for Divination

Upright

Earth: You can move forward if you are flexible.

Fire: Challenge and uncertainty; stress adaptability over and above fixity.

Air: Things are fluid and unfixed at this time; avoid rigidity.

Water: Feelings and intuitions are more sensitive than usual; be present emotionally; release judgements and fixed attitudes.

Ether: Do not expect results; work the process.

Reversed

Earth: You are swimming against the current; do not oppose the flow.

Fire: Enthusiasm and energy dampened; creativity and will somewhat diminished.

Air: You have unrealistic expectations; you are taking the wrong approach.

Water: Emotional issues create complication; you are emotionally disordered; examine and harmonize your emotions.

Ether: you are out of step with reality; your feelings and instincts may mislead you at this time.

Spiritual Meanings for Divination
Earth: Water Energy

Water as one of the four sacred elements is characterized by being wet (or moist) and cool. The wetness of water makes it flexible, fluid, changeable, indefinite and lacking self-control. People in whom these qualities predominate are gentle, conforming, passive, yielding, accommodating, weak, sensitive, tolerant and kind, empathetic, compassionate and adaptable. Water is also cold, and the ancients associated it with Winter (not Spring as might be supposed). Coolness works to bind things together. Thus, water promotes formation and nourishment of composite entities, and its absence causes them to decompose. The moistness of water brings about dissolution of structure and the loss of form. Water mixes and clings but is changeable in shape. It permits the growth and development of form. It is associated psychologically with emotion, feeling, the subconscious, relationships, a nurturing matrix and a creative impulse. Some of these qualities apply in the Lake rune, but the Water rune is more an image of rushing water being channeled through a deep chasm where it seethes and toils downward. If you find that water energy is coming to the fore at this time, you can foster its desirable and useful qualities and become more aware of the aspects which are unsuitable to your needs.

Fire: Danger

The danger that could arise in this circumstance is an emotion which suggests giving up or rebelling against the slow, steady and patient perseverence by which lasting change is effected in the deep, resistant parts of the being. When consciousness enters the deep chasms and abysses of the being, as it often does in deep sleep, we may not be conscious of visible progress. Only a faithful commitment to our higher nature and a disengagement from the binding elements that are being worked out will succeed in the end. The best counsel at this time is: "keep still". Efforts to change things based on our own notions may only worsen the situation. We must continue to relate properly to the higher ideal that we cherish, and to detach from the forces of chaos and confusion. It is useless to think of escaping the situation, rather we must face it squarely and persevere.

The Water rune in Fire is a sign of deep, toiling energy that touches the bottom of our nature and flows where light has not yet penetrated. The way beyond difficulty is not through emotional disturbance. When we pander to our wants, fears and reactions, or when we feed our ambitions, we strive restlessly against the unpleasant aspects of the situation. But the transformative processes that the deep waters bring about are slow and enduring. Thus, to look deep within and abide in stillness is the best counsel.

Air: Dissolution

The Water sign in Air teaches us that progress has a price. It is necessary to set aside or dissolve all the old formations, let go of preconceived notions and the old, habitual mental constructs which have been part of our outlook for so long. It is natural to desire a rest, but at this time it would be a mistake. Much better to see the meaning of the present difficulties. All the elements of our experience can be means of progress, including the obstacles, contradictions, misunderstandings, the blockages and the interruptions – they all provide means for us to grow and develop in awareness, light and love. It is mostly the surface mind which sees the contradictions and difficulties; for the aspiring soul these things can be blessings in disguise. When an open space has been created by letting go of everything that obscures the light, a new consciousness can take birth.

Water: Providence

One who has faith can face all difficulties, even the most trying, without despair. It is necessary to persevere to the end, and this takes immense courage. Despair is a sign of weakness. Pessimism indicates a lack of faith. If one were able to place the consciousness at a higher level and see things from that perspective, one would recognize that at every moment everything in the universe is exactly as it should be. The Water rune in Water brings up the difficulties that must be faced and released; like water from a tap running into an old ink bottle and flushing the dried residues to the top, it churns up and washes away what is no longer needed in the nature. Reactions of anger, unhappiness, disgust and self pity are based on a lack of determination, an insufficient courage, as well as an inability or failure to see life from a higher perspective. The Divine Providence arranges all things for the purpose of progress even when we see only the problematic immediacy of the issues.

Ether: Sincerity

The Water rune in Ether tests our sincerity. To embark on the journey of self-transformation, at least a minimal sincerity is needed. But as the journey progresses, and we move deeper into the process, ever greater degrees of sincerity are needed. To be sincere means to make a constant effort to live in the light of the highest ideal, the inmost truth of one's being. This must grow and develop into a constant attitude that is present in all one does, says and thinks. Sincerity cuts through egocentric motivations and falsities of all kinds; it demands that the mind, vital and body live up to the ideal cherished by the heart and soul. The Water rune in Ether places us in situations that test sincerity. If we have personal preferences, emotional attractions, desires, dislikes enmities, attachments, foibles, or eccentricities, they will be challenged. Unless there is a firm decision to remain sincere, it might seem impossible to be rid of all these internal contradictions. But where the deep action of water churns up the things that need changing, the grace is present, and provided we maintain and increase the quality of sincerity, a way through will open up.

Crisis

The Archetype

The "Crisis" rune shows two lightening bolts. This rune indicates stress, disruption, an unpredictable or unfortunate event, a radical intensification of some challenging kind that may crop up suddenly like a "bolt from the blue". In this, it somewhat resembles The Tower in Tarot, with some of the same opportunities behind all the turmoil. There is a need to open to Truth in order to pass through the difficulties. There is an experience of pain, possibly resistance to spirit or resistance to healing. But the requirement for one who draws this sign is to hold to Truth while facing trials and passing through all difficulties into a place where harmony is re-established.

Standard Meanings for Divination

Upright

Earth: A challenge can be turned into a success; gear up for an intense time.

Fire: Be aware; be alert; high energy present; be fully engaged.

Air: This is a turning point; focus attention and will completely.

Water: Keep cool, as emotions may be challenged.

Ether: Judgement and justice come a-knocking; a powerful input energizes the situation.

Reversed

Earth: You seem to be unprepared for wht is coming.

Fire: Get with it!; it may already be too late!

Air: Do not be complacent; exercise clear judgement.

Water: A disaster looms; your response is inadequate.

Ether: Retribution; you stand to lose.

Spiritual Meanings for Divination
Earth: Deconstruction

We all structure reality according to our mental conditioning. And we all, from time to time, face circumstances which disrupt the structures through which we filter reality. There are certain periods of stress and change which can re-arrange one's life and one's perceptions in major ways. Examples of this might include losing a job, ending a relationship, the death of a loved one, or a severe setback in business. In a different way, winning the lottery and becoming a millionaire might also re-structure a person's life and perceptions. When life presents us with such crises, we have an important opportunity to re-configure our outlook in fundamental ways. In the intensification of physical, emotional and psychological duress, many things come up for change and release.

When faced with crisis, most people become fixated on the immediate issue that has cropped up, rarely on the transformational energy which is at work. We judge a situation to be "positive" or "negative" based on whether it agrees with the preconceptions and preferences of our normal outlook. But life, or divine providence, shakes up fixed attitudes that have run their course, and challenges whatever is outworn, sometimes long before the individual has recognized the need for change.

The first thing we need to do when a crisis comes up is to let go of fixed assumptions, and see whether it is a blessing in disguise. In the case of a spiritual seeker who places Truth above all else, it is often a test of equality. Imagine what can be subtracted from your life. Take away all the things you fancy that you possess; subtract everything to which you are attached, and see where the pain starts. Everything to which we cling, except for the Divine alone, constitutes an impediment to full self-giving and surrender. In this way, the Crisis rune is a blessing and a teaching.

Fire: Duress

Our first reaction to discomfort is to make an effort to limit or contain it. Wisdom teaches us that all containment is a form of self-limitation, most particularly when it involves strategies of repression or denial. How then to cope with issues that are crisis-like in their importance? One answer is to give the issue all the space it can take. When an issue crops up which has the potential to create emotional and mental disturbance, you may want to take this approach and see whether it is fruitful. Open your awareness as wide as you can until you can allow the process to unfold without any need for containment or reaction or repression at all. When you do this, you reclaim energy that would otherwise be siphoned off into worry. When you let go of the need to react, the old identity reconfigures its boundaries. For many people, a large part of the personality is configured around the things to which they react. This structures, but also circumscribes, the freedom of consciousness. When you expand awareness to give ample space for a crisis-issue to unfold, and forgo any need for personal emotional reactivity, you also dissolve some of the limiting parameters of the ego and its personality-structure. In doing this, you bring about transformation and transcendence.

You may at some point need to intervene or take action, but you will have the capacity to act with inner freedom, detachment and equality; not emotional reactivity. The action will then sow no seeds of future karmic involvement. In this way, the Crisis rune can turn challenges into opportunities and difficulties into blessings.

Air: Limitation

A crisis is an opportunity to bring about the transformation of consciousness. This process is inherently disruptive. On the one hand, there is the Fullness, the Grace, the Primal Light, and on the other, there is the ego-structured personality with its notions, preferences, likes and dislikes and karmic tendencies, all of which may be classified, relative to the absolute Truth, as limitation or ignorance. Compared to the wholeness which the soul seeks, the human self we have created is inhibited and out of balance. When we enter into a heightened state of consciousness, our energy, sensitivity and awareness are greatly intensified, and we see and feel things in a way we never did before. In this awakened state, everything is more intense and clear, and minor imbalances can loom as major disruptions. When the inner harmony becomes more finely tuned, any dissonance seems painful. For example, our motives for self-development may be based on self-serving inclinations of the ego. Or there may be a tendency to prejudge the nature of success in the spiritual life and pre-decide the parameters of what is possible or desireable. Crisis comes to shake up the mental structures which limit and suppress the free action of Grace. The degree of flexibility and transparency with which we respond to crisis is very important. We may, like the great oak tree, be demolished by the winds of change, or we may, like the slender reed, learn to adjust and adapt.

Water: Resistance

The Mother explains how rejection and resistance crop up at the time of crisis:

> ...renunciation can only arise in a self-centred consciousness. Naturally, people – the ones I call altogether primitive – are attached to things: when they have something they do not want to let it go! It seems so childish to me! ... When they have to part with something, it hurts! But this is childishness. The true process behind all this is the amount of resistance in things that were formed on a certain basis of knowledge – which was a knowledge at a particular time and which is no longer so at another – a partial knowledge, not fleeting but transitory. There is a whole set of things built upon this knowledge and they resist the force that says: "No! It is not true, your basis is no longer true, let's take it away!" And then, oh! It hurts – this is what people experience as renunciation.
>
> – The Mother, *Collected Works*, 10: 174

The pain of crisis is often like the pain of a tooth that needs to be extracted, and our attitude to crisis is often like avoiding a trip to the dentist. If we have assimilated the Wisdom rune's capacities, it is possible to see a crisis as an opportunity to let go and to grow. Sometimes we are attached and letting go must be enforced by a deliberate act of will. Then, it becomes an act of rejection. That which holds the consciousness back and limits its expansion must be rejected. The Crisis rune in Water quite often presents us with an opportunity to let go, reject, or transcend some issue of a binding nature, or some rigidity or attitude which has outlived its usefulness. Of course, it is quite common for human beings to see things in terms of black and white, good and evil, and to label that which they want to reject as "evil". Emotional reactivity need not be present, and if it is, may not be helpful. The Crisis rune in Water shows us where our equanimity, patience, wisdom and forgiveness may be lacking, and every difficulty we face in the right spirit can be turned to an opportunity to learn and progress.

Ether: Remedy

Suffering is a means for making progress. If the transforming energy of the Crisis rune brings suffering to our doorstep, and we receive the experience with aspiration and opening to truth, there can be a radical transformation of consciousness and a significant step forward in evolution. When we reach the end of the trial, there arises within us a kind of joy, security, trust and wholeness which offer a foretaste of the heavenly energies of regeneration. Generally, humans regard anything they label "evil" as something undesirable, useless or negative. But crisis always brings its opportunity and its redemption for those who greet it in the right spirit. If we wish to grow, crises are indispensable, because they are in essence a re-arrangement of energy, making possible a finer attunement and a more ordered structure within our being. The cause of suffering and its reason for being can be seen in the evolutionary nature of consciousness, which is always transcending its limits and breaking through its boundaries. If we are open to receive a new arrangement of possibilities, and if we see crisis for the opportunity it is, there is no need for suffering; wisdom will reveal the 'blessing in disguise' and make it operative much more quickly than otherwise. In the end, one question remains, and this is it: "Who suffers?" Only the ego suffers. Only the self-chosen limitation of the human mind can experience suffering. For one who does not cling to ego, there is no suffering; what we call suffering becomes joy. We can remember the words of The Mother:

> When... forces of destruction attack us, it proves that we are ready to be liberated from the ego and to merge con-

sciously into the Divine presence which is at the centre of our being, in full light, in peace and joy, free at last from the sufferings imposed upon us by the ego.

– The Mother, *Collected Works*, 10: 321

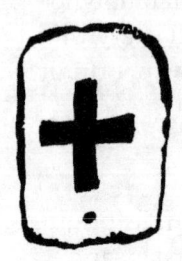

SACRIFICE

The Archetype

This symbol is a cross. A vertical line, which seems to link earth and heaven, is crossed by a horizontal line, which may represent contingency, mortality, limitation or earthly constraint. Under this sign, we experience the need to make a sacrifice, to let go, to make an offering or give a gift. When we do this, we renew our capacity to experience and express compassion toward all sentient beings, and in this we grow spiritually. When the small self lets go of its preoccupation with its own selfish concerns, it can expand to a more encompassing awareness and sympathy, and this is the essence of sacrifice. The lesser is released and we expand to encompass the greater. However, the idea of having, holding, possessing or controlling is also progressively released as we internalize the process of sacrifice, which may be something very close to cultivating non-attachment and desirelessness.

In *The Golden Bough*, (Vol. 4), James Frazer gives us important background about the sacrifice archetype:

> An octennial cycle is the shortest period at the end of which sun and moon really mark time together after overlapping, so to say, throughout the whole of the interval. Thus, for example, it is only once in every eight years that the full moon coincides with the longest or shortest day.
>
> The tradition plainly implies that at the end of every eight years the king's sacred powers needed to be renewed

by intercourse with the god-head, and that without such a renewal he would have forfeited his right to the throne. We may surmise that among the solemn ceremonies which marked the beginning or the end of the eight year cycle the sacred marriage of the king with the queen played an important part. (Vol. 4, *The Dying God*, pgs. 69 and 71)

He goes on to explain how the king was ritually sacrificed to bring fertility to the land so that its vigour did not wane with his own failing powers. In time, a bull was substituted for the king-sacrifice. The bull had long been a symbol of the Mother's powers of fertility. In Egypt, there was a marriage ceremony enacted using costume and masks of a bull, and the Serapis cult and temples were one of the most important institutions in the land. As Baring and Cashford summarize:

> When the priestess-queen 'married' the priest-king, she became the goddess and he became the son-lover, and through this union the earth was regenerated. This marriage of the priest-king and the priestess-queen was also an imitation on earth of the marriage in heaven, when the sun and moon returned after eight revolving years to 'the same heavenly bridal chamber where first they met.'
>
> – *The Myth of The Goddess*, pgs 140-1

After the sacred marriage, the lover must be sacrificed. Later, he is reborn as the son and his life renews the auspicious blessings of The Goddess. The rituals of Baal from ancient Lebanon illustrate this pattern very well. Thus, on earth the sacred ritual of renewal reflects the Lunar Law as it is revealed by the phases of the Moon in the skies above. After the Aryan conquests, the sacrifice of a bull was gradually substituted for the ritual slaying of the king. This sacrifice served to propitiate the darkness that prevailed at the time preceding the New Moon, and it hastened the rebirth of the light.

What was enacted as royal ritual in ancient times has long been an inner, spiritual experience of the mystical life. Many truth-seekers can confirm from personal experience that sacrifice clears a space where regeneration and renewal flourish. It is well known that symbols, archetypes, myths and rituals give outer expression to processes of inner transformation. These latter, however, are invisible because they take place in the formless depth of the human psyche. The Primal Runes and the ancient wisdom which they express can bridge the inner and outer worlds of experience and take us a step closer to Mastery, which is itself one phase of the Lunar Law.

Standard Meanings for Divination
Upright
Earth: Loss becomes gain.

Fire: Accept and sanctify this situation.

Air: Look for the heavenly action in the earthly situation; heaven and earth intersect.

Water: You need to give your best; give from your heart.

Ether: Providence is at work if you can see and feel it.

Reversed
Earth: Opportunity may turn to loss.

Fire: Being uncommitted is your downfall; there is a need for determination and endurance..

Air: The profane is contaminating the sacred.

Water: You stand in opposition to providence; suffering; hardship; servitude, sacrifice.

Ether: You are missing the deeper meaning of this situation; you stand to lose if you continue.

Spiritual Meanings for Divination
Earth: The Lesser Sacrifice
Only by making an empty space inside our own psyche can we harbour the power and presence of the Divine. And in truth, when we see beyond the habits and tendencies that form our outer personality, when we look beyond the noise of our own mental activity, we find that we have no separate existence over and against the Ground of Being. From That we arise, in That we move and

grow, to That we return, and the petty vanities of our ego all melt away as we approach the eternal Source.

This rune indicates a need to undertake self-emptying and letting-go as a necessary preparation for self-transcendence. Themes such as discarding what is superfluous, purification of all that is not in harmony, releasing what is outworn, going beyond, all resonate with this runic symbol. To identify and detach from petty involvements that limit us may be called 'the lesser sacrifice'. Letting go of limitation is, indeed, hardly a sacrifice, but rather a liberation. Only if one clings to what one is giving up is it experienced as sacrifice, otherwise it is a gift. It is only in view of our own propensity for self-indulgence that we form attachments to activities, people, places, possessions and a host of other limited realities. To be unburdened and freed of all attachments is to be given a chance to rise up into a purer, lighter and loftier consciousness. Any sense of sadness, loss or pain associated with sacrifice is a purely human notion based on emotional attachment. The spiritual value of sacrifice diminishes in proportion as it is painful; to the degree that it is a joyous gift, liberation and redemption prevail.

Fire: The Greater Sacrifice

The great myths and poems of all times tell of the hero's journey of return home to his divine heritage. *Apotheosis* is the ancient Greek work for final attainment, when a human being attains the status of a god. After human consciousness attains liberation and rises into the celestial sphere, there may be a call to return to the realm of earthly suffering to help free others from the clutches of ignorance. After the human has realized the divine, there can be a voluntary relinquishing of the bliss of heaven in order to assume the human condition once more, with all its suffering, and serve the spiritual progress of mankind. To give up the highest heavenly bliss from compassion for human suffering is called 'the greater sacrifice'. Only if this is the divine mandate, not a personal choice, is it totally selfless, and only then can it bear fruit. The birth of a saviour is always tied to the theme of sacrifice, and the life of a saviour is always a ritual enactment of higher purposes serving the cause of human redemption. A divine incarnation most often retains the awareness of the celestial fullness while reaching out to touch and transform the sincere seekers who need it.

The original saviour was The Goddess herself. All over the Middle East, in varying forms we have the story of her redemptive sacrifice. The tale, in general outline runs as follows: The Goddess becomes separated from the one she loves (a son, lover, or a daughter). He or she dies or disappears into the underworld. Then the Goddess must descend to where the beloved is imprisoned, or spellbound, or asleep and make it possible for the beloved to return to life and light in the world above. Over and over, in the tales of Inanna, Demeter, Cybele and Aphrodite we read this pattern, but these are undoubtedly based on more ancient prototypes that reach back into the heart of the culture of Old Europe where the Primal Runes were born.

Air: Finding Unity

In the Primal Consciousness, man is one with nature, part of an unbroken whole. Nature is a manifestation of the Great Mother, and man, along with all the animals, trees, birds and fish is one of her tribes. The individual human is a child of the eternal Mother. The unity of all life is a lived perception, not a philosophical concept. Every violation of this unity, such as cutting down a tree, killing an animal, mining for gold, and so forth must be balanced by some form of reciprocal giving, a ritual offering, or sacrifice. If the living spirit of oneness is broken, only disaster can follow, and ritual offering is the time-honoured way of maintaining the spirit of reciprocity or balance between taking and giving. The word sacrifice derives from two words in Latin, *sacer*, whole or sacred, and *facere*, to make. Sacrifice restores wholeness, which is holiness. When adequate rites are performed, the balance and wholeness of life is maintained, and the original fabric of life's oneness is kept intact. But when the human mind comes forward and presumes to dominate and manage nature without any reverence, or reciprocal offering, this arrogant *hubris* ruptures the harmony of the relationship and sows seeds of karmic suffering for all concerned. The Sacrifice Rune in Air reminds us to practice self-giving and honour the primal bond of unity that unites all facets of creation in bonds of oneness.

Water: The Conceptual Net

For approximately the first twenty years of our lives we study to become a full human being, and in this process we accumulate a burden of half-truths and falsehoods which we accept as reality. When we are young, we are open and malleable, but as we get older, the notions, expectations, mental conditioning, social conditioning, and intellectual baggage that we accumulate become fixed into what we call our individuality, or personality. We evolve a belief-system which limits our consciousness, and generates disharmony and blockage with regard to higher domains of energy and awareness. The Crisis rune triggers an opportunity to dismantle this conceptual net in which the mind has been caught, but the Sacrifice rune in Water completes the work and brings about resolution. To unburden ourselves of these accumulations is to release the energy that has been tied down in fixed habits of thought and emotion. When we let go of these conceptual burdens, we begin also to undo their debilitating and deleterious side-effects. Some examples of limiting belief systems might include the following: a) the idea that we are born in sin, a state of existential evil, and that we require redemption from outside ourselves, such as a holy institution, if we are not to end up in eternal damnation; b) the idea that life is a struggle rather than a blessing, and that the benign, harmonious and blessingful appearance of nature is a deceptive mask for something essentially threatening; c) the idea that God is a distant, judgmental and punishing entity who may send us to eternal flames if we displease Him. Of course the very idea that God is masculine in some sense limits the infinity of the deity, and this too is a conceptual limitation. Obviously an individual who thinks this way will be less open and receptive to the infinite variety in which Grace can come from the Source than, say, a mind which had been trained to think in a more open and creative way.

We may at times need to take a holiday from society and from inherited belief systems and open up to a wider set of possibilities which can be sensed by the aspiring heart, if not grasped by the conceptual mind. Withdrawal is sacrifice, but it is also a choice. If we express the energies of the Sacrifice rune by withdrawal, we embrace silence and solitude for an indeterminate period of time.

We become like The Hermit (a figure of the major arcana in Tarot) in order to reclaim an essential part of our own being. In this way, we further dismantle the conceptual net which holds the mind down and chains it to the past.

Ether: Actionless Action

When the Crisis rune is activated, our first impulse may be to react, that is, we start doing something (action) based on fear or re-activity. But the *I Ching* teaches the wisdom of inaction (called *wu wei*). It is wise to wait in the space of ambiguous neutrality for a while, to do nothing. To wait and do nothing, while holding an attitude of awareness and openness is to build up our inner power of Truth. In doing this, of course, we have started to use the energy of the Sacrifice rune in Ether, to let go of reactivity and its roots of fear. Sometimes, it is only by keeping still that we retain the fullness of our inner power and the purity of our heart's essential love. By sacrificing the urge to rush out and do something, we cling to a space of clarity and neutrality from which a higher action can eventually emerge, and this action can restore the harmony of the whole. We hold onto what is good within our own being and refrain from taking part in any negative emotions or thoughts of a reactive nature. Consciously and deliberately, we relinquish or sacrifice our mind's doubt and disbelief of the perceived enemy; we silence any mental dialogue concerning the problem or the individual we hold responsible. We make our inner space of consciousness absolutely empty and neutral, both in the mind and in the heart, and in doing this we invite the entry of Fullness and Grace. Thus, by preserving our own inner dignity and that of one whom we might otherwise perceive as an opponent, we are aligned to powers which can transmute all things to good. This inner stillness of ours acts like a cosmic mirror in which the other person can recognize what is inferior or inappropriate in his or her own being, and thereby make adjustment. This is far better than any strategy of confrontation, opposition or humiliation. We allow a space for the other person's superior nature to regain control and become part of the solution. We are thus no longer polarized into the perceived problem. The Sacrifice rune teaches us that non-action can be as potent as any action in bringing light to a difficult situation.

KNOT

The Archetype

The rune called The Knot shows a cord curved over itself as if knotted. The knot represents a complex problem. The ultimate knot is that of ego. This rune contains the lesson that undoing the knot of ego is the essence of self-transcendence. In the *Tao Te Ching* we read: "The wise, therefore, rule by emptying hearts." (3) and also: "The Tao is an empty vessel; it is used but never filled." (4) The knot is a sacred Goddess symbol from at least as early as Minoan times. As Marija Gimbutas writes:

> In the western wing at Knossos, rooms above the crypts contain round columns, Pillars in the subterranean rooms and the related columns on the floors above are frequently marked with double axes (the horizontal hourglass or butterfly of resurrection) and sacral knots, emblems of the Goddess. It seems probable that pillar crypts symbolized the womb of the Goddess Creatrix, where transformation from death to life took place and where initiation rites were performed. The participants returned to the womb – that is, "died" – and after the ceremonies were reborn again.
>
> – *The Language of The Goddess*, pg. 223

Dying to self, returning to the womb of the Great Mother, and being reborn as her child of grace is part of the mystical tradition of all ages. The Knot rune comes toward the end of the lunar cycle where self-emptying and transition to eternity become absorbing themes. A knot is a karmic energy that has crystallized. It may be a commitment to an ideal, or it may be a limitation which binds and restricts. Consecration is one kind of knot, a pledge of our time, energy and thought to the divine. Addictive habits are a different kind of knot, insidious and constricting. The greatest and often least recognized knot is woven by mind and its thinking activity, and this knot is ego. If you look closely at thought, it is almost invariably self-referring; it is about "me" and "mine", the small self and its preoccupations. Undoing the knot of ego is one of the ultimate spiritual achievements, but it can only be brought about when there is mastery of the mind and its restless thinking activity.

Standard Meanings for Divination
Upright

Earth: The matter is sealed; a marriage or union is confirmed.

Fire: Make a pledge; make a commitment; consolidate; find common ground.

Air: Formulate a resolution; linking and binding are needed; build unity.

Water: Keep faith; maintain integrity; honour your undertakings.

Ether: Emphasize union and continuity; a time for coming together.

Reversed

Earth: You are bound in this matter.

Fire: Your undertaking has, or will, become burdensome; a commitment may be violated.

Air: This matter has become a difficult, complicated bind; obligation becomes onerous.

Water: Limitation; constraint; obligation.

Ether: The situation cannot be resolved as it stands; a no-win situation.

Spiritual Meanings for Divination
Earth: Consecration

In the ancient tradition of the Mystery Schools, the knot was a symbol of consecration. The Mother explains the meaning of this very important spiritual principle:

> Consecration is the culmination, when the Light has illumined all the parts of your being, with a central Will acting on your feelings, impulses, thoughts, emotions, and activities, directing them always towards the Divine. It is when you move no more from darkness to light, or from falsehood to truth or from misery to happiness but from light to more light, from truth to greater truth, from happiness to increasing happiness. ... It is in a sincere consecration to the Divine that we can find relief from our too human sufferings.
>
> – The Mother, *Collected Works*, 14: 105

This consecration is an inner choice of the heart which chooses to centre the life in the ascending light of the soul's aspiration. The heart chooses and wills to be there permanently in the face of all pulls and pushes to the contrary. The decision to consecrate one's life may be triggered by initiation from an external master, but it can only be sustained by a conscious will from within one's own central being. Initiation helps to awaken and reenforce this choice. The Knot rune empowers you to choose consecration and to live in its spirit.

Fire: Flexibility

The spirit of consecration sometimes becomes fixated in the modality through which it is given expression. In fact, any repetitive outpouring of time or energy into a particular form of practice can become addictive of that mode. A certain ritual, a group, a personality, a particular scripture, a holy place or symbol may become a fixation of consciousness. We may cling to such fixations long after they have outlived their contribution to our growth. This can be one way in which we prevent ourselves from moving forward on the path to new areas of development and higher levels of attainment. We are multi-dimensional beings, but we are always at risk of fixation in any area of practice or experience which we find to be good and like to repeat. Especially when we are wedded to inflexible ideas about the formalities of spiritual practice, we risk addiction and self-limitation. A truly transformative process transcends definitive norms, because it is powerfully active at energy levels that the mind cannot control, define, or limit.

If higher levels of awareness are to evolve from our lived consecration, we will need flexibility to adjust and adapt our practice while remaining fully committed to the fidelity and degree of self-discipline that are appropriate. The Knot rune asks us to open ourselves to full consecration to the Source, but does not require us to live our consecration in an inflexible way.

Air: Clinging

Inflexibility often takes the form of clinging. In the words of The Mother:

> To cling to something one believes one knows, to cling loves, to cling to one's habits, to cling to one's so-called needs, to cling to the world as it is, it is that which binds you. You must undo all that, one thing after another. Undo all the ties.
>
> – The Mother, *Collected Works*, 11: 5-6

The Knot rune points to a fine discernment between consecration of spirit and clinging to form. Spirit can be expressed through form, as thought can be expressed in words. But spirit can also be limited and distorted by form. Clinging to a preferred form can arise from insecurity, inertia, or personal preference, but if the individual consciousness is to be universalized, it must widen to first embrace and then transcend all experience and all existence. It is quite a challenge to cling to the spirit of consecration while growing through its many levels and forms of expression, revelation and manifestation and ultimately transcend form itself to attain realization of the Source. This is a journey not merely of years but of lifetimes, and infinite patience must be combined with a persevering will and a fine discernment. The Knot rune in Earth can be a picture of the central consecration of spirit, or it may express a fixation of that consecration into a limiting form. Sincere consecration may nonetheless be limited to a preconceived idea of what is permissible or divinely sanctioned.

Water: Form

Consciousness will continue to empower the old reality until there is sufficient energy and will to release the past. A new level of attainment sometimes comes only through a mystical inner death, so deep are the knots that need release, and so ingrained in all our previous work and progress. The deep knots force us to reexamine our fundamental ideas about life and self and to honestly face all the issues that limit us.

Love itself needs constantly to flow toward higher and freer levels of expression. It may begin as an emotional attachment, but inevitably it will be a pressure to widen into a luminous current that unifies the entire psyche. Love's transformative power can then embrace all aspects of one's being and all forms of experience, and transmute them into harmonies of wholeness. The form of the Beloved evolves also, as our power to love becomes wide and universal. Unconditional love shines its light on all forms, but seeks neither to possess or be possessed by any, and this is its great power for liberation. Divine love is neither attracted by the attractive nor repelled by the repellent; it shines its radiance on all without demand or preference. Love allows the psyche to unify by recognizing the whole within every part, and for this reason it is the master key to liberation. The delight of loving, rather than attachment to the form of the Beloved, becomes increasingly the orientation of a truly consecrated soul.

The Knot rune in Water shows us the binding quality of attachment to forms, all forms, even the preferred form of the Beloved. The Buddha explained the helpful role of forms by analogy. When we have crossed a river in a boat, we do not carry the boat on our back as we proceed onward on foot. We leave it by the bank of the river. Thus, with all forms that serve us well at particular stages of the journey, we move forward with love and gratitude, and release attachment to beloved forms as we grow into the unconditional dimension of love.

Ether: Refinement

The lunar revelation is a progressive refinement of energy and at each stage a new sense of reality comes forward. Unconditional love allows deeper and deeper penetration through the levels of light above and the levels of darkness below. It is the energy that unfolds itself in all the symbols on all the levels of being until we can attain pure being and merge in the Source. Love opens the heart and the consciousness to every facet of experience, and integrates polarities and opposites into a harmonious whole. Many sources of energy, teaching and inspiration can feed this process of being and unfolding, and there is no necessity for fixed goals, still less fixed ideas about those goals. Goals are all relative to the stage of the journey we are currently experiencing, but the overreaching process of transcendence dwarfs our relative goals. Obviously, denial and repression will never release the darker knots into the light of wholeness, yet this strategy is greatly favoured by the mind. In fact, the mind would love to become the doer of the inner work, the guide for the journey and the judge of the results. Refinement is a process of bringing the light of the spiritual heart into the calculations of the mind, and into the strategies of the ego so that they can be gracefully released. Whatever is acknowledged, offered, released and blessed will become a liberated energy which can contribute to the dynamism of our consecration. The Knot rune in Ether teaches us to consecrate the will to a deeper and higher life of the spirit, while simultaneously freeing the mind and life from all manner of knots which would constrict consecration to a limiting pattern and stifle its growth towards Fullness. Refinement of energy requires of us a continuous adjustment, attunement and re-balancing. Judgements, resentments, opinions, and other crystallizations of energy must all be able to release their fixity and flow into wider ranges of expression.

Mountain

The Archetype

This rune presents us with a picture of a mountain peak from which flows a stream that descends onto the body of the earth at its base. The meaning is synonymous with the *I Ching* trigram of the same name: stillness, quiescence, completion, contemplation, established boundaries and introversion. This sign indicates the self-discipline of meditation, introspection and vigilance. It is a picture of the lofty, stable silence and peace that can be created in our inner being. Having turned inward, the contemplative activity nurtures the earth-plane from above with streams of living water. The mountain embodies the power of quietude and the enduring greatness of attunement to Source.

Standard Meanings for Divination
Upright
Earth: A pillar of strength; a secure refuge; a solid foundation.
Fire: High and noble powers at work; a sustaining power.
Air: Faith well placed; higher help; still the mind; turn inward; spiritualize the thoughts.
Water: A haven; sanctuary; emotional and spiritual support.
Ether: Heaven and earth bless and support.

Reversed
Earth: Your support is overturned.
Fire: You are cast adrift.
Air: Reversal of right order; thoughts and ideas confounded.
Water: Your faith is betrayed.
Ether: Heaven and earth withold sanction; you separate from providence.

Spiritual Meanings for Divination
Earth: Stillness
To keep still is to silence the restless and rebellious tendencies of the mind and vital. When we practice keeping still, the nerves are purified and the background noise in the mind diminishes. The ego can only be preserved in the restlessness of the mind. Thus, stillness is a direct preparation for Merging, which is the final rune in the series. The Mountain rune in Earth counsels us to cultivate inner quiet, to slow down the mind, regulate the breathing and turn inward. In doing so, we become more open to the

guidance of intuition and more unstructured in our response to life. Being open and unstructured, we are more attuned to the guidance that comes to us from the heights. The Mountain rune is an image of lofty heights where silence, stillness and snowy purity prevail. By cultivating the energy of this rune, we empty ourself of the false ideas that we have accumulated and stored in our unconscious mind and in the nervous tendencies that have been aligned to the restlessness of our ego's thinking-activity.

Fire: Practicalities

The practice of keeping still is facilitated by yoga exercises to limber the body and facilitate silent sitting. In these slow stretching exercises, we release physical tensions which would otherwise have to be resisted by a mental struggle. The Mountain rune is an image of an erect but comfortably poised posture free of distractions. When we sit this way, we can bring our attention away from the distractions of the external world and turn it to the spiritual, intuitive level of attunement and the empty space of the inner heart. Deep breathing exercises such as those taught in yoga help to quiet the mind and balance the energy of the nerves. Agitation diminishes as we continue to practice in this way and in time we feel a lofty stillness settling in. The top of the mountain is considered a 'sacred space'; it is the final goal of the evolutionary climb. In order to be physically prepared, these practicalities of exercise, posture, breath and silent sitting are most helpful. The Mountain rune requires an integral preparation of body, mind, heart and spirit, but being an earth sign, it points to a foundation in the practicalities. Let us not ignore the physical preparation for the journey into spirit; take the counsel of the Mountain rune in Fire, and align the body with the spirit of meditative silence.

Air: Conquest

Those brave climbers who scale Mount Everest are hailed by the world as conquerors, both for their physical victory with its demanding self-exertion, and for the spirit of courage and endeavour which they display in pushing forward to the highest level of the upward struggle. The Mountain rune in Air is also a sign of victory, inner spiritual victory attained on the heights of being. Through keeping still in the sign of the Mountain rune, the meditator is able to perceive the negative images which the mind and ego still harbour. These are released by opening upward to a higher light and power, the celestial power of Fullness and Grace whose images have arisen in previous runes. When limitation is conquered in oneself, one can then be understanding and forgiving in relation to others who have been caught in similar entrapments of fear and contradiction. We have experienced that freedom comes as a pure gift from on high. Thus, we are not only able but also willing to be of service to others when they demonstrate a sincere will to climb the mountain heights.

The Mountain rune in Air is a picture of the benevolent aspect of a great and lofty spirit who, having been victorious in the ascent and persevered in the struggle then shares the fruits of the victory with others. The vertical line in the Mountain rune stands for a mountain stream. This stream which flows downward from the heights to water the plane below is a symbol of compassion which pours itself out in selfless service to humanity. The victory is not for the small self alone, it is a victory of heaven which is then offered to earth by the compassion that flows from the heights. Only when the snow and ice are warmed and melted do they flow down to nourish the land that rings the mountain. Only love brings the highest to the lowest and joins all planes of being in wholeness.

Water: Reversal

If you have chosen the Mountain rune in Water, you are ready to go within yourself. You must make the mind quiet, open the heart and go deep within to feel the reality which lies at the inmost centre of your being. Then widen your consciousness to become as vast as the cosmos, and lose your sense of boundaries and limitations altogether. In the greatest possible calm, peace and stillness, renew this movement of going deep within and then widening to the limits of infinity. If you persevere in this way, you will begin to become aware of a reality which is other than that which you have heretofore experienced through the outwardly directed mind and senses. The Mother called this a "reversal of consciousness". No longer is awareness turned exclusively outwards. One may be more prepared or less prepared for this decisive and complete reversal of consciousness, but the appearance of this phase of the Mountain rune in Water indicates a call in that direction. There is a call to become aware of the heights of consciousness within. It is something different from the physical notion of height, something which calls the consciousness to rise up in an uplifting flight of silent inspiration, to rise and rise until all the limits of the individual formation fall away and dissolve; then, the energy of the Merging rune becomes active.

Ether: Allay the Inferiors

Earlier, we have referred to 'the inferiors' as the recalcitrant tendencies of our being which lower the focus and intensity of aspiration and dissipate our spiritual energy into dead-end contradictions, antagonisms, stresses, difficulties and fixations. The Mountain rune calls us to quietude. This summons to keep still requires that we deal with these inferiors, and several kinds of strategy may be effective here. We may explain to them our need for quiet, our aspiration for clarity, insight and attunement to the lofty peaks of celestial purity. We may urge the mind and senses not to be drawn into involvement with the superficial appearances of the outer world. We may remind our inferiors of the Buddhist teaching that all things change, and none should be relied upon as a permanent refuge, or indulged as a substitute for our journey inward into silence. We can indicate to the restless parts of our being that a higher power is ready to bless each and every effort toward stillness and to reward our choice of silence with a blessing of immeasurable value. If we can enlist their co-operation, or minimally their acquiescence, we may achieve a decisive reversal of the consciousness inward. The call to meditate can be felt as a deep need of the heart, a hunger of the spirit. The inferiors must learn to trust the Unknowable Source so that its Fullness may take up the work of opening which we have begun. If we prove worthy of this higher help, Grace will enter to effect the full transformation. This inward turning of the Mountain rune may take perseverance, but we should be resolute and persistent in our efforts, willing to stay the course until we come to rest in THAT which has called us to the heights. Keeping still will lead to a state of inner emptiness. In all parts of our being we let go and release agitation. We let go of the restless longings and attachments of the emotional heart, the vanity of the intellectual mind and the ego-bound permutations of energy in our lower vital. In the relaxed but alert disposition of meditation, with the spine erect, we establish quietness and purity in the breath and nervous system. Then, slowly and gently, we turn inward or ascend upward in awareness as the call comes or the inner guidance reveals. Whenever the clamour of the inferiors is noticed, we release it. We continue thus until the Mountain rune energy is established and attention flows continuously like oil poured from a vessel. Then only can we sink into an effortless state of contemplation, for then we are established in tranquility. This is the gift of the Mountain rune in Ether, and this is the inner work to which those who receive it are called. At this point, the Merging rune may come to the fore – but that is another phase of the unfolding cycle.

Transformation

The Archetype

The rune for Transformation is an "X" between two vertical lines. The two lines seem to create a space within which a nexus or crossing of ways is experienced. The need is to release our hold on what we cherish, especially if it is something outward and material. It is necessary to let go and begin to consider what is required for us to merge with the ground of our being. Very often, fear is one of the great limitations that needs to be dislodged, and fear of death is one of its main manifestations. We may consult sacred tradition to learn that transition from a physical to a non-physical form is natural and inevitable, even a time for joyous celebration. Fear is the great enemy, not transition.

This form which I call "myself" is not who I really am. Contraction is as much a part of life as expansion. To experience both and be beyond them is the ultimate test of our mastery and wisdom. In ancient times, the butterfly was venerated (along with the serpent) as a being of metamorphosis. Part of its life was passed as a worm, but after a magical seclusion in a cocoon, it emerged with the power of flight and the beauty of a flower. The serpent was able to renew itself perpetually by shuffling off its skin. The vertical lines represent the principle of containment, the boundaries of the known or knowable self within which a change of being comes about. From the cocoon, from the old skin, a new self will soon emerge.

Standard Meanings for Divination

Upright

Earth: A change for the better; things move to a higher level.

Fire: The situation is advancing favourably.

Air: Turn inward; find, or make some solitude; reflect on the deeper aspects of this situation.

Water: Devotion; a religious calling; do not allow outside interference.

Ether: An alchemical change; an inner rebirth is possible.

Reversed

Earth: The situation is degenerating.

Fire: A reversal; an unfortunate turn of events.

Air: You are cut off and isolated; you face a difficulty which you must try to understand.

Water: A private grief; a disappointment; unhappiness.

Ether: Things will go other than you wish or plan.

Spiritual Meanings for Divination

Earth: Balance

The stress of transformation is not an enemy which needs to be negated, because the desirable outcome of the Transformation rune is not a return to the old balance at all, but a movement beyond it to a new one. The X symbol suggests the stressful aspect of inner change. Our present level of awareness is penetrated by numinous forces that carry us forward to a yet unrealized new level of existence. We are at an interdimensional portal. The old conceptual framework of "right" and "wrong", "good" and "evil" are not that helpful any more. The new balance requires of us a multi-leveled awareness that can simultaneously honour the mundane and the celestial realities as they intersect and integrate. The mind is schooled in old ways, but must become the expression of the new, and our material life which has been a series of practical routines may now be filled with a sense of the inner ritual of things, the magic of the unseen that fills the earthly rounds with deep meaning. This awareness of inner change is not attained merely by altering attitudes and vocabulary. The Transformation rune in Earth puts us on the threshold of an immensely alive and energetic state of being, touching the whole of one's self, not only its parts, with an awareness of the sacred mystery of being. The new consciousness into which we are being born can experience all aspects of life, all people and things, as part of the whole, without the need to label, judge, react or reject. The effort of transcendence can no longer be for the individual alone, because the collective is increasingly seen to be the wider reality. In this sense, the X denotes the effacement of the small ego and the coming to the fore of the Higher Self.

Fire: Mystery

In ancient times, the Mystery Schools were places where spiritual seekers had guidance through successive stages of initiation. In the modern world, many times a soul navigates the same inner experiences as the initiates of old did, but without support or guidance. Where our inner experience is leading, we cannot know. The rules seem to have changed, and a new discernment is required. Our intuitive valuation cannot be based on the old intellectual scaffolding, for this only delays the release into the new freedom and poetry of being. Only by abandoning the old, relative viewpoint can we go forward into the depths of the mystery. We are stalled in an ambiguous space of transformation where the signposts fade away and the path is not clear. To the ordinary mind and ego, this can be fearful, paradoxical, frustrating. We may ask: "What, after all, is real?" Our subjective, ambiguous and uncertain viewpoint is all part of the mystery that surrounds or cocoons us as we move from old to new awareness. But we know that when we emerge from this process, we will no longer crawl on the old superficial surfaces of being, we will fly in the sky of a new inner freedom. The paradox and mystery are only in our perception. The resolution is a leap of consciousness to a higher level, and we are standing at the precipice. This is the message of the Transformation rune in Fire.

Air: Ambiguous Hiatus

At some point in the past, I made a commitment to explore life in its depths and not to imitate the models that authority presented to me as the approved way to go. I somehow sensed that the given model was a pale imitation of the real journey in consciousness to which I was called, and that I had at all costs to awaken a more essential level of my own inner being. I had to seek and live a far larger relationship to existence than any I was taught or shown. I had to allow it to unfold within the old forms that were socially approved. I had to develop a paradoxical and forgiving awareness of contradiction while watching the birth within my own heart of a new inner possibility that I could not fully comprehend or articulate. I had to let go of my fears, especially the fear of change. I had to let go of my old idols and forego the urge to crystallize this new life of my spiritual heart into any form of fixation. Yet there were boundaries in place, allowing a sacred space within me to achieve its refinement, purity and sensitivity. What my mind found empty, my heart could experience as exquisitely full. I was a work in progress, and still am. Where I am now, there is no resting place. There are no fixed goals, and no familiar beacons. My consolation comes from my faith in the inner verity of my experience, seen from the perspective of the eyes of my heart. Although I cannot explain this very well to others, I can at least rest in my own dreams, ideals, hopes and aspirations. These are the matrix of my rebirth. I know that the butterfly who emerges from its long rest so full of colour was once a plain worm on a leaf, even a shapeless tissue inside a woven cocoon.

I think of this place to which I have come and in which I now rest as an 'ambiguous hiatus'. It is the pause before the leap, a time for holding steady, persevering in the rest of renewal and treasuring the liberation of my mind from all that can be grasped or parsed or explained by intellect. When at last I fly free, I will have become a child of the formless air, minus the support of any old ideas or hand-me-down notions. I will be ready for this, because I have learned to wait and to persevere. I am becoming stronger within myself, while remaining vulnerable and sensitive in ways I would never have permitted in the past. I sometimes think of this phase of life as 'time out', but in reality it is the hour before the dawn. The greyness of the sky is already thinning, and the rosy hues of rebirth are ready to leap up along the horizon.

Water: Release

As The Mother describes it, transformation is a radical experience:

> There is a partial change of consciousness which makes you lose all interest in things that you once found desirable; but it is only a change of consciousness and not what we call the transformation. For the transformation is fundamental and absolute; it is not merely a change, but a reversal of consciousness: the being turns inside out, as it were, and takes a completely different position.
> – The Mother, *Collected Works*, 12: 80

Whereas previously the consciousness seemed to be outside and below the wholeness of being, now it is at the heart of reality and has the direct vision of its various movements. It is now within and above, full of knowledge, attuned to the Source. This reversal comes suddenly. There is a rapid opening in some part of the being and one experiences life in an entirely new way. The new state may take time to settle in permanently and become the norm, to express itself in the details of physical life. Nothing the mind can do is capable of generating this state. The mind cannot envision what the new life is like, and mental notions of it are altogether inadequate. Mystics speak of dying to self as the prelude of rebirth, and the X mark of the Transformation rune indicates this self-effacement which precedes the great event of release. This is the spiritual meaning of the Transcendence rune in Water.

Ether: An Integral Experience

Effort and aspiration were very necessary for long periods of time, to build up the capacity for transformation. But as time went on, it became a matter simply of loving well, and remaining in the light of love in all circumstances. The mind had a number of very complex notions about the spiritual life, but the heart discovered that it was simply a matter of living in love. There is higher help, invisible assistance. The various powers and personalities emanated by the Great Mother have their work to do, and their powers come into play at various points in the transformation. The Primal Runes signify the phases of experience that lead ultimately to human transfiguration. They have a pattern of progression leading to the alchemical moment when base matter becomes gold, and human consciousness is divinised. But this transformation of consciousness is only the first step toward an integral transformation of all parts of the being. The mind, vital and body will in time participate in the new life and be attuned to the celestial reality. The material world will in time become an expression of Truth. For long eons, it seems to be unchanging, like the egg that shelters the growing embryo. But then one day, the bird within the shell is fully formed and it breaks through its material casing quite quickly. Transformation is like this. A long gestation with little apparent change precedes a sudden breakthrough and a release into a whole new life. But this release and its wider freedom is only the start of a new and higher stage of the journey wherein all parts of the being, even the most unconscious, will learn to participate in the celestial will.

Merging

The Archetype

The rune-symbol "Merging" has two chevrons pointing outwards as if dispersing energy away from the mark at their centre. Whatever has had form and cohesion is now losing it. This is a time to extract the essence from life-experience, to merge and return to the Source, to enter again into the formless state that is the Ground of Being. The visible falls back into the invisible, goddess Inanna returns to the underground kingdom of Ereshkigal. We are on the threshold of a dark passage, standing before a gateway. We ponder matters of life and death, return to the womb or matrix and the inevitabililty of a passage beyond this world to another which is as yet unknown. We must face these large questions of immortality and destiny, as we come to terms with our inevitable return to the Source.

Standard Meanings for Divination

Upright

Earth: You are protected and sustained.

Fire: Your awareness is growing, deepening, clarifying and expanding.

Air: Keep centred in your inner truth.

Water: You are learning and developing appropriately; expansion is favoured.

Ether: Inner renewal; new life; new growth; self-transcendence.

Reversed

Earth: Your inner and outer life are not in balance.

Fire: You are too extraverted; your energy is unstable.

Air: You are confused; appearance and reality are being confused.

Water: Your mind and heart are not synchronized; your heart is constrained.

Ether: Barriers and boundaries work to your disadvantage; face the challenge of letting go.

Spiritual Meanings for Divination
Earth: Ancestors

The ancestors are those who have gone before us through the experiences of transition and assimilation, and they now rest in the other world. In our day and age, the dead are no longer thought of as ancestral guides and counselors of the living as they were in the age of the Goddess. At a certain point in history, the idea of death changed from transition into the life beyond matter, and was seen as a bitter exile from the joys of physicality. The feeling developed that death brought about a fundamental rupture of continuity, and the result was that communion with the dead no longer mattered. When the Spanish conquered the Incas in the early 16th century, they found a Bronze Age culture fully attuned to contact with the dead. The mummies of the Incas were paraded through the streets of Cusco annually, and each was maintained in a palace as if he continued to live. This culture was snuffed out the by the conquistadors and their Catholic priests, and the bridge between this life and that of the ancestors was broken.

    The Merging rune reminds us that we ourselves will become "the ancestors" and that we should live our life in full knowledge that it moves toward this inevitability. If we live with wisdom, dignity and integrity, perhaps from the life beyond we will be able to see and assist those who come after us. To merge means to become one with something beyond our present form and consciousness. Inevitably, we become what we contemplate or love. Therefore, the Merging rune in Earth points us toward the loving contemplation of our highest ideal and a continuous focus of awareness on THAT towards which our life is moving.

Fire: Kenosis

The Merging rune in Fire is a teaching of oneness. We are capable of becoming anything to which we can spiritually attune. The higher consciousness is like the ocean, and the purified consciousness of the spiritual seeker is like the drop. The Merging rune in Fire points to a time when the drop can fall into the ocean and become the ocean by a process of complete identification. The human mind fears to lose its precious individuality, and the boundaries of its self-limitation. But the heart and soul know that identification is never a loss of selfhood, but a widening of the small self into the vastness of the Higher Self. Merging is based on purity, purity of intent and purity of energy. Character purification is a long process, but in the end it produces a kind of crystalline uniformity of alignment in all parts of the being. A crystal is transparently clear and magnetically attuned just because its molecules all line up in the same way.

When the will is aligned to the Spirit, and the mind and heart take on its purity, this same alignment and purification is effected in all aspects of life. The strategies of ego for self-aggrandizement and self-preservation are exposed as pretentious impurities. Transcending the small self, the ego, is possibly the most difficult step of the entire journey, but it leads in the end to the highest attainment. When we have complete trust in our relationship to the Source and its Fullness, we will be able to die to self and merge with THAT which eternally eludes the mind's grasp. If we have allowed ourselves to be led by faith, sometimes blindly, always with good will and joy, we will be ready for the final letting go, the ultimate kenosis. Resistance perpetuates the life of the ego, but surrender to Source fulfils the Lunar Law and completes the cycle. The Merging rune in Fire tells us that an important stage of inner cleansing and release is preparing us to unite with our highest goal.

Air: Death

The Merging rune in Air is about the death of the small self. It is, as we have said, a drop which falls into the ocean and loses its tiny self-form as it becomes the vast ocean. Merging requires a special wisdom, because it is one of life's most important transitions. A true mystic will die to self before dropping the physical body, and thus the physical transition will be largely ritualistic, an outer sign of an inner achievement already complete and final. Although death is something that cannot be avoided, the majority of people who have no interest in mystical experience deny its implications and look away from its teaching. Death need not be a reluctant loss of the gift of life. It can be accepted, lived and experienced as a culmination and fulfillment of life's purpose and meaning. A good death can complete the soul's self-giving to its ideal. Death can be a victory of the spirit, a final focus of a lifetime of inner growth and achievement. Frequently viewed as a tragically unavoidable necessity, death can nonetheless be welcomed as a summation of the life's purpose. It is in essence a transition or merging of the life spark in the invisible planes of energy and consciousness from which, at the moment of conception, they first emerged. Greeted and accepted correctly, death's desolation changes to bliss, and the normal human response of fear transmutes into gratitude. Because death is final and inevitable, it canalizes the deepest responses of the heart and raises up any residues of fear and doubt which still remain. Often the event is more fearful for those who attend the deathbed than for the person on it. Thus, great strength is needed to go through this transition with equality and peace, strength to endure the fears of others and to trust in the providential ordering of the call home.

In the *I Ching*, the wisdom of *wu wei* teaches us to flow with life, not resisting what happens, not struggling against the inevitable decrees of destiny. Nowhere is this teaching more valuable than when the Merging rune in Air brings us face to face with unavoidable death. Yet that which dies is ultimately reborn, even as low places are filled up and high places torn down. The Lunar Law is a cyclic pattern of renewal. The most challenging phases of its unfoldment often lead most directly to wholeness and integration when their wisdom is embraced and lived.

Water: Dissolution

The Merging rune in Water teaches us that our individual behaviour is no indication of who we really are, rather it is an indication of what we do not dissolve into, and in what way we cherish our separation from a greater wholeness of being. This rune teaches the ego-bound individuality to open itself and to experience a Greater Self beyond its boundaries. It takes effort to maintain the *me* that is separate, and the charade of this maintenance amounts to what the Buddha called suffering.

To merge, we must be pure, and when we live this purity in right relation, we achieve transparency. Transparency allows us to release the limited individuality of our ego. In this way, we can experience broader dimensions of life and consciousness than those which are generated by perpetuating our typical behaviour.

For many lifetimes we have worked to develop an individual mind, a separate will and a distinctive ego, and their formation was a victory of sorts over the collective unconscious. Now, with the coming of the Merging rune in Water, we are called to be present in the matrix of life in a new way. We must now learn to identify with energy and consciousness. In effect, we are being asked to merge with something formless and transcendent, to become something more than the limited self-form we have so laboriously created. Each boundary by which we have defined our psychic structure now becomes a barrier to growth. To maintain the rigidity of these borders is no longer the work required. Rather, their dissolution and transcendence is what the inner guidance now calls us to accomplish. The structures that provided identity at one stage of life (occupation, family, nationality, religion), suitable as they are for living a successful human paradigm, nevertheless bind the energy needed to realize another level of life-experience: the supra-human.

The Merging rune in Water challenges us to dissolve the boundaries of effort-sustained individuality in order to become something far more wonderful than the mind can conceive. There is no denying that faith and trust are needed for this work, and in large measure, but also there can be no doubt of an ultimate, glorious release for those who embrace the requirements of Merging and persevere in the completion of the work. Dying to self means victory over death. There is an old proverb to the effect that the coward dies a thousand deaths, the hero but once. To merge is to experience a kind of death in terms of the lower self, but it is the gateway to rebirth in the eternal Self.

Ether: Defense

It is a natural impulse to defend and preserve what we have created. The life we have created for ourselves is, after all, a victory of sorts over unconsciousness and inertia. Yet the need to define, to compare, to analyze and understand – in sum, the urge to defend one's psychological identity, becomes a liability in the spiritual life. Growth in consciousness is more a calling to let go, to release, to unlearn and to open up to something beyond our comprehension. One of the ego's strategies is to defend and maintain its kingdom, to cherish its creations and safeguard them against all dangers. See this strategy for what it is, the Merging rune in Ether urges us, and then drop it. There is another kind of blessing which is knocking at your door, and only you can make room for it. Be ready to unlearn what you have cherished and to consecrate what you have achieved. In this way, you can be released from the binding power of your successes, victories and achievements and move forward to new adventures of the spirit.

PRIMAL DARK

The Archetype

This rune-symbol shows a vertical line crossed by two horizontal lines. The upward aspiration that moves from earth toward heaven is double crossed by the vertical horizon of mortality and fate. To the human mind, absorbed in the manifold variety of creation, darkness is experienced as a denial of light, and the antithesis of love. It blocks the free flow of benediction down the *axis mundi* from heaven to earth. It is the resistance of matter to celestial influences, the inertia and nescience which manifest as ignorance on earth and stand as an impediment to the flow of the heavenly will and blessings.

Darkness has often, in the ages following the demise of the earliest Goddess civilization of Old Europe, been thought of as evil. But it is better to think of darkness, as represented in the rune 'Primal Dark', as the most devolved, or we can say, most *obscured*, manifestation of light. Light, of course, has always been known as the primal manifestation of consciousness, and in spiritual literature it is sometimes called consciousness-light. The involution of light into energy and then further into the inertia of matter is the original fall by which creation came about. But this fall made possible the universe. Thus, it was pre-ordained and part of the divine plan.

In their original purity, the Primal Light and Primal Dark complement, balance and include one another. The Primal Light is dynamic; it arouses, transforms, stimulates, focuses and directs. The Primal Dark supplies structure, consolidation, spatial extension and concrete expression to the work of the Primal Light. It conserves, limits, binds and specifies. Human experience and philosophy, born from the mind's limitation and ignorance, has sometimes chosen to emphasize the isolation of these polarities from each other, their opposition, conflict and incompatibility. Yet without darkness, there is no backdrop for the self-revealing dance of light, no pair for the dancing self-expression of creation, no lover-beloved, no knower-known - in short, no cosmic play.

From their original purity, Primal Light and Primal Dark give rise to such mutually complementary pairs as action and stillness, creativity and receptivity, firmness and flexibility, strength and yielding, spirit and matter, striving and non-striving chaos and order. Of course when the human mind and ego have come into play, the primal polarities are distorted into imbalanced and stressful pairs of opposites such as impetuosity and lassitude, aggression and vulnerability, self-assertion and dependency, stubbornness and hesitancy. Yang and yin can be seen even here, but distorted by the ignorance of human imperfection.

In the ancient philosophy of India, the pair which we call Primal Light and Primal Dark have been approximated in such dualities as *Purusha – Prakriti*, *Brahman – Maya*, and *Ishwara – Shakti*. Yet these are not perfect synonyms for the Primal Runes of which we speak. They reflect the Aryan mindset, whereas the Primal Runes are from a different, antecedent culture, more lunar than solar, where the original unity and harmony of the whole, not the difference and opposition of its dualities, was of primary importance.

In the path of the Goddess, darkness was used to beckon light. For example, a novice or apprentice who fostered a spirit of humility, openness and receptivity would progress more in the hands of a teacher than otherwise, being more malleable and docile. These three qualities are essentially yin, and are therefore nurtured by earth. The ancient meanings attached to Yin and Yang in prehistoric China are much closer to the meanings of Primal Dark and Primal Light in Old Europe than the Aryan terms which we find in the scriptures of India such as the Vedas and Upanishads. Oddly enough, quite a few of the Primal Runes have been found in the earliest engraved fragments of bone and pottery in prehistoric China.

The Primal Dark is a receptive, absorbing, obscure and heavy earth-power. It allows itself to be acted on by the light of the sun and in time it bears, nurtures and brings to completion the seeds of life. The Moon measures and apportions this gestation from an incipient seed of possibility to fullness and back to death, and its cycle is unfolded in the 28 Primal Runes. The mythic lives of the earliest heroes tell the story of the archetypal human child of light. He leads the way for others. His life and reveals the archetypal stages of human experience from the original Seeding of the Field to the final Merging in the darkness of the unknown.

The Mother explains how the light enters into the darkness and liberates the sparks that have been smothered in obscurity:

> In the very depths of the nucleus of these atoms I have kindled a flame which awakens with a quiver like a palpitation, in this inert mass of inconscience imprisoned in an immobile spiral of forces, as in the obscure eternity of ignorance. It reveals a world where nothing was. In these blind realms of matter where it lay inert and mute, in a deep slumber without life, there comes a vibration emanating from the Supreme Will and matter trembles, shudders and awakens in an ecstasy. It is a mystic influence, a spiritual Will which has gone out from me and has

> penetrated even into the subconscient, into the inert inconscience, to act and to awaken the divinity which is hidden in this dark, obscure and black Inconscience. It is because it was there, hidden, - this divine spark, - that the world was saved; without that it would be the end of everything, of this universe. Then with the liberation of this force and light, the atoms regained courage to face this obscurity of the ignorance, the falsehood of the world imprisoned in the darkest inconscience. And with this emergence, we see everywhere sparks of this light which wants to establish itself.
>
> – The Mother, *The Supreme*, p 64

When the Primal Dark manifests in the consciousness of Mother Earth, it takes form as The Field. Here there is a consciousness of receptivity to the Higher Power of spiritual light. It is more than grudging compliance, it is a willingness to foster the good. Humility, patience and endurance are qualities which Primal Dark reveals through the Field rune. The cave was an original womb of darkness, centrally important in Goddess ceremonies of impregnation, birth-giving and initiation. Death and rebirth rituals were often celebrated in the womb-like darkness of the bowels of the earth. Therefore, Primal Dark had a place of honour in the ancient runic world because it made possible the dance of light, the revelation of celestial power in the ground of being, and the evolution of consciousness by incremental stages on earth.

As with Primal Light, it should be recognized that Primal Dark is pre-archetypal, anterior to the 28 stages of the Lunar Law, and not directly involved in terrestrial manifestation. It comes into existence immediately after the Source, the One, has uttered the primal Word and thereby created the matrix of time and space, the electric and magnetic polarities and the original duality from which multiplicity came into being. The Primal Runes are archetypes. They are the Lunar expression of the Solar light of spirit, revealed in 28 forms, phases of unfolding experience in the dance of light and darkness in the cosmos. The Primal Runes are ancient proto-types, semi-divine original possibilities from which terrestrial manifestation produced its multifarious outgrowths, called in the *Tao Te Ching* the 'ten thousand things'.

The dance of light and dark gives rise to all things sublunar. But the action of the divine Mother, and her epiphany the Moon, nurtures the Solar seeds of spiritual light and brings them to their highest evolutionary expression. To Her, the dark is as sacred as the light. Light and Dark are the warp and woof by which She weaves the destinies of all living beings. Each human being is a microcosm whose pattern, expression and ultimate fate originate in this loom of creation.

The Primal Runes are tools to glimpse the unfolding patterns which are taking shape here below, and to move more consciously to a harmony and perfection of attunement to the Source. They manifest as the 28 phases of the lunar cycle, but behind this cycle we should envisage the Source, and its first self-revelation as Primal Light and Primal Dark.

Standard Meanings for Divination
Upright

Earth: Make fundamental changes.

Fire: Loss is gain; less is more.

Air: Re-examine; re-assess; reconsider.

Water: Make a strategic sacrifice.

Ether: This challenge can be an opportunity in disguise.

Reversed

Earth: Cut your losses; try to foresee and prevent a looming disaster.

Fire: An insurmountable obstacle; your endurance and energy are challenged and drained.

Air: Ignorance brings unfortunate results.

Water: Failure; suffering; hardship; trial.

Ether: A no-win situation; watch out for malice, antagonism and inner attacks.

Spiritual Meanings for Divination
Earth Primal Dark
The original spirit of yin sensitivity is obscured, and the discriminating mind veils it. Intuitive attunement to the real recedes and recognition of the false comes to the fore. Intellect presumes to take the lead and is open to error. Under the appearance of being clever, there is darkness inside. The light of pure essence is obscured and a false glitter of mind-play substitutes itself. Be careful. Ego can assert itself. If you are not careful, you will become conditioned by externals and consumed in ignorance.

Fire Primal Dark
There is a spark of light in the darkness. Discern if it is the light of spirit, and if so, become silent and attune. Take this opportunity to withdraw from false darkness, the obscuring intellect, into true darkness, the cloud of unknowing which is original innocence. Keep the heart open. This is a time when you can nurture the light in darkness.

Air Primal Dark
There is a darkness that takes you back to the Source, and it is the darkness of innocence. If you can enter this darkness, you are moving toward the origin, the point of creation and beginning. You cannot claim innocence by formal effort, because it is not related to forms. Innocence will find you if your heart is open.

Water Primal Dark
If external influences have entered into you, you must re-discover the depth of your natural darkness again. Be calm and open, ever responsive; it is a space where external superficialities cannot abide. Find your innate naïve innocence and do not let yourself be pulled away from it. Turn inward to the deep cave of the heart to nurture reality. The false darkness outside you can help you to discern, and you can be more aware of the true darkness of your heart-cave.

Ether Primal Dark

When darkness is aware of its darkness, it becomes innocence. There is no need to shine in the external superficialities. Be happy with the darkness of innocence. Be still, but aware. Look inward.

Primal Light

The Archetype

The chevron is one of the most widely used symbols of The Great Goddess from the very earliest times. It has been seen as a bird-symbol because of its resemblance to a bird's beak. Writing in *The Myth of The Goddess*, Anne Baring and Jules Cashford say:

> The bird, since Paleolithic times the messenger of the vast incomprehensible distance and so of the whole invisible world, was taken by the Minoans, as by many another culture, to constitute the supreme image of epiphany. ('Epiphany' in Greek means literally the 'showing forth' of the sacred, which is the presence of the divine recognized as *immanent* in creation.) (pg 124)

Again, the chevron has been considered a symbol of The Goddess because its shape suggests the female pubic region which is the passage for the Goddess to birth the creation from its womb-matrix to its physical manifestation. This is an icon which seems to open upward while at the same time pointing (and possibly directing energy) downward toward the earth. The light, which is being directed into the earth atmosphere through this symbol, connects humans on earth to the Divine grace and blessings on high. It is a spiritual manifestation of the Supreme, illuminative and creative. Physical light corresponds on the material plane to spiritual Light, which is the celestial consciousness at work. This light is the illumination that comes from above and liberates the being from obscurity, limitation and darkness.

In the Solar tradition, light descends from the celestial heights to conquer darkness, transforming ignorance and inertia into fullness and perfection. The Lunar tradition, however, is better expressed by the circular symbol of the Tao, where two swirling patterns, one in white and one in black do a rotating dance. Inside the dark side, at the very centre, is a small circle of light, and inside the light side in the same placement is a small circle of dark. The Lunar tradition is a cycle of revelation in which both light and dark are necessary to the dance. Through the various Lunar cycles, the light of the Sun, the message of spirit, is communicated to earth, and those who are open and attuned take in the energy and consciousness for their inner development. The Lunar revelation makes the purity and intensity of the Solar energies accessible to living beings on earth. It is a progressive cycle that nurtures the pace of evolutionary consciousness on earth. The Primal Runes are an expression of this Lunar Law.

As the sign of the chevron indicates, this Primal Light is the white light of the Mother. It comes, not to destroy darkness or conquer it, but to penetrate, uplift, inspire, redeem and divinize life in matter so that it can find its path to enlightenment.

Primal Light and Primal Dark are not in the sublunar realm of evolving creation. They are the western equivalent of Yin and Yang. They may be thought of as states of conscious energy from which the dance of creation comes into being, the raw material from which archetypes take form. They are the original polarities that give rise to creation, the original duality that emerges from Oneness. The *Tao Te Ching* says that in the beginning there was the One. Then came the Two. Then emerged the three, and from this the ten thousand things. The interaction of light and dark gives birth to life and love. It undergoes an experience of involution and evolution. Our climb in consciousness to a realization of the Source is the evolutionary spiral of earthly destiny.

Primal Light and Primal Dark may be considered the "archetypes of the archetypes". They have a special role to play in divination or initiation, but they are beyond the relativity of earthly, human destinies. They are impersonal, anterior to manifestation, beyond mental conception, not seizable by the human will or ego, but indispensable to the cosmic play.

The work of light is to penetrate and transform darkness. The Mother describes this process very well:

> ...it is the force of transformation, that is why it is dynamic. There is the light that penetrates to illumine the mass in the Inconscience, the force to stimulate the *tamas*, and the joy to make it conscious. This force must penetrate this solid, obscure, rigid matter which is obstinate in its perversion and engulfed in falsehood, in order to bring light into the very bottom of this mass of inconscience, of this eternal obscurity that opposes with its immense and impenetrable energies their unrelenting dynamism. There is a Presence which is bound up in matter by millions of cords. It is imprisoned there by an occult power from which it is very difficult to be free. Immobile, it rests in matter, forced by a blind compulsion In the insentient depths where nothing moves, where nothing ever can, thee where everything disappears in a resistance that opposes with an invincible force. That is why this transforming force must act with a sustained power till matter feels and is made more conscious of my presence, of the light that is spreading. I force it down until the light penetrates into the very heart of matter.
>
> – The Mother, *The Supreme* pgs. 59-60

This passage is not only a remarkable description of the dynamic action of light, it also indicates the Mother's work as light-bringer. It portrays how darkness (the Primal Dark Rune) acts to bind light and impede its transformative power. The progressive awakening of matter to its most luminous possibilities is part of the divine, evolutionary plan for earth, and the law of the Moon is a picture of how light emerges from darkness into fullness and returns in cycles of birth, growth, fulfillment, waning, death and rebirth.

Standard Meanings for Divination

Upright

Earth: An object of quest; a grail; illumination on the path.

Fire: Your way is well lit; auspicious developments and favourable outcomes.

Air: Proceed with confidence; circumstances are proptious.

Water: Balance, harmony and wholeness are present.

Ether: The Mother blesses and supports; higher help is present.

Reversed

Earth: You are heading for problems.

Fire: You are moving away from the light.

Air: Reconsider, pause, and reflect.

Water: Elements of disorder and untruth are present; misunderstanding is present.

Ether: You are lacking higher sanction in this matter; you are going against the heavenly will.

Spiritual Meanings for Divination

Earth Primal Light

The light has sunk into the earth. It is covered over at present, but it can be uncovered and released. The density of the covering depends on our on choices. The mind, the emotions and the use of time and energy can all be applied and focused to releasing the light. It would be wise to do this.

Fire Primal Light

In order to generate light, fire must cling to its fuel. Clarity of mind comes from clinging to the Way, because the fund of truth in the Way cannot be exhausted. If we cling to the power of truth as fire does to its fuel, we will be able to radiate light into the world. However ambiguous and disruptive the outer circumstances are, holding to the way keeps the light undiminished.

Air Primal Light

Air is a perfect medium for transmitting light. It is transparent and neutral. If the mind is transparent, the light will shine in thoughts, bringing order, clarity and harmony. Light shining through air is an auspicious image of harmony and perfect attunement.

Water Primal Light

Water reflects light most perfectly when it is still. The mind's stillness comes from the harmony of the emotions, the central stillness of the vital energy and the feelings is a necessary underpinning. Picture a pond under moonlight. It is like a mirror and it can reflect the light of the stars and the moon which are high above. Water can hold the reflection of Primal Light if it can master the art of perfect quiescence.

Ether Primal Light

Ether is the medium beyond the four elements, the subtle matrix of the *axis mundi*. Primal Light wants to descend through the ether and penetrate the areas of our being where we are receptive. Ether is closely aligned to the spirit level of our being. If the light of spirit is not obscured, it can suffuse the mind, will, emotions and body and shine in all parts of our being and life.

The Source

The Archetype

The symbol used to express the 'Source' theme occurs frequently on the most ancient carved stones, not only in Celtic countries, but across Eurasia and into what is now called Siberia. It is sometimes called the "cup" glyph, as if to express the idea of the symbolic cauldron from which all life comes. The point symbol is often carved into megalithic stones in conjunction with spiral symbols, which radiate inward and outward from a central dot or axis of origination. A symbolic point, which is one way of expressing the concept of "The Source", is also present at the centre of a *yantra*, which is a sacred geometric pattern used for meditation.

In the Tantric tradition which comes from India, a *yantra* is considered a doorway into another domain of consciousness, and is used as an object of concentration. The point in the centre of the *yantra*, called the '*bindu*' is considered the connecting link between the finite world of form and the infinite world of formless consciousness. A true point has no three-dimensional size, but when the concept of the point is expressed as a symbol, the representation is given the smallest conceivable magnitude. This point is understood to express the origin and source of all that has come into existence; it is the first and fundamental symbol of energized consciousness.

In the *Upanishads* which, after the Vedas, comprise some of the earliest scriptures of India, we read: "God, being the immovable mover, the One behind all events in the cosmos, is the still point around which everything revolves." From this infinitesimal point comes the dance of nature, the manifestation of everything created. In the Primal Runes, therefore, the point has become the symbol of The Source.

The Source stands above and beyond the lunar influence, being as it were the Mother of the Moon. When the Supreme projects the infinite consciousness into physical, three-dimensional expression, the world of names and forms comes into being. This creative and expressive potential of the Supreme is often referred to as 'the Word'. The gospel of John, for example, begins with the well known passage: "In the beginning was the Word. And the Word was with God, and the Word was God..." While Christianity has interpreted the expression 'Word' to refer to Jesus Christ, claiming that he is the firstborn of the Supreme (who is called the Father) the most ancient tradition equates the Word to the Mother. She is considered to be the creative power of the Supreme. From Her the cosmos comes into existence, and into Her at the end of its physical manifestation in time and space, to Her the cosmos returns. She *is* the Supreme writ large in time and space, the Supreme with form. Sri Aurobindo expresses it in this way:

> It is at once clear to the experiencing soul that here is a conscious Power of one substance and nature with the Supreme from whom she came. If she seems to have

plunged us into the Ignorance and inconscience in pursuance of a plan we cannot yet interpret, if her forces present themselves as all these ambiguous forces of the universe, yet it becomes visible before long that she is working for the development of the Divine consciousness in us and that she stands above drawing us to her own higher entity, revealing to us more and more the very essence of the divine Knowledge, Will and Ananda. Even in the movements of the ignorance the soul of the seeker becomes aware of her conscious guidance supporting his steps and leading them slowly or swiftly, straight or by many detours out of the darkness into the light of a greater consciousness, out of mortality into immortality, out of evil and suffering towards a higher good and felicity of which as yet his human mind can form only a faint image. Thus her power is at once liberative and dynamic, creative, effective, - creative not only of things as they are, but of things that are to be; for, eliminating the twisted and tangled movements of his lower consciousness made of the stuff of the Ignorance, it rebuilds and new-makes his soul and nature into the substance and forces of a higher divine Nature.

– *Synthesis of Yoga* pp 116-17

The indivisible point as a symbol of infinite consciousness is not unknown in the West. In *Gnostic Secrets of the Naassenes*, Mark H. Gaffney quotes from the Gnostic scriptures of the Naassenes and draws parallels with the spiritual traditions of the East:

> The concept of the indivisible point is well known in the Eastern yoga traditions, where it is referred to as the *bindu,* the point of maximum focus and concentration in which duality is compressed into singularity. Although bindu has no size, no dimensionality and no mass, it is quite real and in the East is considered the threshold between the physical world and the spiritual domains. Operationally it functions in both directions: From the standpoint of Creation, *bindu* is the source of spiritual light, the Logos principle, and the first sound (*nada*), but moving in the

reverse dirction it is also the entry point into the spiritual world. The *bindu* is associated with a spiritual centre, or chakra, located between the eyebrows, the *ajna* chakra, but the field of *bindu* is said to lie above *ajna*, in the crown chakra (*sasharara*) located just above the head. As one-pointed meditation deepens and the disciple penetrates *bindu*, the thousand-petaled *sahasrara* begins to unfold: The disciple begins to experience unitive states. (pgs 158 - 9)

All of these meanings stand behind the symbol of the point, which is the Primal Rune that conveys the meaning of 'The Source'. Because Source is prior to and beyond Creation, it also eludes the mind's grasp. Source can not be defined or explained as can Creation. It contains all potentials and all qualities, being Itself unlimited and infinite. The power of the Source can be seen in Nature, whose ordered unfolding on earth is regulated by the Moon. The dual polarities of yin and yang, the four sacred elements, the phases of the Moon, and the archetypal symbols of the lunar law all reveal the working of the divine plan as it unfolds in the physical world. For the mystic, nature is a book full of hints about the glory of creation's eternal Source, and the Primal Runes are a language by which the Divine achieves revelation.

Standard Meanings for Divination
Upright
Earth: Sealed and confirmed.
Fire: Providentially arranged; empowerment.
Air: A sure thing; light and harmony prevail.
Water: Auspiciously aspected; moving the right way.
Ether: Divinely aligned; Truth.

Spiritual Meanings for Divination
(No reversals are possible with this rune.)

Earth Source

As I examine the question of right relation to Source, I ask myself: Is my life grounded in this relation? Does awareness of relation to Source shape my use of material things? Does it guide me in my practical and worldly affairs? Does it extend to my notions about supply? Is there a disharmony or a disconnect between my earthly nature and my divine potential? If the runes point me to consider the Earth aspect of the Source rune, I will remind myself that a spiritual life in the world *is* possible, and even necessary, if I am to honour my soul and its mission. My spirituality cannot consist only in a quest for personal liberation, although this may be its first and indispensable phase. Its real mission is to change the material life into its own image, the image of the Divine. Therefore, Earth and Source are not opposed. They await mutual fulfilment in me, my conscious choice to use time, energy and intention to realize and manifest the dream.

Fire Source

Is my central will in right relation to the Source? Do I draw strength and creativity from this relation? Is my dynamism and drive centred on my personal desires, or on my self-giving to something larger than my own ego? Do I have a good relationship with the eternal and transcendent realities? If the Fire aspect of the Source rune comes up, I am reminded that my creative and spiritual potential as well as my vital energy need to be aligned with the Source to fulfil the divine plan.

Air Source

Is my mind open to the Source? Do I cultivate the inner stillness and peace which could reflect the light of truth? Is my philosophy wide and continuously growing? Beyond my efforts at effecting a mental and moral self betterment, do I embrace the challenges of spiritual self-transcendence in my thought-life? Do I preoccupy myself with thoughts that are negative or stressful, rather than releasing them into the Source? The Air aspect of the Source rune makes me aware of my mind's role in attunement to the Supreme.

Water Source

In my emotional life, am I harmonized with the Source? Do my emotions flow in peaceful patterns of right relation? Is love present in my words and acts? Do I remain close to my intuitive feelings and follow their guidance? Can I accept a call to surrender myself in my heart to the Divine?

Ether Source

Am I attuned in spirit to my eternal reality, my Source? Is Spirit real and living in my personal experience? Do I make room for Spirit in all parts of my being? Am I transparent and pure in my intentions? Do I live a spiritual life in which the Source is something real and important? The Source is my true Self, the Self in all things. All things are none other than this Self, becomings of the Self seeking its full expression.

CHAPTER 9

Making The Runes

One of the first things to consider is the material out of which you would like your runes to be made. In the Futhark tradition (Germanic and Viking Runes), wood comes highly recommended. There are a number of trees that were traditionally used, each with its own energy. The oldest evidence suggests that runes were carved into the bark of the tree, and that the pieces of wood were elongated slips of branches that still had the young bark intact. The image was created by removing the bark so that the white wood beneath stood revealed. These days, when wood is used, it is more common to paint or etch the image of the rune on the surface of a symmetrical and often oval tablet of wood. Tree magic was prevalent in Celtic Europe before the advent of the Romans, and in Teutonic Germany as well. Rune magic and tree magic were very likely mixed together, with the timing of rune-making and the appropriate chants and rituals being elements of considerable importance.

The Primal Runes come from a time that predates the arrival of the Celtic and Germanic tribes in Europe. They were Indo-Europeans, with their own pantheon of gods and their own languages and spiritual traditions. In the earlier age, the earth deities were as important as the sky deities, if not more so. For this reason, stone is a very appropriate material for use in making Primal Runes. The symbolism of colour can also be important, as the runes are very likely to be coloured, even if they are also engraved. And timing, ritual and focused intent undoubtedly go a long way to heightening and focusing the energy and linking the runes with their future user.

Here are some elements to keep in mind:

1) The New Moon is an ideal time to make your runes.

2) Stone is a preferred material for making Primal Runes.

3) You can acquire an engraving tool and drill bits suitable for the job at a fairly modest investment; diamond tipped bits are the best in that stone is quite hard, and the drill tips will last much longer, should you do more than one set.

4) You may choose several colours of stones, such as black for earth runes; red for fire runes; white for air, etc. Or you may have all the stones of a matching colour, and vary the colours with which you illustrate the forms of the runes. For example if the stones are black, you might choose brown or green for earth, red for fire, white for air, blue for water and white for ether. Or you may use once colour, such as gold.

5) Spend time in advance of the engraving event studying the meanings for each of the runes so that you are fully aware of the different energies that you are bringing down into the stones at the time you engrave them.

6) You may want to neutralize or purify the stones several days in advance of engraving them. This can be done by placing them in dry sea salt, or in salt water, or smudging them.

7) The act of engraving, if done ritually, is the act of invoking a living archetype, or if you will, a god, and bringing its powers into manifestation. Therefore, it links the engraver, who ideally will also be the user, to the consciousness and energy which is being evoked as the inscription is done. You should not be involved with such work unless you undertake it in a spirit of dedication and respect. Visualize and feel the runic power for each rune you engrave, and direct this power through your arm, through the engraving tool, and into the stone on which you are engraving. Allow all your knowledge to flow into the form. Remember that when you chant the sounds of the runes, you actualize their vibrations and link them to the carved form of the rune. Be convinced of the identy of the sound and the sign you are engraving. The sound is a vibratory expression of the runic form, and the form embodies the powers of the sound. In similar fashion, when the time comes to paint the colours into the engraved forms of

the runes, visualize a flow from the fiery core of your heart imprinting itself on the stone. Visualize a flow of energy coming from your heart down through your arm, through the brush in your hand and into the runestone. Re-inforce this with the sound of the rune by chanting, and pour all the energy and knowledge you can into the completed engraving.

8) Plan some way to bring your full concentration into the work of making the runes. For example, you may chant the name of each rune repeatedly while engraving it. Feel and visualize the form and the energy of the rune permeating the material on which the rune is being engraved and/or painted. Feel that the vibration of the rune is being sent out into the stone via both the engraved form and the chanted sound.

9) Engrave the runes in order, beginning with Field, and finishing with Primal Light, Primal Dark and Source.

10) Give the runes a home in a suitable box or pouch, and do not let them be handled by anyone but yourself, unless it is at the time of divination.

11) See and feel that they are a living family of energies which have consciousness and identity, and which will serve you well, if respected.

12) At the end of the engraving session, offer the runes as a whole to the prevailing divinity which you see as the guiding spirit behind your work, whether it be in the field of divination, pathworking, magic, or whatever future use you will have for the runes.

13) Once the runes are carved and empowered, you may want to let them rest in darkness until the Full Moon before "awakening" them and giving them their first use. You may choose to delay painting them until that date, and make the painting into an awakening ceremony. You could place the form of the descent rune on top of the box of newly carved runes and invoke its sound while visualizing the runes coming to life at the time of awakening.

14) Remember at all times that the engraved stones have become magically alive, and must henceforth be treated with respect, and cared for with devotion.

CHAPTER 10

Using the Runes

One important point to clarify at the outset concerns the notion of 'usership'. The user of the Primal Runes, the "doer" of divination, is not and cannot be a human individual. The human mind, ego, and capacity are simply unequal to the task. The revelations of divination come through those human microcosms who have made themselves clear channels. In this matter, generally speaking, those who choose are chosen; they are overshadowed by the archetypal powers and become conduits of information, knowledge and guidance. Thus, the real question is not "How do I learn to use the runes?"; rather it is: "How can I become a clear channel?" If we would become proficient with the runes, the very first consideration must be this. There can be no satisfactory interaction with the runes until human ignorance begins to open itself in favour of the guiding light, action, power and wisdom of the Goddess and her epiphanies. This means that the apprentice must develop the requirements of the path and develop the qualities needed for the work.

It helps to understand that one who would use the runes must become in some measure a clear channel. The Moon manifests the light of the Sun when it is nowhere to be seen in the nighttime skies. The Moon, in ancient times, was considered to be one of the foremost revealed forms of the Goddess, showing forth her power and presence in the celestial realm in the darkness of the night. She mediated the guiding light of solar spirit when darkness prevailed. Luna was not herself the totality of the Great Goddess, but rather one of her full revelations, whose totality could never be encompassed by the human mind. Mother Earth was another manifestation of The Great Goddess who was the Source of creation. So also were sacred trees, animals and persons as well as holy springs, mountains, gems and herbs. A high priestess, both in Aryan and pre-Aryan times in the Mediterranean world, was widely believed to be a partial or full incarnation, and thus also an 'epiphany', of the Goddess. Human beings who were gifted with the second sight, or with prophetic and poetic skills, or who had preternatural beauty, wisdom, or physical strength, (or other remarkable endowments) would be considered as vessels of manifestation for the Goddess. They were held to be sacred because they revealed or embodied some aspect of Her power or presence to a remarkable degree. One who consults the Primal Runes can receive guidance from on high, and by doing this such a person becomes a channel for sacred wisdom. If by thought, word or deed such an individual offends the celestial powers, either the higher action is withdrawn, or worse, it becomes a source of bewilderment to the offender. This confounds the minds and lives both of those who offend and those who continue to consult them, so it is something quite serious.

All of which brings us back to the theme of 'usership'. One who practices divination mediates the gods (or, to use more modern parlance, the archetypes). One who dabbles with occult powers, or who practices magic (and the runes do admit of this use) either follows higher guidance and thus remains free of fault, or else exercises self-will in such a way as to obscure or obstruct the divine will, thereby incurring karmic debt. So the real question changes from one of *using the runes* to *becoming a pure instrument* of the powers they symbolise, which is to say, in the specific case of the Primal Runes, a channel or instrument of the Divine Mother and her action.

The first step in this undertaking is serious study. One must read deeply and widely, and one must reflect on the tradition. One must understand the fundamental principles both of spirituality and occultism and live the teachings of The Way with integrity. This is no small matter, indeed it is the work of a lifetime.

Beyond the need to inform the mind through study, it is necessary to contemplate the fundamentals of the particular tradition or traditions in which one specialises. In the case of the Primal Runes, this might include building up an inner connection with the Mother in one or another of Her aspects. It should include meditating on each of the runes in turn to the point where they reveal their meaning and convey some of their energy or power to the seeking mind. Contemplation leads to revelation, and this revelation takes place in two ways. The more common form is purely personal. One finds a meaning or use for the rune-symbol which differs from that which is being done by others who similarly study and use the runes. The other kind of insight is universal and it arises from contemplation in which one attunes to the archetypal reality and power of the rune, and discovers something of its timeless truth which is valid in all places and for all people. The ancients would have said that one makes contact with a god (or goddess); but we might equally say that we tap in to an archetype. Both kinds of revelation, the personal and the universal, are necessary if one is to become proficient. It is by building up knowledge in this way that one becomes wise and skilful. Thus, the second step in learning to use the Primal Runes could be summarised as meditation, or contemplation leading to direct insight.

One form of meditation, not too difficult for the western mind, involves reflection on scripture. One of the most important Mystery School scriptures is the Emerald Tablet. It should be pointed out that Gnostic teachings similar to those of the Essenes flourished for millennia prior to the Christian ascendency, at which time they were labelled heresy and condemned. According to the Mystery School tradition of the West, when the dead body of Hermes Trismegistus (also known in Egypt as Thoth) was found at Hebron by the initiate Isarim, he was holding a tablet of emerald, inscribed on which were a few sentences that distilled the essential wisdom of the Hermetic tradition. These are the words (numbers added):

1) What is below is like that which is above, and what is above is similar to that which is below to accomplish the wonders of one thing.

2) As all things were produced by the mediation of one being, so all things were produced from this one by adaptation.

3) Its father is the sun; its mother is the moon.

4) It is the cause of all perfection throughout the earth.

5) Its power is perfect if it is changed into earth.

6) Separate the earth from the fire, the subtile from the gross, acting prudently and with judgement.

7) Ascend with the greatest sagacity from the earth to heaven and then descend again to earth, and unite together the power of things inferior and superior; thus you will possess the light of the whole world, and all obscurity will fly away from you.

8) This thing has more fortitude than fortitude itself, because it will overcome every subtile thing and penetrate every solid thing.

9) By it the world was formed.
– The *Wordsworth Dictionary of the Occult*, pg. 50.

Read the text several times, slowly and carefully, without too much mental activity, letting its deep meaning of the text sink in. Then, allow the inner knowledge to emerge as you reflect, gestate, mull and consider how these words might reveal something important about the runes. What really counts, of course, is not what any commentator has to say, but what your own higher mind reveals to you.

We have seen, as the third passage of the Emerald Tablet states, that the Moon is the mother of the runes, but we have not reflected much on the fatherhood of the Sun. In ancient tradition, the Sun is considered to be the eye of the divine, the symbol for our solar system of Spirit,while the Moon stands for soul, the evolutionary form that translates spirit into expression in time and space. But the Tablet is talking about "one thing" which is the cause of all perfection throughout the earth. What might that "one thing" be? And how does it relate to the Primal Runes? Passage 6 has been used by alchemists from time immemorial, not only in their attempts to transmute base metals into gold, but more importantly in their spiritual work of raising consciousness to the level of spirit. How might the runes assist in this work? Clearly, if they are a primal revelation of spirit through soul, solar wisdom as mediated by the Moon, then they provide a key, or several keys to the great work. How can the runes help one, as passage 7 phrases it, to "ascend with the greatest sagacity from the earth to heaven, and then descend again to earth"? In what sense are the runes "the light of the whole world"? These and other questions are a very good starting point for meditation on the runes, because the Emerald Tablet is one of the very oldest and most venerated passages in the entire Mystery School tradition of the West.

While mental reflection can contribute to the process of meditation, one only begins contemplation of truth when the mind falls silent and a higher state of consciousness emerges, a unifying of mind and heart in rapt attention to a single truth, or to a formless power. The state of contemplation is often, in Christian mystical writings, referred to as "infused", meaning that it is not generated by self-effort, but descends from on high, as a pure gift, with downpourings of power, light, love and wisdom far beyond the capacity of the individual who experiences and receives them. Meditation may lead to contemplation, or it may not; one may have the gift or capacity, or one may not. But if it is possible to contemplate the deep meaning of a rune, there is much greater likelyhood of penetrating its secret power and releasing its energy.

When your study and meditation have progressed, it becomes important to personalize your relationship with the runes. While studying the runes, you should have their forms in front of you, and it helps greatly if you look at the form of the rune you are reading about as often as you can, loading it with all the associations and understandings that you are gleaning. You begin to see the runic symbols as expressions of various aspects of yourself and of the cosmos.

One valuable exercise you can do along these lines, to personalize the meaning which the runes hold for you, is to write down an inventory of your strong points and your weak points, the elements in your character that you can build on, and the ones that need to be improved. On the left side of a sheet of paper, list your deficiencies and weaknesses. On the right side, list your strengths. Set the paper aside for a day or two, and then reconsider it. A list of ten or twelve points for each column would be appropriate, although you may have more or fewer.

Next, determine which rune represents each of the qualities you have listed. For your strong points, the rune in question will be an upright rune, but for your weak points it is going to be a reversed rune. You may have a weakness that is not listed as one of the reversed rune's qualities, but your own intuition will suggest which rune best expresses the deficiency you have in mind. For example, laziness is not listed for any of the reversed runes, but it could be considered the opposite of fiery dynamism, and hence be the Fire rune reversed. If it is inertia of the physical body, it might be Field reversed; if it is difficulty starting a project, a case of procrastination, Seeding reversed might be the choice; or if it is based in fear, Courage reversed might be the best rune. It will depend on your own intuition, but you will be using the runes in a more personal and intuitive way, and gaining insight into your own personal makeup at the same time.

When you have a clear picture of the strong and weak points in your makeup, you can begin to meditate on the forms of the runes that will assist in tranforming weaknesses into strengths. It is fundamentally important to understand that a challenge is an opportunity. A challenge is a reservoir of energy which has not yet been mastered and integrated. You may first want to meditate on a rune that appeals to you, without any sense of needing it for changing weaknesses into strengths. When you meditate on runes that represent your strong points, you are building up strength. When you take the upright form of a rune whose reversed form represents a weakness that you want to change, you can use it to infuse you with energy and power for inner self-transformation. Meditate on the form of the rune, possibly painted on a plain white surface, or even as it is on your rune-stone. See the form as being full of life, light and energy, and assimilate this into the very fibre of your being. The form of the rune is identical to its inner power. Use this understanding as a key to tap and assimilate that power into yourself.

Thirdly, after meditation and contemplation, comes practice. Many eager souls prefer to skip over steps one and two and get right into practice, and some modern books unwisely condone this. However, practice can only be successful if it is founded on solid background, and there can be no substitute for the days, weeks and months of study, reflection and meditation encompassed by the first two steps. The two most common fields of practice for users of the runes are divination and pathworking. Divination means seeing beyond the surface appearances of things into their deep inner currents so that the past and future stand revealed, and the understanding of the present moment is clarified. Pathworking means learning to apply the powers of the runes. For example, the rune for Fire has great power. This can be directed in quite a few different ways, particularly through the rune's associated sound. One can purify, illumine, empower, dispel obstacles, or dissolve karma by the application of the powers of the Fire rune. However, study, contemplation and repeated practice are required to attain this proficiency.

While it would be best to recommend that you approach a master in person and ask for guidance, there are, unfortunately, few masters available, and they do not advertise their services. Thus, for the most part one must make use of books and one's own inner guidance. Here we come to the "hands on" part of runelore, (not excluding the very physical ritual of making the runes in the correct way).

A Simple Reading

The most important step in divination is to discover the right question. First you must discern what it is that you need to know. You should not presume to consult the higher powers with trivialities, but if you really do have something important in need of clarification, the next thing to do is put the question into words. Finding the right question and putting it into words is the best preparation for a successful reading. If possible, express your question in writing in a sentence of not more than a dozen words. Determine whether your question is spiritual or mundane in nature. This will affect which section of the text you consult, whether 'Mundane Meanings' or 'Spiritual Meanings'. Silence the mind. Open the heart. Meditate, or otherwise connect with your higher guidance. Then, reach into the box or pouch containing the runes and stir them about in a clockwise manner. You may also wish to impart your own energy to them by breathing into them. Finally, choose one rune. Without looking at the symbol, feel which side is engraved and place it face up on the table in front of you. The dot will be at the bottom if the rune is upright, and at the top if it is reversed, however you should not attempt to feel the dot or place the rune upright since this constitutes interference.

Before you consult a manual concerning the rune's meaning, look at the rune you have chosen and note what you feel. Keep your mind completely clear of any preconceptions or notions, and simply note your first reaction. Then you may read about the rune's archetypal meaning, which is the relevant background information in a condensed form.

Next, in order to determine the meaning most appropriate for you, select a second rune and note to which family it belongs. It will either be Earth, Fire, Air, Water or Ether. You are not interested in the symbol *per se*, or the meaning of this second rune, only the family indication which will point you to the specific meaning that most applies to the question you have asked. You may then consult the *mundane* or *spiritual* entries in the book *The Primal Runes* and find which meaning corresponds to the rune you have just chosen. In general, Earth entries are practical, Fire entries have to do with will, energy and dynamic creativity, Air entries concern the mind, Water entries concern emotion, and Ether entries concern things of the spirit. You might want to choose a second rune to check on a secondary level of meaning which may be at work, although this is generally not necessary. In any case, consulting a second level should not be done because you are not happy with the first meaning you have received, but only if you feel the need for more knowledge.

In this reading, the first rune contains the answer you seek, while the second rune points you to the most relevant and specific of the rune's several meanings, in relation your question. Finish the reading by thanking the inner powers that have been at work, and then replace the runes in their box or pouch.

A Detailed Reading

Formulate the question as you did previously. In your mind, determine that the first rune you choose will stand for "shaping factors", which means things from the past which generate the present situation. Intend that the second rune will represent "the present situation". And lastly, resolve that the third rune will reveal "the resolution" or "the solution" to the question you are asking.

Move into the right consciousness for divination, as explained above, and then place three runes on the table in front of you, face up, but either upright or reversed as fate determines. The first rune will comment on the "shaping factors" which make the situation what it is; the second rune will speak about the present situation, and the third rune will indicate how things will turn out. Look at the three runes and intuit what you feel they are saying, both individually and as a three-part statement, and note this down. Here is where your previous study, reflection, synthesis and meditation proves invaluable. If you are drawing on your intuition, this stage of the reading will be rich with meaning, and it will become progressively enriched the more you practice.

Finally, for each of the three runes you have chosen and placed, determine the level of meaning that applies, whether Earth, Fire, Air, Water or Ether, by choosing a second, "qualifying" rune. At this point, you can study the text for specific indications. Put together everything you have learned, and synthesize the answer to your question.

Other ideas for three-part divinations:

a) The Inner Process; b) The Outer Process; c) A Recommendation.

a) The Worst That Can Be; b) The Best That Can Be; c) Advice.

a) The Challenge; b) The Opportunity; c) Pay Attention to This.

a) The Origin; b) The Development; c) The Likely Outcome.

a) The Yin Side; b) the Yang Side; c) Consider This.

There are many possible categories, and the question you have in mind may suggest other useful categories in addition to those mentioned above. You might elaborate from three to four, five, or more positions, with designations appropriate to the aspects of the query in hand. The important point is to formulate in advance of choosing the runes what the meaning of the first, second and third positions will be, much the same as is done in a Tarot spread.

A three-rune reading may be elaborated into a five-rune reading quite easily. Place a rune above the middle rune to represent 'help that you may receive'; place a rune below the middle rune to represent 'things that are fixed and unchangeable'. You may also vary the meaning of these two extra runes to provide the most relevant commentary on the question being discerned.

Casting the Runes

Formulate the question, and if it helps to make it clear and succinct, write it down.

Put your energy into the runes through the breath, or by stirring, or both. Take all the runes in your two cupped hands, and drop them onto a white cloth on which a circle has been drawn, a circle of about 18 to 24 inches in diameter. Alternately, you may take just one handfull of runes, or you may reach into the pouch or box and select nine runes at random and use these for the cast.

Take out the runes that are face down, without disturbing the positions of any of the remaining runes. Then, begin analysing the remaining runes in the following stages:

Those runes nearest to you represent energies which are closest to happening in the present time, or runes seriously affecting the present time, so that their influence should be considered to be 'immediate' in impact.

The very closest rune to you, physically speaking, should be interpreted to mean the primary factor at work in the present circumstance. It may have originated in the past, but it is most strongly at work in the area you seek to understand.

The next rune, in order of distance from you, may be taken as the *current manifestation* of the energies at work (as distinguished from the primary energy itself).

As the runes move into the middle space, and the area most distant from the reader, they describe the near and distant future.

An Idea: At this point, you might want to consider using a cloth with horizontal lines which designate, or divide the cloth, or the circle you have drawn on the cloth, into three bands, representing past, present and future. This could serve to clarify and specify the timelines at work. The closest band to you would then represent 'past', the middle band would represent 'present' and the most distant one would represent the future.

You might also want to use a pattern of nine squares, each with a number. This is accomplished by dividing a large square surface (perhaps eighteen inches square) into nine smaller boxes by drawing two parallel lines horizontally and two parallel lines vertically. The top three numbers, from left to right, are: eight, one and six; the middle three, from left to right are: three, five and seven; and the bottom row are four, nine and two. This forms a magic square. The number and its box describe an area of life-concern. For example, eight designates power and authority, influence and achievement and victory and success; one refers to will, individuality and ego; six refers to harmony and balance, responsibility and service, family and community; three refers to creativity, self-expression, expansion and manifestation; Five refers to freedom, communication, and adaptation; seven refers to wisdom, seeking, detachment and introspection; four refers to work, security and foundations; nine refers to altruism and compassion, attainment and completion; lastly, two refers to relationship and choices.

The distances between runes (as they occupy the near, middle and distant ground of the cloth onto which they have been dropped), stand for amounts of time unfolding as the issue in question works itself out. Distances small and great, as the runes spread away from the reader, represent smaller and greater amounts of time. Runes placed closely together in groups suggest many things happening in a short time.

Clusters of runes indicate related groupings of energies in time, the probability being of an interconnected sequence with causal relations, or at least concomitance.

The left side of the field, (the cloth on which the runes have been dropped) represents *things of a passive nature*. This would include things that *occur to the person* for whom the reading is being done, or things that are *done to the querent* or *attracted by the querent*. Also, the left side *represents the inner, the psychological, the emotional* or *the mental domain*. The right side represents the outer, active domain, including activities which the querent will undertake or initiate, dynamisms which he or she will project into the outer world. Runes falling on the right side indicate occurrences which take place in public where they can be seen outwardly. The number of runes which occur to the left of centre, when compared to the number occurring to the right of centre, indicate whether the subject being explored will happen predominantly as an inner, psychological unfolding, or as a sequence of outer events. Roughly equal numbers on each side of centre indicates a degree of balance between inner and outer factors.

Runes which are in close proximity affect each other. Their energies blend to a degree and interact. Thus, the dynamics which they describe must be considered as a mixture of energies.

Note the location of the three runes: Source, Primal Light and Primal Dark. The Source rune indicates the action of the Divine at its strongest. It influences situations or runes by proximity; in other words, the runes which it touches, or near which it falls will be beneficially aspected, provided of course the Source rune is face up. If the Source rune does not fall face-up, it should be removed. Primal Light also brings a beneficial influence which lightens, harmonizes, blesses and clarifies the energies of any runes or clusters which are nearby. Primal Dark, on the other hand brings heaviness, resistance, obscurity and confusion to any runes or clusters that are nearby. Read the profiles of these three runes to get a clear understanding of their meaning and action, and then see this energy as being applied to runes or clusters that occur in close proximity.

A line of runes indicates a pattern of connected flow, either a temporal flow if it moves away from the reader, or a flow between the inner world and the outer world if it moves on a right-to-left (or left-to-right) axis.

Geometric patterns such as triangles, circles, or squares should be noted. The rune energies which constitute such patterns should be seen as interrelated. The symbolic meaning of a triangle is, of course dynamic, especially if it points upward. A circle is harmonious and spiritual. A square has to do with physical manifestation and boundaries. A little research and a little intuition will help in the analysis of such patterns. Other patterns may form as well, for instance the pattern of a rune such as the cross for sacrifice, or the T-sign for grace. The meaning of these rune energies should be seen as an overall shaping influence at work beyond any of the individual runes that constitute the formation, and adding up to something more important than any individual rune, or indeed any individual cluster.

The Master Oracle

A very detailed and complete reading can be generated by throwing the runes onto their natural matrix, which is a circle divided into four quadrants which follow the runes' progression through Earth, Fire, Air and Water. Additionally, a circular space in the centre of the mandala should be left to represent Ether, the symbolic *axis mundi*. Thus, any rune which falls 'face up' will automatically be placed in one of the five phases of its expression. If, for example, the Growth rune falls face up, it will be either 'Growth in Earth' or 'Growth in Fire' or one of the others.

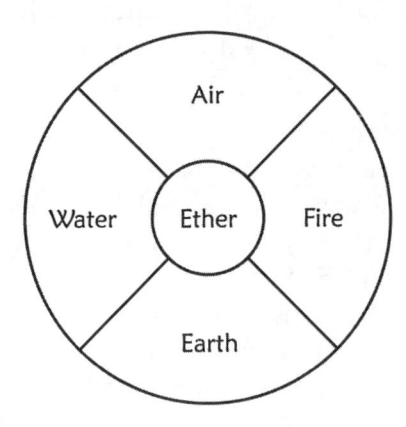

Master Oracle Matrix

When you use the Master Oracle, it is not necessary to follow all the earlier guidelines, you may be selective according to your inner guidance, incorporating those which you feel work for you, as you feel appropriate. Certain concentrations, or clusters of runes falling face-up, can be an indication of where things are most active in your life. Geometric patterns, similarly, can be a clue, or an intuitive catalyst. Since the central area (Ether) represents the spiritual core of the microcosm, then stones falling closer to it can be read as indicating matters close to the heart, and stones falling closer to the outer edges can be interpreted as relating to the outer life.

In order to toss the runes in this way, it is necessary to prepare the background pattern, and this can be done on any surface you choose, although a cloth which can be folded down would be the most portable, and is also quite traditional. The pattern could be stitched or applied with an indelible marker in a colour of your choice.

It is always good to concentrate before you toss, holding the runes in your two hands or in their box, and then pouring them quickly, at the moment you are most focused, and in such a way that there is a random, but fairly even scattering across the background pattern. You should not strive to scatter them randomly, however, for the toss should be fast and uncalculated. You could have your hands cupped with the runes inside, and then simply open the hands from the bottom. Runes which fall well outside the pattern may be discounted from consideration.

Pathworking

In pathworking, the consciousness and energy of the rune can be applied in such a way as to bring about change. This magical application of the power of the runes should only be taken if one has higher sanction. Traditionally, an apprentice would learn by consulting his or her master, and undertake projects on an ascending scale of difficulty, under constant supervision and with many opportunities for correction. These days, however, more responsibility is placed on the reader-practitioner's individual discernment and ethical integrity because information on occult subjects is widely available in books that can be purchased by anyone with the funds. Still, the individual who can actually read a book on occultism and then put it into practice is a rather rare breed. This feat requires considerable intelligence, talent and self-discipline. The willpower and the understanding of such an individual must already have been motivated and developed to a high degree.

If you intend to use the runes for magic or pathworking, it is better to build in all the safeguards possible. It is very obvious that occult power should never be used to harm anyone. Powers thus misused rebound and destroy the perpetrator. But it is also important that magical ability should never be exploited for one's own personal benefit, or merely to satisfy one's curiosity. In support of this, it is very helpful to resolve never to accept payment or reward of any kind for any inner work you may be called upon to perform, so as to separate it entirely from self-interest and to sustain purity of intention, which is indispensable to remaining in the favour of the divine powers. Undertakings which have the nature of selfless service carry far less serious karmic consequences than those done for personal gain. You never know when you may cross a forbidden threshold or transgress a karmic law. Therefore, the best approach is to have a method by means of which to discern that the inner work you do is blessed and sanctioned by the divine. Dowsing or some form of divination may be a means of cross-checking this; but prayer, meditation, contemplation and spiritual discipline are indispensable if you are not to go astray in this matter.

It will help to recall the preconditions which must be met if the runes are to embody their full magical potential. They should be created at an auspicious time, in a context of carefully planned ritual and with the highest of intentions. They should be purified, and their inherent powers should be invoked through the seed sounds which they each embody. They should be awakened by means of a catalyst, and they should be fed from time to time.

The most auspicious time in general for engraving a new set of runes is the New Moon. However if you are versed in astrology, you may be able to make use of special astrological configurations and create the runes at other auspicious times. The ritual which you use while engraving the runes is a very individual matter, but it may include an initial fixing of intention, prayers, an offering of the construction materials (be it stone, wood, ceramic or other) to the divine, consecration of the results, chanting of the rune names while the engraving is being done, visualization of the rune coming to life and a closing ceremony of further purification and prayer. It would be best to meditate for several days in advance, possibly also to undertake a fast in preparation for the work. Once the runes are created, they must be awakened, and this is a magical process whose details should only be passed on by a master to qualified students whose integrity is assured.

Once awakened, the runes may also be fed on a regular basis. There are a number of ways to do this, but some of the simpler ones include chanting their names while holding them, one by one; filling them with the energy of your life-breath; sleeping with them under your pillow; carrying them on your person, or placing them under direct sunlight, or in moonlight. Other ways of feeding the runes more powerfully and occultly may also be conveyed from master to student when the conditions have been met.

In ancient times people lived in villages generally confined to a few hundred or a few thousand people. The village shaman would choose his students carefully. There might not be more than a handful, and not all would pass his tests. Only when tried and tested would the trainees be inducted into the mysteries of power. In certain cases, the apprentice would have to endure severe tests of endurance of a life-threatening nature and not all of them would pass the tests. The runes were considered to be the living embodiments of the powers of the gods, and one who mastered their secrets became, in effect, a living embodiment of the divine action. In the Teutonic tradition, for example, the initiated shaman would incarnate Woden or Freya at the time of doing sacred work. In other cultures, the name and identity of the divinity might differ, but the principle was the same. The worker of rune-magic had to prove worthy of the powers he was being granted, or his own survival and that of the entire community as well might be put at risk. Whether through ignorance or ill-will, any transgression of the laws could invite serious disturbance which was not always confined to the wrongdoer, but might extend to his family, clan or community. To mediate the energies of heaven and earth was the highest and most dangerous of callings, and for many early societies the runes were the prime instrument not only of divination, the way of determining how to proceed, but also of initiation, pathworking and of magic. Those who learn from books rather than directly from true initiates lose a very important component in the formation of their character and outlook. Words on a printed page can never substitute for the sequence of inner experiences and lived challenges that result in real initiation; nor can the trial-and-error process of self-teaching substitute for the direct transmission of power that comes from a master.

All of this being said, one must make do with the tools given, and often this is reduced to the book-in-hand and the will to succeed. Magic is about power. The powers of the Primal Runes exist self-contained in their own world, on the plane of the archetypes. But we have access to these powers in two ways: by means of sound and by means of symbolic form. Beyond its name, which indicates the kind of power inherent in the rune, its seed sound is keyed to the essence of the rune's power, and is a means of invoking, focusing, and directing that power according to intent. The visual form of the rune is also a means of summoning and applying the rune's power. For example, if you visualise the triangular form of the Fire rune, preferably in a fiery colour like red, and superimpose it with your mind on a person or situation, you can apply the energy of the rune and bring about change. Or, alternatively, you may draw the form of the rune with your mind's eye, or even with your hand in the air, sending this form out so that it superimposes itself on that which you wish to change. When you project a rune in this way, draw it from right to left, and from bottom to top, except in the case of runes like Descent, Crisis or Wisdom where the line of energy is obviously descending.

The effectiveness of projecting the energies of runes depends in large measure on the clarity of your intention, your power of concentration and your innate capacity. If you want to enhance the effectiveness of your work, intone the seed sound of the rune while sending out its form into the ether. For example, if you are sending out the Fire rune, quietly within your mind, or even audibly if circumstances permit, intone the sound "I" (as in "eye"), with full concentration and directed intent, as you project the fiery triangle. In the matter of intent, you must be very clear about what you are doing and why. Take time to study the powers of the various runes so that you know which one to choose for the work in hand.

CHAPTER 11

Chanting the Primal Runes

*I*n the subtitle of this book, "Archetypes of Invocation and Empowerment", a unique prospect is touched on, the possibility of accessing a higher realm of reality and applying its power in this world. To express it at greater length, and with more clarity, the claim is this: firstly, that the runes are archetypes; secondly, that these archetypes can be invoked, or called into manifestation; and thirdly that they have powers which can be accessed and applied. This chapter will go into this process in greater depth.

An extended discussion of Archetypes has already been presented in Chapter 5, and there is no need to repeat or summarise it here. What we might draw attention to at this point, however, is that archetypes are not vague abstractions in some other-worldly realm of philosophy. They are living powers, available to those who have the knowledge and capacity to access them. The dynamic aspect of archetypes is often forgotten in speculative writings such as that of Jung, because a system for reaching and using the archetypes has never been widely known or accepted. When we use the word "Invocation" as part of the subtitle of this book, it is implied that there is a way to call down the archetypal powers, and that sound is the key. Again, the word "Empowerment" suggests that, having invoked the forces of the runic archetypes, an individual has more power at his or her disposal. Power manifests in the process of application. It is something that humans normally use to change the way things are, either in the inner or in the outer worlds. Rune magic sets up powerful vibrations in the inner world that can then be directed to a desired result, and this result may very well be intended to precipitate into physical manifestation. Again, it may only be a change of attitude, or a release of blockage, or healing, or blessing which is intended, in essence, an inner change of disposition or energy or consciousness. A few words about invocation are in order, to suggest how the power of the runes can be called down and applied.

Quite a few books have been written on the subject of magical invocation, and it is a topic on which much can be said. We can only hope to review a few of the salient points here. As with divination, the clarity and purity of intent are of the utmost importance. Whenever you work with power, the laws of karma apply. You will, sooner or later, reap what you sow. Clarity of intent means that your idea of what you want to accomplish is well defined in your own mind. Often, the measure of clarity is whether the intent can be expressed succinctly in a single sentence. To this end, it is often recommended that the intent be written down on a piece of paper, and for beginners this is a good idea.

Purity of intent is of the utmost importance, if only as a form of self-protection. Naturally, there should be no possibility of harm resulting from the invocation. If anyone or anything is harmed, one is karmically responsible and the price will eventually have to be paid. Beyond this, there should be no motive other than selfless service at work in the practitioner. Karma arises from desire, and the desire for gain inevitably generates earthly bondage. On the other hand, compassion and service are liberating in their effect and they are striking examples of what is encompassed by the term "purity of intent". Other motives of a pure nature might include self-giving, dedication to duty, idealism, selfless love, divine guidance, inspiration, or justice. However inspired one may be, however, the ultimate measure of pure intent is surrender to the divine will. Only if one's thought, action and intent are aligned with this higher guidance can one proceed safely to work with the archetypal powers of the runes.

What this means, in effect, is that magical invocation should only be taught to, and practised by people who are deeply immersed in the spiritual life, and who have made significant progress in the process of inner purification. In actuality, the full power of the runes is successfully called into play only by those who have a gift for the practice, along with the self-discipline and dedication to devote time and energy to practice. Such individuals are rare, and it is for this reason that information about magic has not created more havoc in the general public than it already has. Sometimes people with the ability to call down the rune powers and put them to work lack the maturity and wisdom to steer clear of negative karma. It is for this reason that runic pathworking, in its higher levels, is best taught only to those who are qualified, (ie. clear and pure intent) and only by a proven master who has genuine attainment, both occult and spiritual. For all others, we must say : Beware!

All of this having been said, should you feel drawn to the practice of invoking the powers of the archetypes, keep this in mind:

1) Timing is important. Consult an astrologer, or study astrology sufficiently to time your practice with favourable planetary aspects.

2) Work with runes that have, as mentioned earlier, been properly *awakened* and *fed*, as well as *purified* and stored in a place free from negative outside influences.

3) Prepare yourself by prayer, meditation, bathing, and study of the ritual you intend to enact before you actually begin your invocation. A short fast can also be helpful for the 24 or 48 hours preceding the invocation.

4) Be aware of the notes you use as you intone the sounds of the runes, and their relationship to the chakras. For this purpose, a set of seven crystal bowls attuned to the chakras can be helpful, or Tibetan Bowls made in the right way with seven metals, and similarly attuned. A small keyboard, natural or electronic might substitute. Again, you are well advised to settle upon a set of correspondences of musical tones with runic sounds that you believe to be correct, and for this purpose there is no substitute for deep study. The author is not supplying this information here because it can be misused if the trainee has not been correctly initiated by a living and qualified teacher – as explained above with reference to 'clarity and purity of intent'.

5) Establish a place which is dedicated to sacred ceremony, ideally with no other kind of use permitted, and with no random coming and going of outsiders. Usually a locked room is set aside for this purpose by serious practitioners. Take the phone off the hook and arrange not to be interrupted for the duration of the invocation.

6) Either verbally or in writing, state the intent of the ceremony at the outset. If you open avenues of energy, be sure to close them again at the end of the ceremony. Make sure you have done good background reading about magical ritual, but then go with what is simple, clear and feels good for you, according to your own understanding.

7) It is helpful to have special clothing which you reserve for sacred ceremonies, whether or not anyone but yourself is there to see you. The point is that the power of association enhances the power of your own faith and conviction and thereby brings about better results.

8) Have your runes with you, and if possible visualize and hold the rune which represents the energies you are working with. See the rune as the physical embodiment or temple of the archetype. Feel that the rune-form and the stone it is engraved on are the living energy of the higher being or force which you are calling down. A rune which is correctly made and handled is a real talisman, and an object of magical power. Your runes are tools of empowerment if you use them correctly as part of your invocation.

9) You may want to use an incense or oil whose properties correspond to the work you are doing. Again, this is an extensive topic to research, but the effort is worth it. Similarly, jewelry made of real crystals or precious stones can be an asset for sacred ceremonies, and an altar may have several such pieces along with candles or flowers, all dedicated with conscious intent to heighten the energy field within which the invocation is to take place.

These suggestions are of a general nature. As you work with the sounds of the runes and continue to read and study, you will evolve your own personal approach. Although it may differ from the way that others go about their practice, its validity will be sensed by you as something that "feels right". It needs always to be borne in mind, and therefore frequently repeated, that careful and deep study of the tradition must be the foundation for your choices of style and ritual. In other words, it is not good enough to find a personal style that you happen to like, but based on your ignorance of the tradition. You may be comfortable with something that is cosmologically incorrect, simply because you don't know better. Why? Because you did not take the time to study. Then, you will pay the price. Either you will be ineffective, which is the most common result, or you will cause harm. Remember, when you begin to study, that some writers such as Rudolph Steiner and Franz Bardon are occultists of genuine, high and pure spiritual attainment, whereas others such as Aleister Crowley were fatally fascinated by the dark side. Be wise in the wells from which you draw your water, because your choices and actions determine your spiritual fate.

CHAPTER 12

The Sacred Sounds

In the following notes on the sounds of the runes, several key words are given at the outset and then a more detailed description of how the rune-sound works, and what potential it has for bringing about results. In the early stages of practice, one is building a bridge, connecting with the powers that be. In time, when the connection is established, the results begin to flow. Take the time that is needed to develop a strong link with the archetypal powers of these runes, and to the degree that you honour the universal laws that govern their use, you will have them at your disposal for the rest of your life.

Field

Applications: To stabilize; to settle; to materialize; to solidify; to reify.

The sound of "U" helps us to experience the silence of the inner depths and to enter a prayerful consciousness. It brings us into the inner darkness, the deepest space within our being. This darkness is clear and safe, it is the inner womb or matrix. It is sweet and timeless. When we chant "U", spirit surrounds us with energies of rebirth, and infuses the space of the matrix with potential for future growth and expansion. In this inner sanctuary, we experience our spirit smoothing away the old and tired parts of our human existence, leaving instead a consciousness of clarity and direction. Meditate with the sound "U" to enlighten your heart and enter the space within yourself which you feel to be your true inner 'home'. With this sound, you will pull in light, open the heart, and be enabled to assimilate information from Spirit.

Seeding

Applications: For new beginnings; for fertility; to persuade or convince; to send energy to another person (or to a situation in the inner world).

The sound of "SU" seeds and anchors light in our being. Its energy brightens our auric fields, opening a portal into divine consciousness and facilitating our entry into higher worlds. With this sound, you can intuitively sense whether your asking is aligned with the divine will, and you intuit how to ask in the right way for what you need. With "SU", you can make a good beginning, open a portal into a holy place and access the energy and awareness to cross through that portal into a higher world. In crossing over, you know: "I am the seed. I am the Light. I am the knowing." "SU" produces a mandala of light and energy in the mind, and if you go to the centre of this mandala, you can access many regions of sacred experience. In these regions, you can receive more detailed knowledge about your holy sounds, or your sacred lineage, as well as many other aspects of your inner makeup.

Gestation

Applications: For healing; to maintain good health; to shelter or protect; to conceal.

The sound of "LU" helps us to focus attention and become aware of anything discordant that we may be holding inside ourselves, whether in thought or belief. We are able to observe the makeup of the small self more clearly. You have the feeling of opening your awareness so that you can see yourself inwardly, outwardly, above and below. You can observe yourself in all ways. Recognizing what is being held in your thoughts, will and intentionality, you can ask for the changes that are needed. With the conscious perspective that "LU" provides, you can attune to your inherent perfection and call it to yourself. With the conscious perspective that "LU" provides, we can embrace the limited self with unconditional love. We are better able to intuit how we may best receive the gift of inner wholeness from Spirit, and how the small self may best reflect the Truth it has been shown. "LU" organizes the energies and thoughts, preparing us to seed the future with greater awareness in the emotional body (sometimes called 'affective intelligence').

Emergence

Applications: To attract new energies into one's life; for a fresh start; to release or liberate; to launch a project; to infuse fresh life-energy.

The sound of "KU" helps us to release karmic disharmonies and emotional residue, and to be replenished with vibrations of wholeness. The energy released by the sound "KU" transforms and arranges the aura so that it resonates with higher and more harmonious frequencies. "KU" can be used for healing, meditation, ceremony or prayer. When chanted on a high note, it opens the crown chakra; a low note opens the root chakra; and intermediate pitches work on the chakras between the crown and the root.

With "KU", you can open any chakra and invoke light, healing and blessings. Express a clear intent to the Higher Self and ask for inner guidance to transform the energies involved. "KU" aligns you with the Higher Self and helps you to direct energy to the area that is being transformed. It relaxes the structures of the human microcosm so that they are more receptive to the spiritual forces which have been invoked.

Thunder

Applications: As a catalyst (to activate); to initiate a new circumstance; to empower by will; to bring about a swift change; to release energy suddenly; to empower; to destabilize; to precipitate upheaval.

"WA" is a sound of awareness. Its vibration helps us to become aware that we are multi-dimensional beings, and that as such we can draw toward us a wide range of energies using the power of sound and attention. "WA" helps us to become one with the divine power of sound. Thus, we become conscious of the many vibrations which we can access in this state of inner attunement. Thunder rune energy helps to balance our masculine and feminine polarities so that we can move to a place of inner wholeness and stillness. "WA" is also useful to empower sacred objects which have a place in healing, ceremony or ritual. It is a sound of power. It activates and charges objects with liquid light when we direct it with conscious intent. "WA" centers us and activates us so that we can penetrate the core of our own being and enter the dimension of infinity. The sound of "WA" moves energy from Heaven to Earth, bringing about powerful transformation in all it touches, and catalyzing consciousness to its full potential.

Growth

Applications: To bring about increase (for example of wealth, or of power); to remove obstacles; for fertility; for transcendence; for male vigour.

The energy of "TI" (pronounced 'tie') harmonizes our inner world and makes us more aware of our soul's path in life. It initiates the journey of self-discovery, unlocks our ancient memory and creates grounding with inner assurance that we can go forward confidently in our quest. When we are rooted, we can journey inwardly in realms of self-discovery, undauted by the perception that we are potentially limitless. It is excellent for releasing karmic residues that are ready for release. The sound of "TI" helps to balance the aura so that the inner and the outer areas of life-experience flow smoothly together. It also aligns mind with Spirit, giving us a basis to settle into life freely and willingly in our striving toward self-mastery. This energy breathes with us, and facilitates our inner blossoming into a harmonious wholeness.

Challenge

Applications: To disrupt; to mediate, where one is called to intervene; to forestall or delay; to reconcile opposing forces.

The sound "WI", accompanied by the symbolic form of the Challenge rune, places the energies of the human microcosm in a situation of receptivity and growth. As the sound of "WI" consumes the energy of chaos, it fuels our potential for enlightenment and we are opened up to higher knowledge. This sound has fire energy in it, which facilitates our self-opening and self-offering to the Divine. The fiery energies of progress are awakened when we intone the sound of "WI", and we are enveloped in a vibratory field of wholeness and knowingness. We become more aware of all aspects of self. We can challenge ourselves to embrace the fullness of creation, not only the challenges of the material life, but the lofty adventure of spirit and consciousness.

Fire

Applications: For protection (of self, or valuables, for example); to halt unwanted forces; to empower or energize; to focus and direct the will; to alter, change or transform.

The Fire energy initiates an auspicious beginning. The sound of "I" is the eternal light of the Creator, and it is within each of us, waiting for release so that it can effect a transumtation of our being and guide us home to Source. This sacred sound ignites the soul and aligns us to Spirit. It is luminous and vibrant, penetrating and enveloping, warm and supportive. The fiery sound of "I" opens and clears the way. It purges and activates. The capacities of the soul can then be applied to our life purpose so that we carry out the Divine Will in every area of life. "I" is one of the master sounds when we are working to expedite spiritual progress.

Choice

Applications: For the faculty of discernment; to gain insight, or an overview; to shape or project intention.

The sound of "RI" activates a cellular code which allows the body to restructure itself and move toward transformation into a light body. The death cycle is released and the imprint of a new light body is rceived. The energy fields become alibned to Source, and the consciousness becomes centred in the 'I AM' awareness. We are able to read the records encripted in the DNA and view both the ancient records of our past experience and our future live. The solar plexus chakra opens up by the power of the sound "RI", as well as the crown chakra. This sound can also bring the imprint of the soul into the mind so that we can interpret and assimilate the wisdom of past lives and ancient records. "RI" is a gatekeeper sound for the portal of the solar plexus region. It is one of the best sounds for accessing past lives.

Karma

Applications: To harmonize the direction of one's destiny; to seal or re-inforce; to bind; to project intention; to superimpose an influence; to place a force.

The sound of "MI" enables the mind to see its beliefs for what they are and then support or release them. When limiting notions have been released, the spiritual heart and the psychic being (the soul-child) are less constrained. New vistas of inner freedom open up, and the soul can replenish itself with new information which serves its further progress. Certain dogmas and beliefs are inherently limiting, but the sound of "MI" sustains and nourishes the inner being as it lets go of the past and opens to the future. It is a vibration of wholeness and completeness that helps us to be centred and grounded, and aligned to Source.

Creativity

Applications: To develop and apply creative will; to elevate any energy; to raise consciousness or energy to a higher level; to create an opening; for attunement to spiritual planes of reality.

The sound of "SI" envigorates your imagination and supports your capacity to create. The light of the higher mind is brought into the human mind, and consciousness expands to a place of artistic inspiration and skill. Mind becomes multi-dimensional. Symbols and images that carry inner teachings become accessible to you, there is a new ability to form and shape your world using the insights of the intuitive heart. The infinite mind of the Creator overlights your path and reveals to you many gifts which had previously been hidden to your recognition. "My mind and God's Mind flow together" - this is what you feel in your heart when you access the power of the sound "SI". The brain re-aligns with the core will, whicn in turn orients itself to God's creative force. You can let go of blockages and weakness to become fully creative as you travel in expaqnded mind to a place of new energy, new creative potential.

Grace

Applications: When you need good fortune; for circumstances beyond normal means of control; to mark and protect; to seal; to affirm; to claim; to protect or shield; as a protective amulet or talisman.

With the sound "NA", the Higher Self blesses the soul with the energy of inner awakening. The inner depths stir and waves of long-forgotten thought begin to caress the aura. "NA" brings many subtle colours into the energy field, colours that are gentle and beautiful. There is a sense of softness, along with an infusion of golden light that speaks of the Creator's love. We feel and know that we are truly and deeply loved, and this enables us to open more fully to the inner magic of existence.

Love

Applications: For love magic; to find a lover; to improve or elevate or spiritualize love; to improve a relationship; for protection (uses the heaven-earth axis); for binding (the "so be it" effect).

The sound of "WE" (pronounced 'way') releases us from the limitations of conditional love so that we can better appreciate how unconditional love can ge given and received. We know how to release the restrictions which we have placed on love with our dogmas, notions and social conditioning. Through the power of the sound "WE", our capacity for divine love is awakened and revealed to our inner understanding. We see a pure way, a pure kind of thinking and a direct route to the fullness of divine love. We are able to receive love more fully and offer it to the world more freely. We let go of the need to suffer, and we see that suffering is not necessary for our inner growth.

Courage

Applications: To push an issue; to take initiative; to augment; to strengthen the life-force; to enhance the fighting spirit; for recuperation; to lift emotions, fortify spirits.

The sound of "RE" (pronounced 'ray') communicates strength. When we chant it, we come to know that we are strong. Thus, we are able to let go of insecurity, and release fear. On the physical level, the energies of "RE" support the spine and nervous system. This energy helps us to experience our full potential, full knowing, and also enables us to share it with others. We are opened up to experience more, to let go of whatever limits or binds. With the vibration of "RE", we release restraints, separations and burdens. We recognize our imperfections and have the power to make changes. We remember our inherent perfection and are empowered to manifest it.

Fullness

Applications: For safe travel; for justice; for success; for financial increase; to achieve a satisfactory conclusion; for blessing; to promote enlightenment; for fullness; to clarify or reveal.

The sound of "E" brings in purification. The universe loves this sound, because it is a heart-building light. The "big bang" which we understand as the beginning of creation resonates with this vibration. It harmonizes you, and tunes you as if you were becoming like the strings of a harp, able to resonate in harmony with many octaves of vibration. The sound of "E" resonates sympathetically with the heart in all creation. You feel : I AM and I AM COMPLETE. The resonance of "E" sings us into evolution and enhances our creativity. It shows us the core roots of the primordial sounds and syllables. "E" connects mind to the power of manifestation. You remember that your soul has promised Source that it will manifest in harmony in creation. In the sound of "E", you are gathered into a place of hope, celebration and closure.

Descent

Applications: When a tangible result is looked for; to actualize; helps bring events to pass; to call down higher help; to call higher powers to witness; for oath-binding.

This sound directs my consciousness to descend to a place of focus. My will descends into its inner sources of power. "TE" leads the way and takes me to a sacred place from where I can descend into matter. This sound also evens out the flow of energy in my aura. I am shown the way to completeness. This vibration resonates with rainbow medicine. It makes miracles possible. The divine consciousness shows you the way to completeness through the energy of this sound. As with other sounds, chanting this sound creates an opening. You go through that opening and have an experience of the infinite. The process is subtle, so you need to focus your intent. "TE" opens a link, an inner portal, and you go through it and see infinite possibilities. "TE" makes you aware of where you need to go.

Wisdom

Applications: Protection; defense; convincing and powerful speech (eloquence); to gain wisdom; to shed the light of wisdom on a situation, or into the mind; for good luck in exams; to contain or balance a powerful energy; to delimit the boundaries of a situation.

The sound "NE" directs you inwardly to know that you have the inner answers to your questions and to become aware that you have, from inner sources, the sustenance to take care of all your needs. "NE" is one of the holy names for the Creator. Through this vibration, you can talk to Creator, and the voice of Creator shows you the sacred path that leads to inner oneness. The space in consciousness created by the vibrations of "NE" allows you to receive fast answers to the questions which you bring to Creator.

Mastery

Applications: To neutralize an enemy or hostile force; for protection; for increase of magical energies; to ward off negative energies; to empower.

The sound of "LE" shows you how to enter into yourself and claim your inner mastery. You become aware of yourself moving through initiations and linking to Source through the power of knowing. "LE" can take the form of a flame, and illumine or show you other forms of yourself. You can link, in the inner world, to others who are like you. "LE" opens you to further degrees of mastery; it is a gate-opener to mastery. The energy of "LE" is very human, it relates to you as a fallible human being and helps you consolidate your mastery.

Lake

Applications: To promote harmony and wholeness; to unify; to include, or bring together; to reconcile or unify; for alliances and partnerships; for family stability, or marital harmony; for social order and oneness.

When you chant the sound of "RA", you feel like you are looking directly into the living face of the Source, and being reflected back to yourself as Creator sees you. In this reflection, you sense your fullest potential. You know what you are and what you can manifest. There are many ways to be and to experience self. In this sound, you experience the androgynous nature of spirit, but also see how masculine and feminine express it in incomplete ways. You become master of your process of self-creation as you see yourself mirrored in the face of God. You can then be all you want to be. The aspect of the divine you touch here is playful and childlike. It encourages you to open into your infinite play. You are also given power to manifest things on the three-dimensional level through the energy of the sound "RA". It was not only one of the most important Egyptian names for divinity, but a syllable of magical power in ancient times.

Transmission

Applications: A sending rune; to change someone's attitude; to make someone more receptive; to harmonize differences; to distinguish; to dissolve resistance.

The sound of "MO", when chanted silently or vocally makes a gate open in the inner world of consciousness. You can then move to a place within your own being where you become much more of who you really are. Very gently, even playfully, this energy harmonizes various parts of the being until you feel that you are made whole again. You see and sense how to interpret your experience and how to transform yourself. The sound "MO" encourages you to wait on directions which you will receive from within. When you chant this sound and wait, you begin to draw in energies that will transmute you for the better. There is a clear inner arrangement of the parts of your inner being. Your peripheral vision opens wider. Vibrations move up and down the spine to release crystallized thoughts. You will have a sense of something very beautiful and magical unfolding within you.

Dreamweaver

Applications: To contact your intuitive faculties; to stimulate the imagination; to invoke the muses; for channelling; to open a portal.

This sound of "NO" takes you into the dreamscape and the

dream time. Here you can weave a thought into reality. In this space, you see your choices more clearly. You observe how you weave thoughts through time and you become much more conscious of the choices you have been making. Thus you become more conscious of your weaving, you weave with knowing and inner direction. This sound brings in butterfly medicine and a variety of colours. The right and left hemispheres of the brain are taken into a balanced centre. You can see sacred geometry from this centre. You feel that you have been placed in your inner seat of power, and here you become more aware of yourself as a multidimensional being. The possible ways you can travel and the choices that are yours to make are revealed more clearly to your understanding. Creator gently guides you through the available choices, you see the richness of possibilities and you move to make a better next choice. With the vibration of "NO" you can open up a new path in the inner worlds, and you can tape the infinite wealth of the inner life for a richer and more beautiful experience of existence. "NO" purifies you. It empowers you to work out your choices with more clarity, and thus move to a better future.

Water

Applications: To generate flow and movement; to dissolve; to blend; to efface or obscure; to cloak; to allay; to wash away; to purify.

Through the vibration of the vowel sound "O", you can experience creator in liquid form, as liquid light, and you experience how creator flows as creation in a liquid way. You open your own records, and you access primordial records within yourself, your watery matrix. The sound of "O" moves you into various layers and places you within your inner self to interpret your experiences. This is a soft, gentle, velvety, warmly knowing vibration. It feels comfortable and supporting. You come to see clearly your birthright, and to experience your passage through life as a journey of infinite knowing. You can build up the sound until it becomes more full of power and thus increase awareness of what is around and within you. A gate of knowing is opened. You can be quiet and still, or you can see and interpret more information as it comes through that gate. Thus the "O" vibration can be a place of rest, or of infinite supply, should you wish to absorb more.

Crisis

Applications: To inject energy; to direct conscious intent; to seal success; for victory; for success; for strength and confidence (see also Courage rune); to empower; to activate; to arouse; to enhance initiative.

The power of the sound "ZO" opens you to the four sacred elements. It also connects you with your inner pilot, your Higher Self so that you can move deep within and know how your inner divine guidance would direct you. Mind receives directions from Source within the energy of "ZO". Creator directs mind so that self-empowerment becomes possible. Consciousness comes into the mind from Creator and focuses you and makes your highest potential available to you. You align with the infinite, and seem to light up from within. The conscious mind then knows what to do in order to bring information through; you are aligned and fully open to receive from spirit. In consciousness, the "ZO" energy takes you high above the normal human ranges of consciousness and you float in the plane of *buddhi*, or illumined intellect; there you can gather information at your highest potential. In the vibrations of "ZO", you move through your impediments, they do not restrict you, and you ascend to your most illumined level of mind. This is a good sound to work with when you want to recover from crisis or stress. We can use the sound of "ZO" to connect with healing energies, and these can be assimilated and drawn through the body or placed in the aura, or in a chakra. With this sound we can rise above the body to view it with the inner vision, and from there we may direct the healing energies as needed.

Sacrifice

Applications: Banishing; protection; to seal; to bless; to bind.

Chanting the sound of "LO", I align with Source, and become centred in Source. Then, I flow out from Source. I see my spirit come out into the NOW of time and space from the Centre. I draw knowing from the centre. I am opened to sky and to earth simultaneously. I see how all things meet in the centre. Through the sound of "LO" it is possible to invoke the breath of God and activate it to descend into human consciousness. You can chant this sound silently, or audibly, but either way, it will help you let go and move freely in the inner world. You are empowered to release and to create. Your heart and mind open to each other and you become aware of Source Energy, Source Power. If some energies are disrupted or broken, you are shown how to sacrifice self to the Source and offer yourself to wholeness. You open to abundance if you have the intention to receive help, inner help. "LO" gives you empowerment direct from the Source, rather than from an inner guide. You will receive an infusion of Creator's will to work with this symbol. Being connected to Source, you can see how it originates Male and Female energies and flows them into manifestation. The awareness of how Source manifests as creation comes to the fore, and you see how the polarities express Source in creation. Through the vibration of "LO", you can access information and receive answers so that you can move in a sacred way from the centre to be in creation, conscious of what you manifest, holding the hand of the Creator.

Knot

Applications: Binding; love unions; when luck is needed (calls in the help of the Goddess); to promote unions and friendships; to protect possessions; to seal a spell; to re-inforce a union.

"RO" unblocks you so you can tap the information you have gathered, your lineage and spiritual bloodline. "RO" is physically healing. It can be used to heal the liver, kidneys, throat chakra and brain. Healing can also take place in the chakras and subtle energy fields. The soul-energy is focused on parts of the body, including the subtle bodies, that need healing and balancing. By chanting this sound, you may release pain and even out areas of imbalance. The passages through which the soul's light should pass are unblocked. "RO" clears the way. This sound opens you to channel from a deep place, moving you into equilibrium of mind, steadying the nervous system and creating an energy field around and within you which is evenly balanced. The breath is charged with spirit, and the consciousness is opened to Source. As with certain other sounds, past lives may be seen. You come to know how your soul exists in matter, in material manifestation, and you also see how spirit is awakening in matter. The energies of the aura are more closely identified with the soul. "RO" connects you to the core of the planet and links you to collective consciousness. It brings in other sounds. The *Tan Tien* centre below the navel is energized by this vibration. "RO" shows you the way to connect successively with soul, then spirit, then Creator, then earth.

Mountain

Applications: Protection; to make secure; to empower; to purify; to elevate energies; for contemplation; to spiritualize.

"KA" reveals to you that you are master of yourself. It reveals the "I AM" presence within. You know and feel that you are inherently perfect and complete. You travel to an ancient place of knowing where the elders are, the well of spirit where the energy is pure. You can also use this sound to tap the wisdom of the elders at ancient ceremonial sites. The information there is pure, it has been preserved in sacred continuity and not corrupted. The resonance of "KA" contains the elder, the wise one who speaks. You experience your inner self as wise, and you can contact the ancient wise one within yourself. You experience life as an unfolding of providence at work, and you open yourself to its providential flow. The heart child can approach and meld with the awareness of the elder. Your innate innocence is allowed to play, and you see that where you are now is perfect. You will be able to play with your inner child inside the resonance of "KA".

Transformation

Applications: To integrate two different energies; to focus magical intent; to direct magical energies; for all issues of partnership; to focus intent and direct energy.

The sound of "MU" sings you home. It shows you the way home to a place within your own being that knows no separation. You feel like you are sitting on the lap of God. You are in a place where the energy is even, gentle, caring, friendly, supportive, and you feel that you are being suffused inwardly with courage. Here, you replenish yourself and seed yourself into what you need to know. "MU" can move forward or backward, or in all directions.

It stimulates the imagination and helps you to move forward in a playful way. "MU" shows you your child self, your heart's inner child. It brings you dragonfly medicine. If you want to come out of your body, this sound will show you how. "MU" also opens awareness of past lives.

Merging

Applications: For mental and physical equilibrium; for fulfilment (in career or love); for protection, especially in cases of emotional vulnerability; to mark (with intent, ownership or energy); to reconcile.

The sound of "PU" links you to the future. It moves you into future knowing. You move forward in right choices. "PU" links you to a good future and provides you with an open gateway to move forward. "PU" is the energy of providing, and also the power of explaining. Things that need to be explained can be illumined by the energy of "PU". This gives you confidence to cross barriers and choose a better future. With "PU", more information and energy are processed through the solar plexus and root chakra. All processes having to do with the mouth and tongue are also infused with light and power through this sound.

Primal Light

Applications: To strengthen (for example to enhance a previous rune); for healing; for love and good relationship; for success and safety in travel; to encourage a positive or fruitful result; for fertility; the sign of the Great Mother; protection; to seed with light; to invoke light.

The sound "MA" is the invocation of the white light of the Divine Mother. It purifies and uplifts all parts of the being.

Primal Dark

Applications: To disable; to incapacitate; to obscure; to make heavy, dense or slow; to cloak; to invalidate.

The sound of "PA" is a sound which can be used for going deep, for entering into darkness, for covering and concealing, and for burying.

Source

Applications: To invoke the Divine; to consecrate; to spiritualize.

The sound "A" is spiritually creative and empowering. It is a true mantra for invoking the Divine presence and power. It can be considered a seed syllable for Source, and used when we want to align all parts of the being with our highest inner guidance.

The Wisdom Cycle

We have seen that the Moon is the Mother of Time. She imparts to each phase of time its quality, its potential for expediting the evolution of consciousness. One way to live in harmony with the celestial wisdom is to follow this pattern, and one very good way of doing this is by reading or meditating on the lunar qualities which are active on any given day.

The lunar cycle begins with the New Moon and comprises 28 days. The first day of the cycle, the New Moon day itself, will be expressed by the runic energies of The Field. The second day of the cycle will relate to the Seeding rune, followed by Gestation, Emergence, Thunder, and so on.

All of this plays out against the backdrop of changing pattern of the heavens as described by astrology. This pattern flows as follows:

Sign	Dates	Element
Aries	March 21 – April 19	Fire
Taurus	April 20 – May 20	Earth
Gemini	May 21 – June 21	Air
Cancer	June 22 – July 22	Water
Leo	July 23 – August 22	Fire
Virgo	August 23 – September 22	Earth
Libra	September 23 – October 22	Air
Scorpio	October 23 – November 21	Water
Sagittarius	November 22 – December 21	Fire
Capricorn	December 22 – January 19	Earth
Aquarius	January 20 – February 18	Air
Pisces	February 19 – March 20	Water

The 'Wisdom of the Day' is to be found by determining which of the 28 lunar days has arrived, then checking which of the four elements is prevailing, by referring to the table of astrological signs above. For example October 21, 2004, the day on which this chapter is being written, is day ten of the lunar cycle. This places it under the rune Karma. There is a handy computer program which can be downloaded for free, which tells you the day of the lunar cycle you are in, with the dates of the New Moon, First Quarter, Full Moon and Third Quarter noted as well. One has only to click a lunar icon and all this information comes up. Now, October 21 is still under the sign of Libra, which is Air. Therefore, the reading for the day is that of the Karma Rune, with the energy of Air prevailing. First, read the mundane associations for the day, under the heading "Standard Meanings for Divination" and then the spiritual message for the day, under "Spiritual Meanings for Divination" – in both cases, refer specifically to the subheading for Air.

In this particular case, for example, October 21, 2004, the mundane or standard level of meaning reads:

> "Inconsistent expression (or manifestation) of core values; your heart is not centred."

The spiritual lesson of the day begins:

> Karma is a construction of the ego. It arises when ego pursues its own self-serving motives in thought and action. When ego abdicates its pride of place and is replaced by a higher and more spiritual guidance, karma comes to an end... etc. (page 129 – 30)

These two readings together inform you of the prevailing pattern which is at work on the cosmic level. This is the backdrop against which the individual's highly personal experience is being played out.

The reading for the day is an excellent way to make yourself aware of the prevailing influences at work, and to be conscious of the archetypal lunar forces as they move through their various phases. Beyond this general reading, you may want to draw a rune for the day in order to be aware of some of the factors at work in your own particular case. Having drawn the rune for the day, you may draw a second rune to see what aspect is at work, whether earth, fire, air, water, or ether. Being aware not only of the cosmic pattern which sets up the prevailing influence, but also your own individual situation and the issues you must face due to personal karma, you are well equipped to face the coming day.

Attunement to wisdom may, of course, be enhanced by holding the Wisdom rune and chanting its seed syllable several times. This is best done before you study the reading for the day. Also, when you have completed your reading, or readings, and see the nature of the difficulty ahead of you, you may choose an appropriate 'remedial' rune, visualize its form and chant its seed sound in order to clear the way forward. Runes not only advise you of what you face, they also provide you with energy to tackle the situation and to bring about positive change. Because each of the runes is also a talisman, you may carry your remedial rune in your pocket throughout the day, and from time to time hold it in your hand and chant the appropriate seed syllable.

From this practice of attunement to the lunar law, many good things flow. We are re-connected to the ancient powers that govern the unfolding of life on earth. We are re-integrated into the living influence of the Divine Mother. We remember our place in the patterns of providence and destiny which are weaving their way forward in our minds, hearts and bodies through the action the Moon.

One of the greatest dissociations we face in this modern age is a separation from nature, and from the divine power that is behind nature. Our earliest ancestors saw nature as the primary gospel or revelation of the divine, and they saw in nature a Great Mother. In our own day and age, we have created a society based on industry, technology and the scientific paradigm, all of which relegate the divine in nature to the remote background of our awareness. This is what makes it possible for us to destroy the environment without compunction, to obliterate eco-systems and entire species without remorse. To remember the wisdom of the Divine Mother as it is revealed through her archetypes is to be re-established in our rightful place, in right relationship to the Source and its unfolding plan in time and space.

CHAPTER 13

Bard of Runes

When I went to live in the forest, I had no idea that the Muse was going to pay me a visit. But I should, perhaps, have foreseen it. Many years previously, when I first took up the celtic harp and began composing music in the ancient vein, I had a dream vision. I was taken up into the world of the Moon and given the most beautiful melody imaginable. It was music that would melt the heart of anyone who heard it, and flood the heart with bliss. When I received this gift, I looked back down onto the earth, knowing that I would have to descend into the normal waking consciousness, and I said: "Why bother to remember this music when I come down again through all the stages of return and finally wake up? No one cares; they just do not care. It's not worth the effort." And so I left that piece of music where I found it, in the world of the Moon. There were other times over the intervening years when I received music during sleep, in a dream, and would awaken to transcribe it, but nothing like that direct experience of being transported into the world of the Moon. From this experience, I came to know directly that the Moon is indeed the mother of poetic and musical inspiration.

Time passed, and during a visit to Peru in 2003, I began to feel the need to understand divination with stones. It was one of those compelling urges that just had to work itself out into direct experience, and in the end would generate a book. And over a period of many months, on my return to Canada, an inner understanding of the Primal Runes emerged. It was not what I had initially been looking to do at all. Actually, I had no interest in the subject of runes before this body of understanding knocked on the door of my higher mind and asked to be given expression.

When the idea of divination with stones first came knocking on my door, I believed I was looking for a simple system of casting stones on a cloth for divination. Also, I had just completed a book and was in no mood to shoulder the job of writing a new one. I had been leading a group of meditators in a Full Moon meditation for several years, often with harp music in the Celtic style, and the call of the ancient wisdom was growing in strength through this period of time. The impulse to go more deeply into the runic symbols of Old Europe kept growing and growing until I knew it would be my next book. The completion of this book, entitled *The Primal Runes*, finally pulled together and gave full expression to this need and pressure I had experienced for so many months. Now, when I look back, I believe that it was an impulse from the Muse, a revelation from the inner worlds of a very lunar inner vision. As I shall explain, this rediscovery of the runes of lunar law has much to do with my proclivity for composing bardic poetry and harp music.

Now, I can understand that the Moon's gift of a most beautiful piece of music was not only a melody for the harp. It was, more importantly, a gift of inner seeing and feeling, an infusion of capacity which would enable me as a writer and contemplative to bring down and give expression to some of the essential lunar archetypes. I believe that the wisdom of the Primal Runes is an exquisite music of the soul, a patterning of energies and forces that are the matrix and birthplace of the instrumental music we hear on this earthly plane. Our music, here-below, translates parts of that more perfect music which is heard in the higher worlds. Poets and musicians, bards of all stripes, are wayfarers between the worlds, bringing auditory treasures from the beyond. I believe that there is a constant singing forth of light, beauty and joy that fills the spaces above us, the spaces between the stars, the darkness that we imagine to be empty. And when we hear or overhear that music, the music of the cosmos, nothing will ever be the same again. Of course, this is a conviction that the ancients held as well, and many mystics and meditators have apprehended this 'music of the spheres' in their own direct experience. What we have lost is the paradigm, the cosmology, which would enable us to recognize and live in the light of the cosmic music which surrounds us. We have lost the bardic touch.

For some time, it has concerned me that the feeling and the vision which would make a higher attunement possible is systematically eradicated by our society and its preferred educational system. Beautiful young souls come into life with hope and freshness, but by the time they are young men and women, they have been changed into cautious, skeptical adults. How and why does this happen? It happens because the old traditions and cosmology, the old attunement to Nature, and the folk art and oral traditions that arose from contemplating Nature, have been replaced by a 'corrupted myth'. It is worth considering how this impacts us, how it cripples us and prevents us from living in right relation with the Moon, the stars, the sacred elements and the music of existence. Why? Because in a sense the Primal Runes are the remedy for this dissociated sensibility which is our social inheritance. They are a sacred gift of the Goddess, the Moon with the power to change life for the better and in some measure rescue us from our self-created crisis.

Let us consider, for a moment, the 'corrupted myth' which I alluded to above. We grow up being taught that Reality can be quantified, measured and divided into increasingly more basic (and intrinsically more real) units. What can be measured, we learn, can be controlled. We come to believe that Reality is material, that it is comprehensible and that it unfolds according to fixed laws. We thus think that all problems are solvable if we make full use of intellect, or our brains, which we believe to be the most highly organized matter in our bodies. We are, after all, physical bodies; simply put, for most of us, this body is 'who I am'.

We are taught that mental intelligence will provide us with knowledge and power which are the keys to success in life. This is what we have in mind when we urge young people to get "a good education". The original meaning of the word educate, from the Latin *ex* and *ducere*, is to lead out of ignorance and darkness, in other words, to guide toward enlightenment. But now, we mostly relate education to the process of getting "a good job", which means we can become one of the knowledgeable, powerful (good jobs generate wealth, which is power) and dominant individuals of society, a leader of others. In this process of getting ahead with self-enrichment, and self-advancement, we learn that emotion is irrational and unreliable; 'affective intelligence' is unimportant, if not totally irrelevant. We hear words like "imagination", or "fantasy" talked of in disparaging terms, and we gather that intuitive feelings are primitive forms of thought, immature levels of consciousness that are hardly worth paying attention to if you have the higher powers of logical reasoning at your disposal.

As for Nature, we are taught to think of it as a rather imperfectly organized and chaotic relic of evolution that needs to be shaped by humans, in support of their goals, to supply raw materials for human projects. The kind of projects which would be considered worthwhile have to do with the increase of wealth. Wealth is generated by processing raw materials into useful products. The production of goods is the basis of prosperity, so Nature has some value because it supports industry. Of course, money is the prime measure of value. Not beauty, or goodness or harmony, but money. We organize society around the dynamics of the market place. Economics has replaced religion as our primary concern, and since throughout history so many people killed each other under the name of religion, we have a collective sigh of relief over that. Now we can all get on with the sensible business of making ourselves prosperous – so the common sense philosophy runs. Even a brief study of television will prove that the chief motivation of modern humans is the desire to accumulate and consume. In the modern paradigm, society can be described as a consumer-oriented arrangement of personnel adequate to the requirements of the market place. Education can facilitate the process of getting ahead in life by generating wealth, and in this sense it is a 'good thing' and leads to personal happiness. Having possessions is, of course the way to be happy. It's good for the economy too. We take it for granted that our opinions, desires and goals should be exposed at every waking moment to advertising, and thus we are willing to be bombarded with it from every direction, all the time. More could be said, but this is a brief outline of what I call the 'corrupted myth.'

Is it any wonder that the spirit of the bards has been lost? How contrary our modern, secular mythology is to the ancient patterns of the Lunar Law. We deny our sense of the sacred by learning to doubt all experiences based on intuition, inspiration or faith; they are not taught as valid sources of educational input.

They are completely ignored by science. The triumph of science, the scientific paradigm, and the scientific method, are taken as a vindication of the secular mind, and the current world dominance of Western civilization is often interpreted as validation of the superiority of this secular way of being.

However, the triumph of one part of the human psyche (rational mind) over all others cannot be an unqualified victory for mankind, since it is achieved at the cost of integral balance. It is not only in our minds, but also throughout our bodies, our vital energies, our emotions and in our inmost souls that the totality of our being is distributed. The so-called victory of the mind over life as championed by science has not brought us lasting happiness, either as individuals or as a society. We are facing problems on a scale never before imagined, to the extent that life on our planet, as we have known it, may cease to exist if present trends continue. For many people in the world, especially the majority of people who live below the poverty-line, the modernist promise of heaven on earth is bankrupt. Not only is nature reeling from our pollution and destruction, but significant numbers of children and adults are plagued by obesity, weakening health, mental imbalances, stress and attention-deficit disorders.

Science is the most powerful myth that the human mind ever created. But it is ready to be replaced. There is a new vision waiting in the wings. It is an intuitive, creative, vision that arises from attunement of the heart. And from this vision will arise a new myth, the myth of *eros*, or love. Long ago, the Greek philosophers clearly saw that *eros* is the prime mover of stars, acorns and the affairs of human beings, that it is the force of motivation that links us to the whole of life. Fascinated by power, the human mind seeks to divide and control; but the loving heart joins and completes. It is moved by an instinct for wholeness, and it finds expression in harmony, melody, poetry and beauty. Love is not something we make, or do, it is something we are. *Love is Being becoming itself.* Love links the separate self to a deeper reality, showing the deep truth of existence beyond anything that can be known through the filters of mind, personality or ego. Love is prior to knowledge; *we love in order to understand.* Love is the intent of life itself. We do not define it so much as it defines us. Love is the deepest yearning to achieve a re-union of what has been separated. When we choose love as the organizing vision of our life, we begin to create new words, new images, new paradigms, and we being to live in a new way, free from the tyranny of the past.

The nature of love is perhaps better expressed with the rhythms of poetry than with the plodding measures of prose, something which I attempted in these lines:

> Love comes down to express itself in form.
> Love goes up to lose itself in spirit.
> Love smiles to awaken slumbering hearts.
> Love weeps to remember itself when overcome by slumber.
> Love moves to share itself;
> Love moves not to realize itself.
> The mind of man and the spirit of God are united by love.
> This love and that love are not different realities,
> But parts of a single whole.
> Love makes all parts whole.
> Love is all in all.

I have experienced in my own life that the magic of moonlight is somehow mysteriously linked to the opening of poetic and mystical awareness, and the renewal of spirit. Over and over again in the process of composing music, writing poetry, or meditating on wisdom, cosmology, creativity or beauty, the subtle influence of the Muse, the lunar power of inspiration, is present. The *Night of the New Moon* is a time of conception, followed by three days of *Emergence*. The *Day of the Crescent Moon* sees the *Emergence* complete, and three days of *Expansion* follow. Towards the *Night of the First Quarter*, the momentum is tested, and the growing independence and confidence in the new life-direction is confirmed. It becomes definitive. After this comes three days of *Action* leading to *the Day of the Gibbous Moon*, where the commitment is tested by productive activity and struggle. Three days of *Overcoming* lead to the *Night of the Full Moon*, which is the culmination of the cycle. What was vaguely *felt* in the past is now clearly *seen*, having become a revelation or illumination. The symbolical seed planted at the time of the *New Moon* now flowers into clear vision. *Three Days of Fulfillment* follow, a time of assimilating the experiences of the first half of the cycle, refining and universalizing the forms that have been built; also, the talents used to build forms are further evolved. *The Day of the Disseminating Moon* comes and then three days of *Sharing* the widened vision, not necessarily in words, but in manifestation. The experience is furthered at this stage by connecting it to the world. What has been understood and assimilated is now demonstrated, and if necessary, reformed.

If *The New Moon* is the implantation of a seed, and *The Full Moon* is the flowering, *The Last Quarter* is the fruit, the harvest of the cycle. *The Last Quarter* tears down whatever has not served its purpose, or whatever has become obsolete. It is a time to let go. Three days of *Re-Orientation* follow *The Last Quarter Moon*, a time when results must be assimilated and understood. Whatever does not harmonize with the growing consciousness must be repudiated or dissolved. *The Day of the Balsamic Moon* moves us toward a closing. It is followed by *Three Days of Release*. The essence of the experience is now distilled to become the foundation of a future cycle. This can be a time of introspection or withdrawal, a time to empty the old and prepare for transition.

As a student of the bardic tradition, I feel that one of the most convincing ways to show this process at work is to express it in the rhythms of revelation, not merely as reflective prose, but in the poetry of ecstatic revelation. When the Muse speaks, she reveals her powers in rhythm, in the urge to create, in something formless seeking form, pressing forward in order to be uttered or "outered" in words or in music. When these rhythms are translated into words without interference from the mind's logic, you have incantation, speech with the power of magic, - and this is true poetry. The seeding power of the New Moon makes itself known in the first place as a secret voice or whisper within you. Here is one example of its self-revelation:

A Voice

Only a voice that no one can hear, my love,
One voice alone, in the core of my heart,
Calling to me from deep in my soul, my love,
Calling my name when the night is so dark.
Whose is the voice that I hear when I dream?
And who calls my name in the bosom of sleep,

Knowing the tears I never reveal, my love,
Deep in my soul, in the stillness so deep?
Moonlight dances on the meadow,
Starlight dances in the sky,
How I long to join the revel,
How I long to rise and fly.
Flying in the sky of spirit,
Far beyond the sleeping valley,
Flying where the dreamlight leads,
Beyond the starlit sky.
There is a time to rise and fly,
When dreamlight fills the night,
When spirit does the ancient dance
That makes the world grow bright,
When dreamers dance the night away,
And sleepbound hearts rejoice,
When earth and heaven show the way,
And wonder finds a voice...
Only a voice that no one can hear, my love,
One voice alone, in the core of my heart,
Calling to me from deep in my soul, my love,
Calling my name when the night is so dark.

I have called this stirring seed of the "bardic" touch a Voice and a Whisper. The 'Whisper' aspect comes through in these words, which I wrote in my cabin in the forest, prior to my first visit to Peru.

Whisper

Listen to the whisper that lives in the breeze,
Hear the wind sigh in the ancient trees,
Feel the gentle teardrops that fall on the dew,
Tears that are being wept for you.
In the ocean of dreamlight, the timeless womb,
Where the Moon bewitches the sea,
From a sky of love that is far above,
The whispering comes to me.
In the deepest night, when the stars are bright,
When the heart is at rest in the soul,

> From the mystery of eternity
> Comes a call to a distant goal.
> Silver is the moonlight, and deep her spell,
> Lost is the world in its sleep;
> Fated is the tide where the dreamers dwell,
> Precious are the tears that weep.
> I have no understanding, my eyes are blind,
> I am held by the Moon as a thrall,
> But I long to fly in my heart's own sky,
> To follow a whispered call.
> Listen to the whisper that lives in the breeze,
> Hear the wind sigh in the ancient trees,
> Feel the gentle tear drops that fall on the dew,
> Tears that are being wept for you.

Unfortunately, poetry, like imagination and fantasy, has been devalued and discredited as a way of knowing. But in ancient times, it was THE way of knowing, *par excellence*. Prophetic, revelatory speech was the sacred specialty of bards, oracles, seers, sages and holy men. Their judgements and sayings were sought after and considered more precious than gold. It greatly debases poetry to think of it as a form of entertainment. Originally, it was the embodiment of the power of incantation, which is invocation, the calling down of divine beings or powers into the earthly atmosphere. Robert Graves, and a number of other modern writers, to their credit, have recognized that poetry assumes its full power and moves into its true home as it approaches the status of mantra. Word of power *evoke* the realities they describe by a magical working of rhythm, cadence, sonority and imagery. The magic that true poetry can work is felt in the affective and intuitive part of our nature as a thing of power and beauty, something capable of energizing and elevating the consciousness. This is the skill we find in parts of Shakespeare, Homer, Virgil, Valmiki, and other great bards of the past, and this is what we have lost in our neglect of the Lunar Law. We have forgotten the beauty of poetry, we have forgotten what the role of bards originally was, and why in ancient societies they were accorded places of honour, second only to the king. Not only the sweet, the pleasant and the reassuring aspects of life find their way into the music of the bards, they also evoke the fearful, the awesome and the dreadful aspects of the Goddess, as in the following:

> The Lady advances from sickle to crest,
> Unfurling her standard, invading the West;
> In silver and silence, the witch is unveiled
> As queen of the spheres where sunlight has failed.
> The clashing of kingdoms, writ large in the stars
> Foretold the conjoining of Neptune with Mars;
> In the fields of the restless precursors of day,
> Her magical spellcraft is passing away.
> The balsam is dripping like dew from the trees,
> The cedars and hemlocks perfuming the breeze,
> And mist is as incense aswirl in the glades
> Where darkness is dying and prophecy fades.
> Arachne is spinning a filigree web
> Ensnaring the souls from the waters that ebb,
> And fireflies are swarming where water lies still
> In the eyes of the doe that the hunter will kill.
> The virginal bride who will end as a crone
> Kneels down at the feet of the porphyry throne,
> For the birth of her babe is foretold and ordained
> And the flowing of blood from a heart never stained.
> Where seeds of imperishable light have been sown
> By the chords that the mystical spirits intone,
> The Lady prevails in her dance with the sun
> In the wake of the worlds she has done and undone.

Rarely does the bard explain to the listener what he is doing, or why he feels called to his craft of words and music, devoting so much precious time to the art of word-weaving. But if a bard did explain why he does what he does, the explanation might run something like what follows. These words come from my inner feeling of why I am drawn to play the harp and to write poetry.

> My words are for the dreamer in your heart,
> My music is for the lover in your soul.
> What I have to say, I dedicate
> To the dreams you will ultimately realize,
> And what I have to sing, I consecrate

To the love you will finally actualize.
I try to dedicate what I have
So that the love of our dreams
May blossom within our hearts.
I try to consecrate what I am
So that the dream of a perfected love
May unfold within our souls.
I speak only to invoke the silence of love's sacred dream,
And I sing only to awaken the wonder of dream's secret love.
My speech and my song are unnecessary,
For love needs no expression,
    and dreaming requires no explanation.
Their perfect eloquence has no equal
Either in the world of our soul's solitude,
Or in the homeland of our heart's intimacy.
We share an inexpressible vision,
And we live for the impossible reality.
Although what we have and what we are
    may not be understood by others,
Still, we see what we must do,
    and we sense what we will become.
There is a deep necessity behind the music of our lives,
And there is a high possibility beyond the words of our speech.
In the heart of dreaming,
We see the birth of that inner necessity,
And in the soul of love,
We witness the unfoldment of that utmost possibility.
Beyond the world of speech, and behind the universe of song,
A new wonder is alive because we have come together.
Together, we will transform what now lies
    beyond us into a reality.
Together, we will widen what now waits
    within us into a destiny.

The bard is thus more than a mere entertainer. He translates inspiration, prophecy, revelation and divine beauty into the perfection of sound, so that these living energies can be transmitted from heart to heart and thus replicated in lived human experience.

There is a world beyond this world,
A sea beyond this sea,
And a heart that is bound beyond the beyond
To the shores of Eternity.
Within the void behind this world,
At the portal-gate of form,
A sacred need is born in time
And the pain of quest is sown.
Music comes, but void of sound,
And a voice in noiseless song,
A melody of the secret soul
As deep as the world is long.
There is a time for dreaming dreams,
A time to give them wings,
And a time for flight in the crystal light
Where the voiceless singer sings,
A time when dreams must come to life
In a world that dreams no dreams,
A time for sleep to awake in quest
And brave the ocean streams.
Eternity is awakened here
On the shores where visions beach,
Where formless light forsakes the beyond
And the quest achieves its reach.

The Primal Runes are the alphabet and the grammar of the plot of archetypal experience. In some way or another, all true poets have felt and acknowledged the magical power of the Muse, creative energies whose source the ancients believed to be the Moon, the Goddess. What is this Primal Power? In looking back over a number of prophetic pieces of writing that came to me in the bardic way, one in particular approaches the answer:

I am that Primal Force
Moving in wind and water,
I am Lord of the Mystic Deep,
The Sovereign Eye that visions forth
Creation and dissolution,
I Am That I Am.
I am the script and the reader,

The subtle movement of mind;
I am the tracery of fate in the ether,
The ascent and the fall;
I am that, and more.
I Am That I Am.
I am the eternal life,
And I am the change called death.
What moves and moves not
Inheres in me,
And touches m not.
I Am That I Am.
I am war and harmony,
I am music and destruction;
Light and dark abide in me,
The high, the low, and the wide sweep,
The mortal and the immortal.
I Am That I Am.

In deep contemplation, one can enter a state of consciousness where all that exists is this Primal Being, and one knows IT as one's own Self. Only much later, when one comes down from the heights of mystical experience, is it possible to find words for what has been known, felt and seen.

When the primal force touches the heart and the mind, what happens? It is a touch of fire, an illumination of understanding and will that brings on the urge to press forward. Something of this archetypal momentum can be felt in these words:

Let Us Go

Weave the dream in the fire
In the heat in the ancient desire
And feel the magic burning, burning,
Higher and higher and higher.
Feel the spirit arise
In the gleam in the eye of your eyes
And see the ancient power climbing
Up from the earth to the skies.
Once there were forests high and noble,
Once there were rivers clear,

> Once there were springs where ancient music
> Sang for all to hear.
> Once there was time to dream the magic,
> Once there were dreams to see,
> Once there was fire to feed the spirit
> Strong and true and free.
> Alas, the times are changing fast
> And the fire is burning low;
> In my heart I hear the music calling,
> Come now, let us go.
> Far away and far to go now, come now, let us go;
> Far away and far to go now, come now, let us go.

In *The Primal Runes*, I have reached back into an age of high and noble forests, clear rivers and springs where ancient music sang for all to hear. I have gathered up a long forgotten wisdom tradition founded in signs and sounds discovered at the dawn of human history, and based on the waxing and waning phases of the Moon.

In this final chapter, I am coming back to the music heard and unheard which is constantly being woven by the working of the lunar law in our earthly experience. Even now, when so much history separates us from those earliest times, the powers of magic are at work in the sky and in nature. Those who are touched by the Moon, or who can open to the Goddess in any of Her forms, or in Her formless aspect, will be awakened to a new depth and richness of life. They will become poets, musicians, prophets and sages. For the Goddess pours Her powers out on all who can approach Her the right way. The Primal Runes are one embodiment of the wisdom of the Divine Mother. Taken together as a complete family of energies, whether used for pathworking, divination or invocation, these most ancient runes embody the wisdom of the Moon. Their sounds awaken the soul to its timeless destiny, and their symbols point the way forward through time to a higher plane of consciousness and realisation. If I have selected a few poetic or prophetic pieces from my own writing, it has been to illustrate by first-hand examples how this can indeed happen in the life of one who awakens the process and experiences it first hand. When I say that the Muse changes life and consciousness, it is a testimony of personal experience. There are so many pieces of harp music (as on my CD, *Bard of Hearts*) and so many poems to choose from to illustrate how the bardic inspiration works that the only challenge has been what to leave out. The poems alone could fill a book almost as long as this one. However, in my own personal experience, it is actually in composing and playing harp music that I come closest to capturing and expressing the inspiration of the Muse. Harp music comes very close indeed to being a language of pure feeling, but it cannot, alas, be shared by mere words on a printed page.

We are all gifted with the powers of the Primal Runes. For most of us, these talents and powers lie latent. But they *can* be awakened and actualized. The publication of this book means that magical tools for attunement to the ancient archetypes are within your reach. I wish each of you who feel called to explore the Primal Runes the very best of good fortune. I know we are truly spiritual brothers and sisters going forward together into a future where Providence intends that all good and noble things will become attainable. Merely to look up at the night time sky and see the light of the Moon shining down with silver radiance is to feel, in the core of the being, that although the ancient magic may have dimmed over the centuries, it has never left us. It is here. It is only waiting for us to say "YES!" and it will spring to life once again, to guide us on the long journey home to our Eternal Source.

APPENDIX 1

Old Europe

Between 7,000 and 6,000 BC, agriculture became well established along the river Danube. By the first half of the sixth millennium, five regional variations of the Old Europe civilization had evolved: 1) The middle Danube, 2) the eastern Balkans, 3) the Aegean and central Balkans, 4) the Adriatic and 5) the Ukrainian (or Moldova-west). Among these regions there was a commonly held pattern of Neolithic (new stone age) culture, with distinctive local variations. This civilization continued to prosper well into the copper age (5,500 BC), developing its own self-generated sources of societal organization, art, and a distinctive set of graphic symbols which seem to be the earliest instance of linear writing of which we have evidence. Earlier agricultural urban centres can be found at Catal Huyuk in Turkey and Jericho in Palestine, but in neither of them do we find evidence of writing.

Agriculture in Old Europe was controlled by women. They would also have been in charge of ritual and ceremonial activities relating to fertility, sowing and harvesting. Men, on the other hand would take care of hunting and its rituals. The relationship between men and women seems to have been egalitarian rather than hierarchic, as it later became after the Indo-European invasions. It is easy to understand why an agricultural society would evolve a world-view centred on the Great Goddess. The abundance of female figurines which we find from the third to the sixth millennia BC indicate that women had a prominent, or even dominant role in the religious rituals.

As the sixth millennium progresses, we find evidence of sheep, goats, cows and pigs being raised. Small towns with stone houses develop, along with plantations of fig and olive trees and even vineyards. A site south of Kiev dated to the first half of the fourth millennium BC had about 700 acres of houses and a population of about 20,000 people. Copper, gold and silver were being mined at this period of time, and by the Bronze Age, there is evidence of alloys made with arsenic or tin and the "lost wax" technique of metal casting. All of this was present two thousand years before the rise of the Mesopotamian civilizations. "Through the late fifth and early fourth millennia all aspects of material culture from pottery and houses to figurines and settlement organization demonstrate attempts to use materials to naturalize and mark out the position of women in the domestic context."[1] Artistic forms persisted from the Late Neolithic into and beyond the Copper and Bronze ages, some of them such as the spiral or the meander being traceable even as far back as the Paleolithic age.[2] It is this persistence and continuity of basic forms stretching over millennia which allows us to connect this earliest civilization to the classical world of Greece and Rome, and thence to our own modern culture.

One of the most interesting sources of ancient forms is the set of symbols used for writing. "Archaeology," writes Harald Haarmann, "has confirmed that the pre-Indo-European population in southeastern Europe possessed a script, and that writing was a cultural institution in its own right. ... Inscribed objects from the sixth, fifth and fourth millennia BC have been found in more than two dozen places."[3] The so-called Vinca script stands out as possibly the earliest example we know of a set of symbols used for writing. Many of the signs have exact counterparts in the better known Cretan Linear A script, suggesting a link or cultural affinity between these two regions which may extend as far back as the Neolithic age. The popular misconception that writing originated in Mesopotamia is still prevalent, but the archaeological evidence proves that in fact the oldest script originated in Europe.

From the very beginning, the signs used in Old European writing seem to have been associated with religious ideas, which would include what we today might call cosmology, philosophy, magic, ritual, divination, shamanism and healing. Of course, what we know as religion simply did not exist then. All life was lived in a magical cosmology in which the shaman would be an oracle, healer, teacher, historian and counselor. The script would be a shamanic tool with magical overtones and with applications for divination as well as communication. But the frequency with which it was used on goddess figurines, which were then discarded, suggests that it was a tool for communicating with the gods. It may have served to convey their messages to earth as well as to send wishes and prayers up to the celestial spheres (or deep below to the chthonic deities). We know that there was a cult devoted to the ancestors, that ritual was important in many or all aspects of life, and that holy places were set aside for the rites. The grandiose temple architecture which we find in later Mesopotamia and Egypt did not, however, develop in the culture of Old Europe.

Virtually all the objects which bear signs of the old script played some role in the rituals associated with the Goddess cult. It has to be borne in mind that this was a period of time prior to the advent of the Indo-European sky gods and the patriarchal institutions that history has described in the Mesopotamian and Greek worlds. The Goddess took many forms. It is believed that the small statuettes featuring prominent hips and breasts are showing her as the embodiment of fertility. More than 90 percent of all figurines found in Southeast Europe between 3,500 and 6,000 BC are female.[4] Much of the pottery is also designed to suggest a connection with the Goddess. This is the oldest and original cult of the Goddess, predating its later appearances in the Middle East. Shrines of the Great Goddess and ritual objects related to her worship have been found in many places in Southeastern Europe. Even houses had shrines, some of which have been excavated and studied.[5] We also have clay models of sanctuaries and temples, some of which prefigure later temple designs in Mesopotamia.

Ages of Upheaval

The civilization of Old Europe flourished for two thousand years, from 6,500 BC to 4,500 BC. Then, suddenly, it was shaken to its core by the arrival of Aryan (also called Indo-European) peoples from the east. In Marija Gimbutas's view, these invading Kurgan tribes entered the area of Old Europe in three successive waves, the first lasting from about 4,300 to 4,200 BC, the second from 3,400 to 3,200 BC, and the third from 3,000 to 2,800 BC. They imposed a culture that she characterized as 'stratified, pastoral, mobile and war-oriented' in contrast to the characteristically agricultural, sedentary, egalitarian and peaceful cultures they conquered. The invaders had a hierarchically organized society with male priesthoods and warrior castes who held positions of dominance. They were taller, stronger and better armed than the peoples of the goddess culture. Gradually, the latter were pushed to the periphery of the Old Europe cultural homeland, and came to occupy the Cyclades islands, Crete, Cyprus and a few coastal regions along the Adriatic shore and Anatolia. After about 2,500 BC, the cosmology of Old Europe, including Greece and Anatolia, had become a mixture of the invaders' dominant male deities and solar mythology with some elements of the old goddess religion. The two systems, the indigenous Old European and invading Indo European co-existed and blended to become the culture celebrated by Homer and epitomized in Classical Greece.

The Minoan culture was a kind of rebirth of the Old Europe goddess tradition. On the isle of Crete, three phases of this civilization flourished. Early Minoan, also called Pre-palatial, to about 2,000 BC; Middle Minoan or Early Palatial from 2,000 to 1,600 BC and Late Minoan from 1,600 to 1150 BC. In the middle period, the Minoans used a script called Linear A which has never been deciphered. Between 1,600 and 1,450 BC, the Mycenaeans on the mainland imported a script known as Linear B, which was an early form of Greek. After 1,450 BC, the Mycenaeans became dominant in Crete and by 1,150 BC, the arrival of the Dorians on the mainland had brought their culture to an end.

Both Linear A and the Cypriot script have many resemblances to the Old Europe script. In fact, most scholars believe that both are based on it. In an earlier table, we have seen the high degree of correspondence between the Old Europe script and the Cypriot script and there is a strong possibility that the symbols and their corresponding sounds remained associated continuously back to the very earliest times.

Fig. 5: Map of Old Europe

Pelasgian inscriptions found on the Island of Lemnos suggest that these people referred to themselves as SAKA, and their Sky god was known as "SAIS". It would seem that the Greek god "Zeus" is simply a Hellenized version of the older Pelasgian deity. The ancient shrine of "Zeus of Dodona" is thus the Pelasgian SAIS (who is likely the 'Ais' of the Etruscans, also known as 'AYAS' in Central Asia). The Pelasgians are referred to by Homer, Herodotus, Hesiod and others as the indigenous people who lived in Greece before the arrival of the Greeks themselves. There is a tradition that Pythagoras was Pelasgian by birth, and that the Pelasgians were the last remnants of the peoples who preserved the culture of the goddess in the face of the Greek invasions. It is quite certain that a great deal of Greek mythology (particularly tales of the Greek goddesses) has its roots in the traditions of Old Europe.

We are on fairly solid ground in affirming that the ancient scripts of Old Europe, Crete (particularly Linear A) and Cyprus were a significant repository of the goddess' ancient esoteric lore.

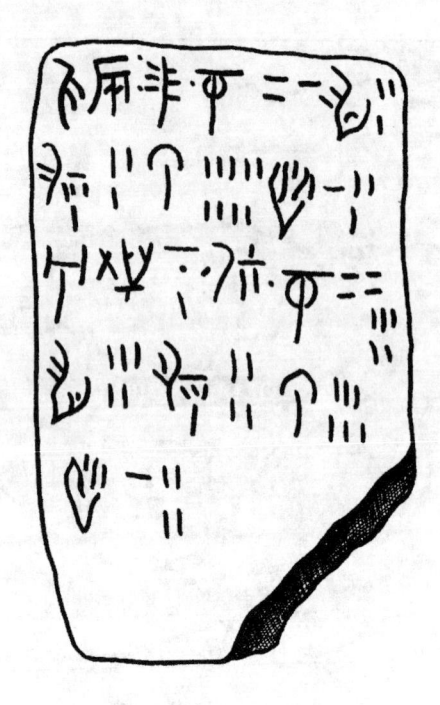

Fig. 6: Linear A Sample

In Old Europe, these signs had a strongly religious association and for the most part were used in sacred rituals. Somewhat modified, they were still in use, at least on the isle of Cyprus, practically until the time of Alexander the Great. It is our great good fortune to have sufficient information to match the Cyprus Script with the Old Europe Script and to know the corresponding sounds. The Cyprus Script was an awkward tool for transliterating the Greek tongue, so when Greeks became dominant in the region, it soon died out. We do not know the language for which it was originally designed, but it was probably not an Indo-European tongue. It could very well have been one of the dialects of the so-called Pelasgians.

---

[1] Hodder, I. *Theory and Practice in Archaeology* (London, 1992).
[2] Gimbutas, M. *The Language of the Goddess* (San Francisco, 1989).
[3] Haarmann, H *Early Civilization and Literacy in Europe*, (Berlin, 1996), pg. 16.
[4] Markotic, V. *The Vinca Culture* (Calgary, 1984) pg. 145.
[5] Gimbutas, M. *The Gods and Goddesses of Old Europe* 7,000 to 3,500 BC (London, 1974) pg. 81.

APPENDIX 2

A Sacred Script

The Old Europe script was used on objects associated with burial-rites as well as votive offerings and pottery associated with religious rituals. It was also used on objects such as spindle whorls and loom weights. In ancient cultures there is a well known connection between spinning, weaving, divination and the theme of fate. Spiritual or religious rites were often practiced in the home.

One inscribed object in particular has received a great deal of attention. A spherical stone found at Lepenski Vir has its surface area divided into forty roughly square segments, and etched into most of these segments are found varied symbols from the Old Europe script. It is not understood how the stone was used, but inscribed turtle shells from ancient China which were quite similar in appearance are known to have been used for divination. The Lepenski Vir stone is the oldest case of writing being used on an object whose function was likely to have been divination.

Most inscriptions consist of one, two or several signs, but when there are more they are arranged in a linear fashion, which suggests writing. The fact that signs were used in isolation suggests that they were symbolic, referring perhaps to one or another aspect of the sacred cosmology which underpinned the cult rituals. We do know many of the basic concepts of the Old European world view and it is thoroughly religious. But we may never be able to decipher the meanings of individual signs because the languages of Pre-Indo-European peoples died out in the centuries following the invasion. Everything we do know suggests that the inscribed objects were used by shamans, priests, worshippers or devotees of the Great Goddess. The Old Europe script seem to have constituted set of symbols of cosmological significance which had application in magic, ritual and divination. It was a sacred script which died out long before it was ever turned to profane or economic purposes such as the earliest scripts we find in Mesopotamia.

The Old European script was frequently set down in a linear fashion, which means it could be "read" from left to right (or possibly from right to left). The limited repertoire of root signs is elaborated, developed and graphically embellished to arrive at over two hundred derivative signs. Many of the primal root signs, such as "X" or "M" or "V" or "O" come down directly from Paleolithic times. The script is full of sacred and geometrical symbols, most of which are abstract rather than illustrative of natural motifs. The illustrative signs seem to depict plants, animals, humans, rivers, the sun, the moon, or simple tools such as we might expect to find in the late Neolithic or the Copper Ages. Because the script was in part pictographic, we can assume that the image of a plant, for example, refers to a plant, and similarly that other naturalistic symbols refer to the things they seem to depict. Sometimes, two signs are blended together to form a composite sign, or ligature, joining, as we speculate, the separate meanings of the originals into a new meaning. For example, "bird" plus "dog" might become "bird-dog".

Strokes and dots were used, possibly to indicate the plural form of certain nouns, or multiples of the object being designated. But there could have been other forms of inflection or alteration of meaning intended by such "diacritical" marks.

The Old European script was actively in use from about 5,300 BC until 3,500 BC. Indo-European pastoralists known as the Kurgan culture pushed into the Danube basin and northern Greece in three waves. The first lasted from about 4,400 to 4,300 BC; the second wave occurred in 3,500 BC; and the third wave took place in about 3,000 BC. The Old European culture was replaced between 3,500 BC and 3,000 BC by the culture of the invaders, and the cult of the Great Goddess began its slow decline. The archaeological record during this period shows "a drastic reduction of religious images in the visual arts."(Gimbutas, 1989, pg. 318) Many Old European settlements were abandoned, and the archaeological record shows that many agriculturally unfavourable locations such as caves, and coastal stretches near the Aegean sea were occupied, likely by the displaced Old European populations. During this period, which was a kind of Dark Age, the old religious rituals, imagery and associated decorative arts fell into decline. Use of the sacred script, which was closely associated with the cult of the Goddess, also declined and eventually disappeared. The signs were probably so closely associated with the rituals and beliefs of the conquered people, with their strong female elements, that the newcomers found it easiest to reject and ignore the system altogether. The story of how Delphi was once a Goddess oracle is well known. Greek myths tell how Apollo came and slew its sacred snake (a goddess symbol) and became proprietor of the place – a tale in all probability often repeated during this time of invasion and displacement.

There is considerable evidence, however, to suggest that some of the Old European cosmology, tradition and writing was inherited by the Cretans and Myceneans as well as Cycladic island-dwellers and even Troy in Asia Minor has yielded articles inscribed with very similar symbols. The Cretan Linear A script in particular seems to have borrowed many signs from the Vinca script, as even a cursory comparison of the two will indicate. Neither Linear A, nor the language of the Minoans who used it has yet been deciphered.

It is of some considerable significance to western students of religion and spirituality to consider that our most ancient ancestors created a symbolic script devoted almost entirely to sacred purposes, and that it was in active use for over two thousand years between the middle of the sixth and the middle of the fourth millennia BC. Scholarly thinking and research in the past has asserted just the opposite, that the light of learning and spirituality was imported into Europe from the East. While the spirit of the West has for much of its history been characterized as secular, materialistic and militaristic, it must now be admitted that prior to the Indo European invasions, just the opposite was true. The Old European civilization seems to have had a focus on the sacred, to have created living conditions of relative peace for two millennia, and to have finally fallen victim to warlike invaders *from the East.*

The fact that early writing in Europe was used almost exclusively for religious and magical purposes, and that it died out before being widely put to any other use, means that it remains a set of pure archetypes whose spirit has never been profaned. And this is not likely to change because scholars have no way, using the ordinary methods of research, to determine what the symbols mean. If the purity of a symbol derives in part from the uses to which it has been put (witness the degradation of the sacred swastika by the Nazis), then the Old Europe script is likely to remain an essentially sacred set of cosmological symbols which preserve their spirit until they are again put to active use.

On the surface this would seem to be something of considerable interest to western students of the esoteric. It is this same character of *primal, sacred integrity* which has made the Viking runes popular in recent decades. Not only are these runes regularly used for divination, magic, and sacred ritual by all kinds of people interested in such things, but they are part of a widespread revival of Germanic Paganism which is active both in Europe and North America. The FUTHARK runes seem to preserve their intimate connection with the living spiritual archetypes of ancient Teutonic peoples.

We might speculate that a more ancient sacred script, which existed in Europe prior to its invasion by outsiders, might similarly be a point of contact with the cult of the Great Goddess and her manifestations. If we discover the core meanings of the symbols, we could put them to use once more, and this might help to bring about a revival of the earliest spiritual traditions of the West.

People everywhere are hungry to know the true story of their earliest roots and origins. A loss of connectedness with ancient tradition, and in particular Pwith *sacred* tradition, and with *nature*, characterizes the malaise of many people in the West. The decline of institutional religion (itself a relatively recent development in history) may indicate that our churches and their scriptures can no longer answer this need and respond to this hunger which people have. On the other hand, popular fiction and cinema like *Lord of the Rings*, which tells a story about the spiritual forces at work in our mythic past, have proved to be vastly popular. One survey has concluded that Tolkein's masterpiece is widely considered to be the greatest piece of writing in the twentieth century. Could this be because it fills a spiritual need?

APPENDIX 3

Cultic Symbols

Those who mastered and used the symbols of the Old European Script, likely a small number of priests or shamans, would have a tool of extraordinary power to enhance their importance and influence in society. Mastery of these signs, and the powers they signified, would enable such initiates to communicate with the goddess and her manifestations and to invoke her assistance and blessings. Religion was not separated from magic at this early point in history. Words and signs of power, and the rituals in which they were embedded, could be used to influence the heavenly powers in the skies above or the earthly powers deep below and to bring about favourable results as needed. The rune-magic might also be used adversely against an enemy. Although the Old European society seems to have been remarkably egalitarian, the mastery of this script could have created a small elite with considerable influence. The cosmology of ancient Europe and the world-view of primitive societies gave heavy emphasis to mystery, mysticism and magic, and a shaman or priest would have known much about healing, divination, ritual, tribal history, the traditional myths, and practical counseling. To our way of thinking, he or she would have been a "jack of all trades". But to know the mindset of those who used the Old European Script, we must firstly understand the Great Goddess and Her Cult.

All available evidence (meaning the artifacts on which we find the script) suggests that it was used to communicate messages of religious significance. But we must remember that the division of life into two categories, sacred and profane, is a relatively recent development in history. In ancient Europe from the end of the

Ice Age to the arrival of the Indo-Europeans, the inscribed symbols were used to represent the names of the Goddess, or her titles. It could also be used for magical formulas, or ritualistic verses, or talismanic symbols of power. It is believed that the signs may have been used also for divination, for protection, for calling down blessings or to invoke the presence of the goddess or the god in the course of specific rituals. Only rarely might the script be used to convey a story or a description or to set down an economic record.

The religion of early Europe focused on "chthonic and lunar spiritual principles strongly related to female divinity. The images portrayed were impregnated with the richness of the earth and were as cyclical as the moon."[1] Because the Old European script is found most often inscribed or painted on objects used in the Goddess cult, we suppose that the names of the Goddess, her attributes, her powers, privileges and functions are their most likely subject matter. The Great Mother ruled over life and the afterlife. She imparted energy for life's continuance and for its regeneration. She set the rhythm of the seasons and brought down the rains which provided crops and human sustenance. The core symbols refer mostly to these and other themes of a primarily sacred nature.

Many miniature sculptures of the goddess in stone, horn or bone have been found in the region between Siberia and southern France, over three thousand in total, and these date back as early as 27,000 BC. There are virtually no instances in Paleolithic art of a father figure.[2] The Neolithic age saw the invention of ceramics, in approximately in 6,500 BC, and from this point on we have thousands of figurines and vases as well as many ritual articles, all fashioned from clay. All of these help us to decipher the icons associated with the Goddess. Many of the images are continuous from Paleolithic times. Marija Gimbutas has summarized our knowledge of this field in her work *The Language of the Goddess*, a definitive contribution to the subject. From her research, and from others who have carried on the work since her death in the early 1990's, we have arrived at a good understanding of the basic elements of the Goddess Cult, the main elements of which can be summarized in outline.

The Goddess is Nature herself. Her representations in art

seem to come in four main categories. First, we have a personification of the generative forces of nature. In this function, the goddess presided over reproduction, birth-giving, maintenance of life and health, and the activation of life energy. Secondly, the Goddess represents the destructive aspects of nature. In this role, she is Goddess of Death and her symbols include a poisonous snake, or a bird of prey such as a vulture or raven. Thirdly, as mistress of regeneration, she manages the life cycles of the cosmos. In this manifestation, her symbols include the pubic triangle, the uterus, the fetus, and such animal totems as the toad, frog, hedgehog and bull, as well as triangles and double triangles. It is also believed that when she is represented as a bee, butterfly or moth that her regenerative powers are being expressed. Lastly, she stands behind the children to whom she has given birth, including the male deities whose death and resurrection are part of the symbolic drama of nature's life-cycle. But such male deities make up only three to five percent of Neolithic sculpture.[3]

---

[1] Haarmann, H. *Early Civilization and Literacy in Europe*, (Berlin, 1996), pg. 16.
[2] Gimbutas, M. *The Civilization of the Goddess*, (San Francisco, 1991), pg 222.
[3] Ibid. pg. 223.

APPENDIX 4

The Lunar Law

"I understand the enigmatic words in the stone engravings from the days before the Flood."

– Assurbanipal, the last king of Assyria

*I*n ancient times, poetry was intimately related to divination and magic. Over the centuries and millennia, things have changed so much that in our day and age, we can hardly understand how this might be. When we begin to study the fundamentals of ancient divination, its relation to word-magic, to myth and to poetry begins to become clear. We begin to see that they all were linked and synthesized into a comprehensive traditional wisdom so that it is hardly possible to alter any of the parts and preserve the integrity of the whole.

Robert Graves has done an excellent job of explaining this interconnectedness in *The White Goddess*, which he calls "a historical grammar of the language of poetic myth". His thesis is that "the language of poetic myth anciently current in the Mediterranean and Northern Europe was a magical language bound up with popular religious ceremonies in honour of the Moon-goddess, or Muse."(pg 9) The Indo-European invasions which took place in waves between roughly 4,300 BC and 2,800 BC, remodeled or altered many of the primal myths and changed the social structure from matrilinear to patriarchal. Marija Gimbutas writes:

> The repeated disturbances and incursions by Kurgan people (whom I view as Proto-Indo-European) put an end to the Old European culture roughly between 4300 and

2800 BC, changing it from gylanic to androcratic and from matrilineal to patrilineal. The Aegean and Mediterranean regions and western Europe escaped the process the longest; there, especially in the islands such as Thera, Crete, Malta and Sardinia, Old European culture flourished in an enviably peaceful and creative civilization until 1500 BC., a thousand to 1500 years after central Europe had been thoroughly transformed. Nevertheless, the Goddess religion and its symbols survived as an undercurrent in many areas. Actually, many of these symbols are still present as images in our art and literature, powerful motifs in our myths and archetypes in our dreams. We are still living under the sway of that aggressive male invasion and only beginning to discover our long alienation from our authentic European Heritage – gylanic, nonviolent, earth-centred culture.

– *The Language of the Goddess*, pg. xx

The early Greek philosophers rationalized mythology and poetic language. They placed poetry under the patronage of Apollo, winnowing out much of its ancient, magical empowerment. Socrates in particular rejected early Greek mythology and encouraged scientific rigour in thinking. By his time, the inner sense of most myths from pre-Indo-European times had been lost, although the Greeks continued to illustrate mythology and to mentioned it in poetry.

For Robert Graves, the function of poetry has always, at its deepest level, been "religious invocation of the Muse" Its use is "the experience of mixed exaltation and horror that her presence excites." (TWG, 14) To understand why such evocations have this primal power that we can feel in our very bones and nerves, we must turn back the pages of history to a very distant time indeed when the Great Mother had unchallenged primacy in the minds and hearts of humanity. The symbols of Old Europe are our most direct link to a culture in which the Great Mother could be experienced as a living power and presence. She was the Earth which gave life and eventually buried it, and she was the Moon, who measured and fixed the life-cycles and the destinies of all beings. In fact, the changing phases of the lunar cycle were and are the primal tale of birth, growth, challenge, initiation, waning, death and rebirth, the core paradigm of all mythology and cosmology.

Robert Graves contends that a true poem is necessarily an invocation of the presence and the power of the Great Mother, and the evidence of its truth is the effect it has on the listener of awe and wonder. The primal story which poetry tells concerns the birth, life, death and resurrection of the Son of the Goddess. This character may be a child, lover or heroic warrior. In facing the destiny he is born to, he struggles with his blood-brother, his other self, his weird, and as the year wanes, he goes down to defeat in a losing battle with his inevitable fate. For the love of the Threefold Goddess who is mother, bride and death-dealer, the hero-son struggles against overwhelming odds, and in the end he embraces or accepts his own death. According to Graves, this tale has thirteen phases and an epilogue, and all true poetry celebrates some incident or scene in its primal plot. The goddess is there at every stage of the tale, since the pattern-of-the-whole is a working out of the destiny she weaves.

According to Graves, when a poet successfully evokes the presence of The Goddess, the listener may feel his or her hair stand on end, the throat may seem to constrict, and the pulse quicken. It is She who abides in the Moon's magic, in the wind's lonely song on the high hills, in the distant bark of dogs on a frosty night, in the hooting of the owl and in all primal, oracular and archetypal epiphanies. Such experiences speak to our innate sense of ancient, magical presence. This numinous power is The Goddess Herself, for she manifests still in all her mystical influence.

"Many myths of the Moon", according to Jules Cashford, *(The Moon, Myth and Image),* "are structured on the distinction between the phases and the cycle, which is also the distinction between the parts and the whole." He continues:

> Yet the etymology of the word 'phase', which comes from the Greek *phaino*, 'to show', suggests that the primary distinction is that between the invisible cycle and the visible phase through which the cycle is manifested. This essential paradox, which leads the mind beyond the frame of the senses, is that the cycle, the whole, is invisible yet

> contains the visible phases, as though the visible comes out of and falls back into the invisible - like being born and dying and being born again.
>
> – (TMMI, 31)

Astrology speaks to us of cycles, while mythology speaks through the actions of characters. But it is the richness of the Moon Mother that has furnished their form and process, fixity and flow. The Primal Runes of Old Europe came to exist in a worldview where The Goddess, through her lunar epiphany, created fate, time and all the players on the earthly stage. These runes express various phases and aspects of this lunar paradigm. Eternity enters into the flux of mutability, and the unfolding of time becomes a story. What we might call "The Lunar Law" gives the Primal Runes coherence, pattern, context, plot, and power. The Moon gives birth to time in such a way that it also proposes how to live that time through its cyclic phases, and when the law is followed man achieves harmony with the heavenly order. The Moon suggests how time may be transformed into ritual. By means of ritual, flux and mortality can be made transparent to the eternal Source, thereby being redeemed and elevated into revelations of a timeless Truth.

The Primal Runes objectify the Moon's ritual progression through phases of brilliance and obscurity. They reveal how earthbound consciousness can participate in the unfolding of the divine plan and thereby achieve a higher destiny. In one lunar month, the Moon reveals an alternation of waxing and waning, blessing and challenge, light and darkness, fullness and loss, glory and decay. To know and live the hidden harmony of this woven destiny is wisdom, and one who masters the law of The Goddess transcends the pull of mortality. The knower of the rune lore becomes a seer, a sage, a bard or a prophet. He has the keys to the symbols and can reveal their hidden power and knowledge, which is that of The Goddess Herself, to the uninitiated.

The Lunar Law held sway, so the ancients believed, over the entire sublunary manifestation. In the worldview of our earliest ancestors, Earth and Moon were one manifestation in dual aspect. The image of the Moon reflected in a pool of water perfectly

THE LUNAR LAW **323**

expresses this. The Moon determined and measured such processes as birth, fecundity, growth, destiny, death and rebirth. The Lunar cross, a widely used design in Neolithic pottery, expresses the division of the agricultural year into four seasons that follow the fourfold cycle of the Moon – Waxing (Spring), Full (Summer), Waning (Autumn) and Dark Moon (Winter). Against this backdrop, the mythic protagonist experiences the phases of a heroic life. The lunar cross is also a picture of a lunar month divided into four weeks, and these have seven days each. Although the exact time that the moon takes to travel round the earth is 27.3 days, and the exact time it takes to move through its cycle of a (Synodic) month is 29.5 days, ancient custom settled on 28 days as the archetypal lunation cycle. The Babylonians, Hindus, Buddhists, Persians, Copts, Arabs and Chinese all divided the wheel of the zodiac into 28 houses of the Moon. When the 28 days of the lunar month are arranged in a circle, and the circle is divided into four parts by a cross at its centre, the result is four units of seven days. Seven became the number of days in the month, and of course the days were named after the seven known planets.

Jules Cashford gives a very interesting summary of just how deeply our ideas of measure are related to the Moon:

> The oldest Indo-Aryan root connected with the heavenly bodies is the root *me*, which means 'Moon', and becomes in Sanskrit *mas*, or *masas,* meaning 'Moon', and 'month', while *mami* means 'I measure', *mati* means a 'measure', and *matram* is an instrument for measuring; *ma* means 'time' and 'Moon'. *Ma* or *matar* also means 'mother', in the sense, perhaps that the mother is the mind and measure of all things for the child, as the primordial Mother is for the race and the Great Mother is for the universe. This is the root of all the subsequent Indo-European languages relating to both Moon and measurement: Greek *mene,* Moon; *men*, month; *metron,* a means of measuring; *metreo*, I measure. Latin, *mensis*, month, *menaeus,* monthly, from which comes *mensura,* measurement, *menstruus,* monthly, *metiri,* to measure and (surprisingly) *mensa,* table for a meal (held at regular, measurable times)... In Old

> English, *mona* is Moon, *monath* is month, *metan* is to measure and *maeth* is a measure.
>
> – *The Moon, Myth and Image*, pgs. 40-41

The ancients believed that the Great Mother, whose epiphany the Moon was, and is, not only measured time, but actually *made* time, and ultimately *was* time, as well as the *source* of time, which is to say, eternity. From the very beginning, the magical idea of tapping a power higher than man is connected to the notation of time. Time, for the ancients, signified not merely a neutral measuring tool, as it does for us, but also a sense of infused value that gives life meaning. The Lunar Law established not only the *measure* of time, but more significantly, its *quality*. It explained why certain times favour certain kinds of endeavour, while other times were less favourable. From the very beginning, the Moon's role in telling time extended to infusing time with its intrinsic meaning. Earthly affairs then became imbued with the energy that the Moon radiated through varying phases and cycles.

One well attested example of lunar meaning can be seen in North America, where the Sioux and Chippewa tribes divided the year into 12 lunar months to which they gave qualitative names. April was The Moon of the Plants; May was The Moon of Flowers; June was The Warm Moon; July was The Moon of the Roebuck; August was the Moon of the Sturgeon; September was the Moon of Corn; October was the Moon of Journeys, and so on. This same attribution of quality to time, (along with measure), is widely evident when the Lunar Law prevailed. The Primal Runes emerge from this worldview where time, its cycles of changing quality, its measure and its meaning, were governed by the Moon.

The first five Primal Runes, from Field to Thunder speak of beginnings. There is hope for things to come, and a tenuous but growing grasp of earthly processes of increase. From Growth to Karma, the runes move through varied kinds experience, showing a general movement beyond the heaviness of Earth into the fullness of Fire. When Fire energy is amplified to its maximum, the runes Creativity and Grace make their presence felt. Then in the house of Air, there is a time of brilliance and fruition. From Love to Lake, this is a phase of glorious possibilities. The light is at its maximum and many dreams can be realised. From Lake to

Mountain, there is first a sharing or giving of the attainments to the world at large, and then a coming to terms with loss and decay. The light is diminishing, and the individual feels a need to discover life's deepest meaning as the life-energy recedes. Runes Mountain through Merging move inevitably toward the dark latency of The Field, where at last a new birth will take place. The Darkness of this time is like an underground cave where the earth mysteries are celebrated in utmost secrecy to restore life and prepare for a new cycle of its manifestation. This is the pattern of sublunar destiny woven by Primal Light and Primal Dark, runes that signify the warp and woof of Fate. Their interaction through twenty eight phases of a lunar month supplies the fabric from which human lives are stitched together, either with grace and wisdom, or in ignorance and desperation, according to the individual's mastery of the eternal Law.

Thoth was a Moon god of the ancient Egyptians, but he was also a god of wisdom and a regulator of fate and individual destiny. In *The Egyptian Hermes*, Garth Fowden writes: "So important were the moon's phases in determining the rhythms of Egyptian national life that Thoth came to be regarded as the origin of both cosmic order and of religious and civil institutions."(p 22) Thoth presided over the civil year, law, temple cults and sacred rituals, texts and sacred formulae (spells). He would have been the god of runes, if the Egyptians had used them, because the Moon, and her ninefold Muses, were widely understood in the ancient Mediterranean world to be the Mother of arcane wisdom. We do not know if the culture of Old Europe had a figure who was the equivalent of Thoth, but we can be fairly sure that broad similarities were present, because the Mediterranean and Mesopotamian cultures for which we *do* have evidence reveal significantly parallel patterns.

The word "rune" comes from Old English and the Old Germanic languages. The modern English word "rune" derives from the Old English *run*. The common Germanic root word *run* has the idea of mystery and secrecy. The Gothic word *runa* signifies "divine mysteries" and in Old High German the words *runa* and *giruni* have similar meanings. In Old Norse the plural word *runar* suggests "secret lore" or "mysteries". In Old Irish, *run* means secret; in Middle Welsh the word *rhin* means "magic charm" and the Finnish *runo* means "song" or "invocation". All these senses enter into our modern English word rune, suggesting a set of spiritual mysteries of a whispered kind that counsel esoteric wisdom by means of secret scripts, symbols or messages. We find similar understandings in the most ancient Mediterranean sources. The word "hieroglyphs" means, in Greek, sacred writings, also known as 'the words of the gods'. They were said to have been written originally by Thoth, with his own fingers, an appropriate role for a god who was at once scribe and the resurrecting Moon. As for the sacred signs of Old Europe, they are the oldest of all known runes, many being in constant use from Paleolithic times. We have no written documents from the time prior to the Aryan invasions. Thus our insights into early runes, their meanings and their uses, must rest largely on what remained of the Goddess legacy in the centuries and millennia following the Indo-European invasions.

For the well known Elder Futhark Runes of Northern Europe, which came into prominence about 2,000 years ago, we have the story of Odin, who hung on a tree upside down day after day to win the rune-lore. Less well known, but closer in time and geography to the origin of the Primal Runes is the tale of Inanna, the Sumerian Goddess of the Moon, which tells how she brought the Tablets of Destiny (or *me*, moon, moon-wisdom) to mankind. It is quite possible that this tale, or its prototype, dates all the way back to the time of Catal Huyuk in Turkey, where archaeologists have found sanctuaries to the Goddess, virtually intact, as old as six or seven thousand years BC. Patricia Monaghan summarizes the tale of how Inanna brought the Tablets of Destiny (equivalent to runelore) back to earth in her book, *Goddesses and Heroines*. The story runs as follows:

> Across the immeasurable distances of the sweetwater abyss lived Enki, god of wisdom, and with him were the Tablets of Destiny and other magic civilizing implements. These were his treasures, and he kept them from humankind. But his daughter, the crafty queen of heaven, took pity on the miserable primitives of earth and fitted her boat to travel to her father's hall. There she was grandly welcomed with a banquet of food and wine. Wise he may have been,

but Enki lived his daughter beyond wisdom, so much that he took cup after cup from her at table and then, drunk, promised her anything she desired. Instantly Inanna asked for the Tablets of Destiny and 100 other objects of culture. What could a fond father do but grant the request? Inanna immediately loaded the objects onto the boat of heaven and set sail for her city, Erech. Awakening the next day from his stupor, Enki remembered what he had done – and regretted it. But he was incapacitated by a hangover as massive as the previous evening's pleasure, and he could not pursue his daughter until he recovered. By then, of course, Inanna had gained the safety of her kingdom, and even the seven tricks Enki played on her did not regain him his treasures.(p 160)

This tale of Inanna reveals a number of interesting details. For one thing, it suggests that The Tablets of Destiny were the root and origin of Sumerian culture. These were a gift from the Moon Goddess, and they were written down in a primal, magical script. Was some similar mythic tale extant in the culture of Old Europe, to explain the divine origin of the sacred signs? Some of the goddess myths from ancient Greece give hints of earlier times, just as the roots of language do. Myths of early peoples from Greece, Egypt, Mesopotamia and India suggest that culture and knowledge of divination were gifts of the Gods (or of The Goddess). Furthermore, archaeologists who have studied the runes of Old Europe mostly agree that they were a sacred script used primarily in rituals, and divination, and the reading of oracles.

Oracles are deliberately generated omens. Interestingly, the term omen comes from two words, *os* and *men,* meaning 'mouth of the Moon'. An omen is therefore an utterance of the Moon, which is to say, the Muse, or the Goddess. This is one example of how language may cast light on the observances and understandings of early times through the root meanings of words. To divine by means of runes would be understood in ancient times to mean seeking guidance from The Goddess, through her very own sacred signs and symbols, within the patterned framework of cyclic time which She Herself had spun and woven to govern creation.

Freya of the Norse runic tradition acts much like the primal

Great Goddess, of whom she is an aspect. Freya taught her magical arts to Odin, who attained the knowledge of the runes and the wisdom them embody for humanity. At one point, Freya had to descend to Svartalfheim, the land of the dark elves, to win a treasured golden girdle. Then, she ascended with her prize to the upper worlds to use the boon for a wider good. Through her pact with the gnomic fertility powers of the world below, she was able to bring fecundity to the land of Middle Earth. The treasured golden belt which she obtained from the dark underworld powers is the archetypal hidden treasure that can bring benefit and blessings to the world, and these blessings Freya generously dispenses after she attains the prize. As Odin's female counterpart, she is deeply immersed in the rune wisdom, and in many ways her epic quest parallels that of the Middle Eastern goddess Inanna.

Like the Futhark runes, the runes of the Goddess (which I call Primal Runes) are more than mere fortune-telling tools. They are signposts of the rich wisdom and cosmology of the ancient world. Each symbol opens portals into the primal mind and sheds light on the archaeology of man's earliest dreaming. Together, the thirty-one chosen rune-symbols constitute an entire wisdom constellation, a teaching of what the Goddess has to say and offer to her children.

Since the Moon allots human beings their quota of time, she is also the source of fate, the creator of destiny. She apportions the good and evil that any given life can embody, which is to say, the *quality* of the given time that a human being has at his or her disposal. The result of the creative activity of The Goddess is sometimes given runic representation as a net or web. The Moon is not only the spinner of the threads of time, but the weaver of the web of meanings and hidden patterns of potential that underpin and overarch the outer manifestations of the phenomenal world.

The three phases of a) lunar waxing, b) fullness and c) waning were interpreted from the earliest times as influences for firstly, growing up; secondly, achieving maturity; and thirdly, growing old, or waning. These were personified by the Greeks as separate goddesses. For example, in Hellenic times Artemis and Kore were goddesses of the Waxing Crescent Moon. Demeter, Hera, Aphrodite and Athene were goddesses of the Full Moon, and Hekate was a goddess of the Waning Moon.

Behind these goddesses loomed the three 'Fates', the *Moirai*, who were older than all the goddesses and gods. Originating in Greek mythology, but doubtless based on earlier traditions, the word *Moira* means 'part', 'share' or 'portion'. It refers to the action of the three phases of the moon, their triple role in assigning to mortals and gods their destiny, and destiny's three phases of beginning, middle and end. Three *Moirai* have different names and functions. *Klotho* spins the life-thread, *Lachesis* weaves its patterns of fate, determining the span of days, and *Atropos* cuts the thread of life with her shears. Homer calls the *Moirai* the 'Spinners', but sometimes he may also refer to a single goddess by using the term *Moira*, especially in contexts where fate means death. Even the gods cannot challenge the inevitability of fate.

The notion of the Moon as a spinner may not be obvious to us in this post-modern, technological age. But we can still look up into the evening sky and observe how the Moon does seem to ravel and unravel its light in a perpetual, cyclic pattern, perhaps suggesting the image of a spinning wheel. The image of Moon as spinner evolved in an age when women were responsible for making thread and fabric, in addition to managing many religious and divinatory activities. In archaeological finds at Old Europe sites dating back to six or seven thousand years BC, spindle whorls and pots are the objects most frequently engraved with primal runes. One of the most ancient symbols which we find inscribed on the earliest pottery is the above-mentioned net, which suggests a fabric of invisible threads binding human life to the inevitable patterns of birth, growth, decline, death and rebirth. The Moon generates, or weaves, the cosmic veil whose intersecting threads establish the knots of destiny. These are woven into the lives of individual human beings by the invisible power of The Goddess in her role of *Moira*. One way to gain an insight into the pattern of a human destiny is by means of divination. From the dawn of history, seekers have approached the Goddess through her oracular icons, casting or selecting the runes to ponder their meaning.

As with many other forms of divination, a moment of synchronicity is deliberately generated when one draws particular runes and "reads" them. Belief in synchronicity makes it possible to see correspondences between a randomly generated selection of runic symbols, and the unfolding events in the outer world. Through long observation, the sages of ancient times traced connections between the phases of the Moon and the patterns at work in the earthly world below. Although we are less observant of such connections and relations, and although much of this traditional wisdom has been lost and forgotten, the fundamental laws that govern the process are still as true and active in the inner world as they ever were. The archetypal energies of the Moon and the meanings they weave into our lives can be still be discerned in the Primal Runes if we understand and use them in the right way. With sound knowledge of tradition and a transparent attunement to invisible energies, we can become quite skilled in the use of these ancient glyphs for divination, initiation, and for a host of other spiritual and magical applications, the only limits being our faith, sincerity and skill.

APPENDIX 5

The Cypriot Syllabary

Serious, in-depth study of the Old European script was not undertaken until the 1970's, but as archaeology and research extended our understanding, a number of things became evident. The first very limiting fact is that we know next to nothing about the language used by its originators, and this is not likely to change. Second, there are no complementary inscriptions in languages we know to help us, nor are we likely to find any such. This script flourished two thousand years before the beginnings of literacy in Mesopotamia and was dying out just as writing became widely used in that region of the world. Third, at this time the number of inscriptions is too small for any meaningful statistical analysis. This may change in the future as more artifacts are uncovered, and more studies undertaken. Fourth, the Old Europe script is "partly pictographic-ideographic, partly stylized-abstract character"[1] and is not the same kind of writing as we are used to, the modern system being based on a phonetic alphabet.

In the Old European script, a sign would often stand for a single word, and this word would be rich in cosmological or religious significance. Each sign was capable of communicating one clear meaning, and many scholars feel that the thirty root signs, mostly geometric forms, do just this. There are syllabic symbols but these are not as numerous as the ideograms.

The sound of the word may have been important for magical purposes, but we have no knowledge of the language spoken by the people who developed this system of writing. But since there is continuity in the use of certain symbols from Paleolithic times up to and through the Bronze Age, there may also have been continuity in their associated sounds. The sign "M", for example, was likely an ideogram for water. In the classical Cypriot syllabary, "M" represents the syllable mi.[2]

The people who lived in Cyprus prior to the arrival of the Greeks are thought to be an offshoot of the Old European culture of the Danube river basin. A certain amount of reconstruction is possible, building on the hypothesis that phonetic values for the key symbols could have been continuously associated with them. The fidelity with which the Vedas and Upanishads were transmitted from thousands of years BC right up to the present time shows how conservative and exact religious traditions can be in preserving their scripture and ritual. Certain symbols might have had a continuously associated phonetic sound for several millennia, beginning at some indeterminate point in the sixth or seventh millennium BC. About one third of the symbols which we find in the Old European Script were used widely throughout Europe, suggesting that their core meanings could have been known and commonly agreed to through large segments of time and territory.

The Cypro-Minoan script dates from 1,500 to 2,000 BC. Both this script and Linear A are descended from a common ancestor. The existence of a bilingual inscription in Cypriot and Phoenician made it possible to decipher the classical Cypriot script in the 1870's. We know that it was used to write Greek and Eteocypriot, a yet unidentified language likely related to Old European. Each sign or symbol in the Cypriot script represents a syllable, not an alphabetic letter. Each syllable consists of a consonant plus a vowel or in some cases simply a vowel. It is speculated that one class of symbols in the Old Europe Script represented words, and others were syllabic.

Because this Cypriot script is not very well suited to Greek, it is believed to have been adapted for the use with Greek vocabulary from an earlier non-Indo-European language (Gimbutas, 1991). A visual comparison of the Cypriotic script with the Old European script suggests that they are related (see Table 1), the former very likely deriving from the latter. We know that the Old European script was amazingly stable and fixed for almost two thousand years, thus there is good reason to think that the phonetic values associated with specific symbols may also have endured, at least in isolated instances such as the island of Cyprus. At present, the Cypriotic Syllabary is our best clue as to what sounds may correspond to certain of the Old European signs.

Very little discussion has developed concerning the magical nature of these signs. Archaeologists, historians and anthropologists are reluctant to speculate about things like this in the absence of specific (or preferably conclusive) hard evidence. The best kind of evidence we have at present regarding the possible magical uses of the Old European script is inferential. We do know that symbols have been mediators of occult power and doorways into altered states of consciousness for as long as shamanism has existed, and there is general agreement that magic and shamanism date back at least to Paleolithic times. Specific sounds may have been associated with written forms from the earliest times, whether the symbol was pictographic or syllabic. Sound has been used to induce altered states of consciousness in all most of the tribal societies that anthropologists have been able to study, whether through drumming, chanting or the repetition of mantras and prayers. The classical writer Hyginus records that The Fates invented the seven letters of the Greek Alphabet: Alpha, Omicron, Upsilon, Eta, Iota, Beta and Tau, which makes them responsible for providing mankind with the vowel sounds. Diodorus Siculus recorded that Orpheus used the Pelasgian alphabet, which is to say the Primal Runes. Orpheus, of course, is considered the master bard of ancient times, whose words and music could charm the heart and create magic.

The symbols of the Old European script, as part of an ancient cult, would have been used in association with magic, divination, invocation and religious ritual. It is quite possible that a wide number of variable magic systems and liturgies arose in different regions or at different periods of time. While the script itself was remarkably fixed and persistent, there could have been fluidity or evolution in the cultural archetypes to which it referred, and variability in the rituals, chants and forms of divination or magic to which the symbols were applied. The Goddess, we know, had many epithets, many manifestations, and her artistic depictions were manifold. We can thus envision a somewhat flexible system of shamanic practice enduring through thousands of years in the Balkan heartland, with varying degrees of regional difference, the whole of it being held together by a core cosmology and a rather fixed system of notation.

A number of studies and books have outlined the likely shape of early European cosmology. Marija Gimbutas in particular has contributed invaluable material in her many books on this period. The use of the ancient signs in modern times for divination or magic will necessitate a close study of what we know about the Old European religion, and the best inferences and applications which we can make, based on that foundation of solid research. We may not want to rule out psychic investigation either, since this would have been considered a perfectly valid way to achieve knowledge by the ancients themselves, although modern scholarship is much less accommodating about its use.

To make use of the religious and magical properties of these signs, it would be necessary to assemble:

a) a comprehensive study of the Goddess Cult in Old Europe, based on the surviving clues;

b) a summary of the prevailing cosmology in Old Europe, from about 7,000 BC to 3,500 BC;

c) an assessment of how the signs seem to be have been used and applied with regard to the objects on which they have been found;

d) a matching of the signs to sounds and to their likely meanings (in the case of the root signs and core ideograms) based, firstly on any available research within the field (the Cypriot Syllabary being one example), and secondly on universal principles which are evident in magical and spiritual systems of ancient origin, and thirdly on intuitive insight and higher guidance;

e) an application of the signs, possibly carved into stones or wood as tools for divination, taking into account what we know of ancient tradition and universal principles that govern the practice.

If we attempt to recreate a complete understanding of the Old Europe Script as its original users knew it, we will be disappointed. The conventional scholarly approach is based on written records, which are absent, and inferences from a very incomplete archaeological survey. There are serious limitations as to what we can learn in this way.

On the other hand, the symbols have much to teach us if we are open to intuitive methods of learning. And if, having studied the historic realities as best we can, we actually begin to *work with these ancient signs* in an open-minded way, there is much that they can teach us. There is a difference between revelations which are true for a single individual, and those which are universal in scope, and the two kinds of knowledge have often been confused. But it is possible to attain and channel knowledge about the archetypal powers and meanings of the signs and symbols of this script. Because the Old European Script had a focused religious application for the earliest millennia of which we have any knowledge in our history, not being widely used in other was that we know, they remain archetypes of our primal roots. Archetypes live in the minds and hearts of those who contemplate them, activate them, claim them and embody them in action. We have in this ancient writing a set of windows onto our distant past, a set of tools for exploring the archaeology of our spiritual origins and the beginnings of our religious awakening in the West.

How far can we go? It is certainly worth seeing what we can make of these primal runes, using all the tools at our disposal.

---

[1] Haarmann, H. 1996. Early Civilization and Literacy in Europe. Berlin. pp. 32.
[2] Gimbutas, M. 1991. The Civilization of the Goddess: The World of Old Europe. San Francisco. pp. 309.

An Invitation

*R*oger Calverley continues to write and to explore the Mystery School tradition, divination, meditation, and the Primal Runes. He has an ongoing program of teaching, study and writing in this area of concentration. He is the director of a meditation centre in Lindsay, Ontario. If you want to share your own insights and experiences with Runes, or have serious questions based on your reading of *The Primal Runes*, or *Ancient Mysteries Tarot*, Roger can be reached by email at: calverleyr@yahoo.ca.

Once or twice a month on New Moon and Full Moon days, Roger may make time to engrave a set of Primal Runes of magical empowerment. Should you be interested in obtaining such a set, or studying this subject in greater depth, feel free to write.

Roger has also produced a CD called *Chanting The Primal Runes*, which illustrates how the powers of the runes can be invoked. Feel free to enquire by email.

Bibliography

Andrews, Ted. *Sacred Sounds*. Llewellyn. St. Paul MN, 1994.

Aswynn, Freya. *Northern Mysteries and Magic*. Llewellyn. St. Paul MN, 1998.

Anthony, Carol. *The Philosophy of the I Ching*. Anthony Publishing Company. Stow MA, 1981.

Bardon, Franz. *The Key to the True Quabbalah*. Dieter Ruggeberg. Wuppertal Western Germany, 1971.

Baring and Cashford. *The Myth of the Goddess*. Penguin Books. London England, 1993.

Cashford, Jules. *The Moon, Myth and Image*. Four Walls Eight Windows. New York NY, 2003.

Eisler, Riane. *The Chalice and the Blade*. Harper. San Francisco CA, 1988.

Frazer, Sir James George. *The Golden Bough*. The Macmillan Company. New York NY, 1935.

Gaffney, Mark. *Gnostic Secrets of the Nassenes*. Inner Traditions. Rochester VT 2004.

Graves, Robert. *The White Goddess*. Farrar, Straus and Giroux. New York NY, 1983.

Gilbert, Adrian. *Magi*. Invisible Cities Press. Montpelier Vermont, 2002.

Gimbutas, Marija. *The Language of The Goddess*. Thames & Hudson. San Francisco CA, 1989.

Gimbutas, Marija. *The Gods and Goddesses of Old Europe*. University of California Press. San Francisco CA, 1982.

Gimbutas, Marija. *The Civilization of the Goddess*. Harper. San Francisco CA, 1991.

Haarman, Harald. *Early Civilization and Literacy in Europe*. Berlin Germany, 1996.

Hodden, I. *Theory and Practice in Archaeology.* London England, 1992.

Jung, Karl. *Modern Man in Search of a Soul.* Harcourt: Harvest. Orlando FL, 1976.

Knight, Christopher and Lomas, Robert. *Uriel's Machine.* Arrow Books. Southend-on-Sea, Essex England, 2000

Markotic, V. *The Vinca Culture.* Western Publishers. Calgary Alberta, 1984.

Monaghan, Patricia. *The New Book of Goddesses and Heroines.* Llewellyn. St. Paul MN, 2000.

Monroe, Douglas. *The 21 Lessons of Merlyn: A Study in Druid Magic & Lore.* Llewellyn. St. Paul MN, 1995.

The Mother. *Collected Works.* All India Press. Pondicherry India, 2003.

Mountfort, Paul Rhys. *Nordic Runes.* Destiny Books, Rochester NY, 2003.

Neumann, Erich. *The Great Mother.* Princeton University Press. Princeton NJ, 1974.

Peschel, Lisa. *A Practical Guide to the Runes.* Llewellyn. St. Paul MN, 1998.

Prechtel, Martin. *Secrets of the Talking Jaguar.* Penguin. New York NY, 1999.

Pollack, Rachel. *The Body of the Goddess.* Vega. London England, 2003.

Renfrew, Colin. *The Emergence of Civilization.* Methuen. London England, 1972.

Rohl, David. *LEGEND: The Genesis of Civilization Vol. II.* Arrow Books. London England, 1999.

Rudgley, Richard. *The Lost Civilizations of the Stone Age.* Simon & Schuster. New York NY, 2000.

Sri Aurobindo. *Savitri,* Pondicherry India, 2001.

Stone Merlin. *When God Was A Woman.* Harcourt Brace Jovanovich. New York NY, 1976.

Thorssen, Edred. *The Nine Doors of Midgard.* Llewellyn Press. St. Paul MN, 1991.

Thorssen, Edred. *Northern Magic.* Lewellyn. St. Paul MN, 2002.

Tyson, Donald. *Rune Magic.* Llewellyn. St. Paul MN, 1989.

Wilson, Ian. *Before the Flood.* Butler and Tanner Ltd. London England, 2001.